THE FIFTH GRAVE

ROB JONES

This one's for Snow-White, again

"Bloody thou art, bloody will be thy end."
Shakespeare

PROLOGUE

Wiltshire Downs, 1992

The young woman scrambled through dead leaves and branches, scratching her arms on a wild blackberry bush as she staggered deeper into the woods. With her heart pounding and her breath clouding in the cold, dark air, she scanned the trees for a way to escape the terror now closing in behind her.

She ran forward once again, the brambles and holly whipping at her legs as she tried to find a path to salvation. Turning, she saw he was still there, closer than ever – stalking forward through the night, made into a silhouette by the blazing fire burning at his back.

Her head swam with the drugs and everything she saw was distorted by blurred vision. For a moment she thought she saw the headlights of a car, a flash of hope – but what would a car be doing out here? Then she realised it was the moon, rising in the eastern sky above the ancient woods, doubled by her inability to focus properly.

Not knowing what else to do, she ran towards it anyway. Perhaps she could hide somewhere further ahead among the trees with the spirits of the dead. With luck, her pursuer would stumble into one of the muddy ditches that were obscured deep in the misty understory and give her more time to flee.

She clambered up a rise until she was at a higher elevation but her view was still blocked by the dense woodland and her failing eyes. A jackhammer heart thumped against her ribcage as she scanned the trees for another escape route. Was it better to run or hide?

Spying a jumble of logs freshly cut from the carcass of a felled tree, she clambered down behind them and prayed for a miracle. Her breathing slowed and her mind raced. How had it come to this? She thought she knew him. She thought she'd known them all.

She was one of them once – a part of all this. But now, the excitement had decomposed to terror, the exhilaration they had known together had rotted away into the horror of being hunted like a lame vixen cowering in a covert. For a moment she wondered if he could be reasoned with, but then the moonlight reflected off the blade in his hand and she saw he was no longer the man she had once known. He was someone else now, or something else. She should have known better.

"I'm going to kill you, *witch!*" His voice split the autumn air like steel. Cold, emotionless and, she realised with panic, a faint tinge of pleasure. He was *enjoying* tracking her, knife in hand. The realisation struck her like a fist – as far as he was concerned she was no longer the woman he had known, but simply prey.

She wanted to scream out and tell him to leave her alone, but she knew the futility of doing so and that it would only give her away. Would the others come to her rescue, or would they join the hunt? If she wanted to live to see another sunrise, she had to fight the urge and stay silent.

She watched as he struggled through the dormant bracken and cottongrass and cursed her name to the moon. He was drawing closer now. Hiding was a mistake and she felt her pulse quicken as she stared at the trees, searching for a way out of this nightmare.

She felt the energy draining from her body as the man stalked ever closer, and now as she spied on him he started to transform into some kind of chimaera – or was it just the drugs coursing through her bloodstream? Her mind drowned with confusion and fear. Perhaps they had done this to her, given something to her to stop her getting away, to sharpen their sadistic pursuit of her?

Now, as the deranged hunter drew nearer, the adrenaline pumping hard inside her gave a moment of lucidity and her mind raced with thoughts of her family. Her mother and father were safe at home in the warm, so near and yet so far. How could she have been so stupid to end up like this? She closed her eyes and mumbled a hopeless prayer.

"Getting closer, witch!" The words leapt from his spit-flecked lips like needles.

She stumbled out of the log pile and made a dash for it down the northern slope of the ridge. Ahead she thought she saw a road and headed towards it, but the man behind her was faster, stronger, more agile. She knew that only too well. Now he was upon her, swearing and cursing as he made his way down the bank, stopping only to kick his leg free of some muddy leaf-strewn ground.

"We're going to burn the witch..." he said, louder now and almost hysterical. "You can finally be with your sisters."

Almost at the edge of the woodland, she felt a heavy smack on the back of her head and fell forward, tripping on an exposed root and going down into a filthy ditch where she struck her head again on a half-buried rock. In the mulch and leaves, she saw stars and realised he must have hit her on the head with a rock. But maybe, she dreamed, she would be safe in here.

Safe from the chimaera.

From Magalos.

Stai lontano, per carità! Please, just leave me alone...

Behind her, she heard the man laugh. Somewhere behind him, the others were chanting as they danced around the fire. It was all a terrible nightmare. Nothing like this could possibly happen to her. There was a crunching sound as her pursuer trampled down the horsetail she was crawling through. Terrified by his closeness, she shut her eyes and stopped breathing.

But it was too late. She felt her heart pounding in her chest, as hard as a tenor drum and like nothing she had ever known before. Now came the dizziness – was it the terror of the night or their poison inside her? She vomited wildly and clutched at her stomach as the agony coursed through her frail body and sent tremors down her arms and legs.

She tried to cry out but no sound came. She felt herself fading away and then she saw he had found her in the darkness. Powerful arms grabbed her shoulders, turning her over in the undergrowth.

"Leave me alone!" she cried out, her voice hoarse with terror. "Please!"

She felt his hands on her as he held her down and looked at her with his dead, dark eyes. He scowled like a devil as he stared at her pleading face, and after glancing over his shoulder he raised the knife in the air. She saw the blade shine in the moonlight as he plunged it towards her, and then her world went black.

CHAPTER 1

Wiltshire Downs
Boxing Day, 26ᵗʰ December 2018

The wind roared across the plains from the west and howled among the tussock grasses. A light mist clung low to fallow fields iced with frost and somewhere behind a thick bank of grey clouds a weak sun struggled to light the day.

Blowing into his hands to warm them, Philip Croft glanced at his watch and decided to get moving before the world and his dog showed up. He had taken a few minutes to rest in the fields to the south of the ancient woodland, but time and tide wait for no man and he had a lot of ground to cover.

His friends were well ahead of him by now and he had to catch up with them or they'd probably be done and dusted and get to the pub before he even started. Sipping some more tea from a thermos, he screwed the lid back down, put it in his bag and trudged up towards the trees.

Halfway up the track, a bitter wind scratched his face like raven's claws. He shivered and pulled down his bobble hat before waving at his friends. They were working at the western edge of the woodland so he decided to search the northern section near the edge of the chalk ridge.

Reaching the woods brought some relief from the northeasterly wind and after adjusting his metal detector, he tucked his chin into his scarf and began slowly scanning the mulchy earth in pursuit of his treasure. With a bit of luck, he'd find something before his friends and then the Christmas drinks were on them.

Philip had been detecting these woods and plains for more years than he could remember, but he'd never taken his equipment to this part of the ridge. Rich in Iron Age and Roman archaeology, the whole district offered treasures of history and gold to anyone with the desire to find them.

The often harsh climate, acid soils and chalk bedrock of the downs produced unique biodiversity and as he swept his metal detector from side to side, the search coil assembly brushed against sedge, rock-rose and knapweed. Clustered around the woodland floor, fragile tufts of cottongrass waited patiently for warmer days when they would burst into snow-white flowers, but Philip enjoyed detecting any time of year. It was all the same to him – now, when the ground was clear but frosty, or further into the spring when the landscape blossomed with butterfly orchids and the tiny purple puff-balls of devil's bit scabious.

With no sign of any treasure yet, he continued to go deeper into the woods. The air was cold and damp in here, and through the bare winter canopy above him, the clouds skipped across the rolling hills of the downs. They moved so fast they reminded him of a speeded-up film.

In the corner of his eye, he thought he saw movement. He turned expecting to see his friends but there was nothing except one of the four notorious beech trees. Like most locals, he knew all about the beeches. The wood sustained countless thousands of trees, many of them beeches, but four of them were different from all the others. Four of them had a very bleak history indeed. Old, and massive and... he shuddered and walked in the other direction.

With the giant beech at his back, he made some adjustments to the discrimination setting on the detector. It was a new present he'd received yesterday and he was still getting used to it. He tweaked it again, varying the quantity of metal it would pick up, and lowering the sensitivity due to the increased mineralisation of the immediate area. After a few phantom signals, he decided to push on to the northern fringes of the woodland.

With the end of the woods almost in sight and the snow-capped roofs of the Langfords on the horizon, he began to sweep the coil around the base of a much younger beech tree. No chance of disturbing anything nasty under this one.

But then he heard it.

The detector started to whine and bleep – he had found metal at last.

As he crouched down on his knees in the dead leaves, he set the detector down and reached for his bag. Trees stripped of their foliage by the winter winds loomed precariously above his head as he pulled out his trusty pinpointer. He used this to refine his search and speed up his recovery time after the main detector unit had alerted him to the presence of metal.

He swept the pinpointer over the earth and his mind conjured images of Roman coins and Iron Age relics, or even more lucrative Anglo-Saxon jewellery. A Roman Road cut right through the centre of these woods, carrying on to the Great Ridge Wood further to the west. With so much history passing over this spot, he knew the chances of a good find were high. The notion of finding a hoard of precious coins quickened his heart.

Then the pinpointer failed. He cursed and searched his bag for a new nine-volt battery. Despite the cold, he changed it with nimble fingers and the device squawked again as it picked up the signal. This time he passed it over the area more carefully and managed to isolate the signal to a few square inches. Whatever he had found, it was tucked away deep in among the roots of the beech, where they disappeared down into the crisp red leaves and the damp loam soil below.

Fumbling for his trowel, he began to dig down into the earth in between some of the gnarled frost-bitten roots, his breath clouding in the air in front of his face as he dug. Working his way well down into the soil around a foot deep, he saw the dull glint of a mud-caked ring. Gold – it was certainly gold.

He moved the trowel away and reached his hand towards the precious treasure. When he finally touched the metal, he realised with horror that the ring was still attached to a brittle, bony finger.

Revulsion drove him away from the grim discovery and he thought for a moment he might be dreaming. Had he seen this or was his mind playing tricks on him? A second glimpse of the shrivelled, skeletal finger gave him his answer. Turning away from the tree in disgust, he tripped over his bag and fell back onto the frozen ground. He gasped for air, unable to believe what had just happened. Staring up at the monstrous, towering nightmare of bare, twisted branches receding in the falling snow, weathered by endless millennia of bitter winds, his head began to swim.

He had to tell someone.

His friends.

The police.

He called out for the others but there was no reply. They must have moved further to the west and were out of earshot. Reaching for his phone, he cursed when he felt the empty pocket. He always left it in the car to minimise phantom signals from its metal housing, plus signal coverage in the woods was patchy at best anyway. Hurriedly packing his equipment back up into his bag, he turned away from the beech tree and headed back through the woods to his car.

CHAPTER 2

Thirty miles to the north, Detective Chief Inspector Tom Jacob recalled the police psychologist's words with disdain as he stirred the milk into his tea. Watching the low-fat milk cloud up in the black tea, his mind drifted back to the tense conversation from the week before.

Trauma.

Grieving.

Guilt.

He sighed and finished stirring the creamy emulsion, turning the tea a smooth tan colour all ready to drink. Lifting his eyes to the window, he saw the world had changed overnight. A crisp frosting of snow from a light fall the night before had turned his garden white, but the weather wasn't cold enough to freeze his river. He followed its path as it meandered through the fields and into his garden. Flowing directly beneath the kitchen of the Old Watermill and right out the other side to the decrepit granary in the front garden, he listened to the sound of the running water as he took a sip of the tea.

A stone-curlew shrieked and wheeled in the sky, tucked its wings in behind its back and swooped down below the canopy of the trees at the end of his garden. When it was out of sight, he sipped some more of the tea and considered if the psychologist had made the right decision in advising him to return to work. Maybe he should have followed his instinct and taken some more time out to process it all.

No. His philosophy was that some things were too bleak to be recalled, but Dr Amelia Lovelace had strongly disagreed. She had told him that repressing memories, no matter how terrible, was unhealthy and bad for you. Instead, he had to talk about them, preferably with a professional, or someone close to him. A great idea, except for a couple of issues – he hated talking about himself and he had no one close to him. Not any more.

Now, he rubbed his face to determine if he could get away without shaving or not. He'd shaved two days ago, so the answer would be no, but he still passed his hand over his chin and cheeks just in case.

The answer was still no.

He walked upstairs and ran hot water into the sink. The steam rose and clouded the mirror, and after crouching a little from his usual six-foot, he squirted some shaving gel into his hands and rubbed it into a lather. After covering his face in it he wiped the steam off the mirror with the back of his hand, leaving gel smudges across his reflection. He sighed and picked up the razor. Ten days old and blunt, he hacked it against the stubble under his chin, nicking himself and drawing blood.

Cobalt blue eyes and jet black hair, some silver on the temples. More grey than a fortnight ago, he noticed with no concern at all and ran the razor deftly above his top lip. Now he stretched the skin down over his upper jaw to make the cheek taut and easier to shave, shaking the cut hairs and gel off in the hot water in a ritual he had done since he was a young teenager. The cold scrape of the steel blade, the sting of the soap in the gel on his lips, the forced study of his ageing face. Those days seemed like another century, which they were, he supposed.

He rinsed the remnants of the shaving gel from his face with a splash of water from the cold tap and patted himself dry with a hand towel. As he put the towel back on the rail he knocked the tea cup into the sink. The price of too much beer the night before and the inevitable consequences the morning after – a sore head, dry eyes and an unnerving lack of concentration.

"Sod it," he said, and fished out the cup, washing the soap out with some fresh cold water and then pulling the plug on the whole damned mess.

He moved over to a lead-lined window on the mill's north side and peered out over the frost-caked garden once again. Damned, it might be, but it was his only sanctuary now. Far away from the nightmare that his life had become in Oxford – but was it far enough away for him to start all over again?

Only if his guilt let him.

He slid on his wristwatch and walked downstairs. What was it they said? *Today is the first day of the rest of your life.*

Something like that, but with less than a week until he

went back to work he was starting to wonder just how many more chances this life was going to give him.

Just then, his mobile chirped. He heard it but couldn't see it. After a brief search, he found it in his jacket hanging over the back of the kitchen chair. The caller ID kept no secrets, and when he saw it was Anna Mazurek he wasn't sure whether to smile or frown.

"I know you're desperate to see me again," he said. "But you couldn't wait just a few more days?"

"Still the same old smart-arse, I see. Your start date just got brought forward."

He smiled. "I missed you too."

"How far is your place from Grovely Wood?"

Straight to business, as usual.

"Around forty-five minutes. Maybe more like thirty if I drive like you. Why?"

"We've got a dead body buried underneath a beech tree. Welcome home, Jacob."

*

He swung open the old, creaking garage doors and frowned. The car was his father's, not driven for years until a few weeks ago and still a bit reluctant to do what it was told. A relic from the sixties, the big powder blue convertible Alvis was most charitably described as a work in progress. Barely roadworthy, he had teased it through the MOT and covered it with classic car insurance to keep the costs down. The plan was to restore it to its former glory and sell it to an enthusiast, and in the meantime, it was the only vehicle he had.

He opened the chunky rust-speckled door and collapsed down on the soft, torn leather seat. It took three attempts to turn over, but when it did, it fired up with an impressive growl and shook the paint cans on his workbench. Driving the enormous beast out of the small garage was like navigating a cruise ship out of port, but he was soon pulling away down his gravel drive and turning onto the main road running to the west of Bradford-on-Avon.

The usual drive into work took him past the Caen Hill Locks on the way into Devizes but today he was going south. This drive to the ancient woodland offered expansive, panoramic views across the far-reaching downs and today the snow had made the landscape seem even bigger than usual. Snow at this time of year was rare but not unheard of, but a lot of people had lost money betting on a White Christmas. According to the news report the snow hadn't fallen until after midnight.

Boxing Day meant quiet roads and he soon reached Cranborne Chase and the chalk ridge where Grovely Wood was situated. He signalled and slowed to make a right turn and reached his destination without a hitch. The canopy of the woods was just visible a few hundred feet to the west and he spied a vehicle parked up at the side of a narrow lane. Drawing closer, he saw people inside it and when he parked up behind the car they pushed open the doors and climbed out.

He emerged into a gloomy and miserable day to find three nervous and confused faces looking back at him. "Are you the man who phoned the police?" he asked.

"That's me," one said, raising his hand. "I can show you where I saw it."

"No, just tell me, please."

He pointed as he described the location and Jacob made a note of the man's number plate. "I want you to wait here. Other officers are on their way. Understand?"

"Yes, of course."

Tucking his face down into his scarf, he started towards the woodland up on top of the chalk ridge. He stopped halfway to the tree line, his shoes already covered in snow from the fallow fields surrounding the woods. He took in the location for a few moments. Bleak, windswept and secluded on the best of days, the light snowfall seemed to have moved the place to a whole new level of isolation. A few villages were scattered around the woods, obscured by the closed-in weather; the only tangible sign of humanity was the ghostly outline of a farm building beyond the railway line to the east.

He walked up the sloping chalk ridge and reached the tree line. Entering the dark woods, he followed the main Roman Road running through the centre, branches interlocking above him like a cathedral's vaulted ceiling. Slowly, he made his way to the area that the man had described.

Leaving the road, he walked down an incline towards a hollow full of fallen leaves and broken branches. His path led him up the other side of the ditch and into a small clearing where he found himself standing in a ring of beech trees, half-bare and obscured in the gloomy forest.

And then he saw it. The scene was exactly how it had been called in. At the base of a beech tree on the far side of the clearing was a freshly dug hole, at the bottom of which he saw the unmistakeable glint of a golden ring on a filthy dirt-covered bone.

He took in the grisly sight and blew out a long, slow breath. From the size of both the hand and the ring, he was sure it was a woman, but how long she had lain under this tree was much harder to know.

Taking out his iPhone, he took some preliminary photos and saved the GPS coordinates of the crime scene. He looked up at the tree's canopy and then followed its trunk straight back down to the shallow grave.

"You wanted to be sure she was never found," he muttered.

He closed his eyes and started to rebuild the moment in his imagination. Night, he thought. Were there just the two of them up here, killer and victim? Or more than two? A shallow grave around a foot deep beneath a beech tree. No, he reconsidered; the tree was an afterthought, or maybe an accident of nature.

A deer barked, hoarse and wild in the distance, startling

him from his thoughts.

He checked his phone. He'd been up here for nearly a quarter of an hour and still no sign of Mazurek or the CSI team. He was considering the likelihood of their being caught in the snow when he saw a pair of LED headlights forming two arctic haloes on the road at the base of the ridge's eastern slope.

It was Mazurek's blue BMW, and behind her, he saw the headlights of other police cars and the CSI team. Now things could get moving.

CHAPTER 3

He pulled up the collar of his coat and blew out another long, quiet breath. It condensed in the wood's cold air, lingered for a moment and then vanished into the grey sky. Down on the road, Detective Sergeant Anna Mazurek was talking with two CSI officers, one of whom was passing her a coffee. She gripped the paper cup and trudged up the hill, looking like she wanted to be anywhere but here. Her blonde hair was tied back in a neat, professional bun and beneath a woollen coat, she wore an expensive petrol-blue suit. As she drew closer he saw the slate grey eyes and the high cheekbones he remembered from so long ago.

"Morning guv," she said, extending a gloved hand. "Christ, you got old."

He gave a nod. "Thanks."

"Before we start, I just wanted to say that it was a privilege working with you before and I'm really sorry about what happened."

"Okay." He looked down at the road. "What is CSI doing down there?"

"They're waiting for their senior officer."

"Right."

He shook her hand and was surprised by the strength of her grip. He'd worked with her many years ago before taking a promotion and moving to the Met, and he hoped she hadn't changed too much. She was tough, she was unforgiving, and as he recalled, she was a very good detective.

"Good to see you again." He fixed his eyes on hers and gave as good as he got on the handshake front. He was still thinking about how she had used the word *privilege* in connection with working with him, and it made him uncomfortable. "Even in these circumstances."

"The pub might have been better," she said, sipping her coffee. "Or even the office."

"Either of those would have done me just fine."

She changed the subject. "What the hell is that parked down there?"

"A 1962 Alvis TD21 drophead coupé," he said proudly. "Why? Do you like it?"

"I wouldn't be seen dead in it. It looks like a skip."

"You have no class."

"If you say so."

"It's a beautiful colour though, you have to admit."

"All the panels are different colours, which bit do you particularly admire?"

Jacob smiled. "The bonnet has just had its final respray," he said.

"Are you sure it's even legal?"

He looked at the old wreck parked up below the ridge and frowned. "Some more work is needed, admittedly."

"It needs a car crusher."

"I'll pretend I didn't hear that."

Her laugh was muted by the cold wind. Down on the road, some uniformed police officers were talking with the metal detectorists.

"Who's with the caller and his friends?" Jacob asked.

"PCs Smith and Cook."

"Okay, thanks."

She glanced up at the bare trees looming out of the weak dawn light. "Now then, have you seen what's ruined my Christmas holidays yet?"

"Yes, skeletal remains buried in a fairly shallow grave," he said. "Problem is we have a tree growing over the top of them."

"That's what the caller said."

"Get in contact with the Forestry Commission," he said. "This part of the woods is owned and controlled by them so call them up and tell them what's happened. Also, tell them to get someone up here with a chainsaw and a winch. I want that tree out of the way as soon as possible."

"Guv." She pulled her phone from her pocket and started to look up the number. After she had made the call, she slipped the phone away and stamped her feet to warm them. "They're sending some people over."

He nodded and turned his face out of the wind.

"So where exactly are these remains, guv?"

"It's just over here. Follow me."

*

Looking down at the skeleton's hand, she shook her head in disbelief. "At the end of the day, you've got to ask yourself if it's all worth it."

"Sorry?"

"I mean if you have to share the same world with the kind of animal who can do something like this." She took another sip of the coffee and stamped her feet once again on the hard ground to help her circulation. "Dumped out here and left to rot like a dead animal. Christ, it's cold."

"You can say that again," he muttered. "And yet people are out here with bloody metal detectors."

"It takes all sorts."

She looked up at the man beside her and tried to work out his age. Word around the office was he was still on the right side of forty, but up close and personal she had to disagree. There was more grey in his temples than she had expected, but it didn't look too bad on him at all. If anything it leant a certain distinguished air to him, as did the crow's feet settling in at the corners of his blue eyes.

"So, what do you think?" he asked.

"Hard to say while there's a bloody tree on top of it."

"Which is why we need one of the foresters up here, pronto. Where the hell are they?"

"Speak of the devil, sir."

Jacob turned to see a Land Rover making its way up the track. When it reached the woods a uniformed constable hopped out and opened the five-bar gate blocking the lane.

Waving the vehicle through, he climbed back into the cab and they drove slowly over to the crime scene.

The PC climbed out again, as did a younger man in a green body warmer, followed by the driver, who slammed his door and trudged over to them along the track. He was wearing a crumpled waxed jacket, a pair of brown corduroy trousers and green wellington boots that had seen better days. The picture was topped off by a woollen flat cap pulled down low to stop the bitter wind blowing it away.

He drew nearer now, his hands shoved down inside his jacket pockets.

"How do?"

Anna spoke first. "Neil Talbot?"

"That's me," the ranger said, pointing to the sign painted on the door of his Land Rover. It read *Forestry Commission England*. "That kind of gives it away, I suppose."

Jacob said nothing.

"And this is Adam Dawes," Talbot said, pointing to the younger man. "This is one of my assistants."

Anna sniffed and took out her notepad to make a note of their details and registration number.

Dawes craned his head to peer over shoulder. "Don't often see much action around these parts."

Anna ignored his comment. "I'm Detective Sergeant Mazurek and this is Detective Chief Inspector Jacob. The situation here is that a body has been found in these woods, just behind me in that hollow over there. The problem we have is that it's caught up in the roots of a tree and we can't get the body out until the tree is removed."

Dawes stepped forward and sniffed. "I bet that doesn't happen every day."

"Leave it, Adam," Talbot said gruffly. "Let them get on with their jobs."

Jacob's eyes sharpened. "Thank you both for getting here so promptly. What with it being Christmas and everything."

"No trouble at all," Talbot said. "I live local and come up here most days anyway to make sure everything's all right and no one's been messing about up here."

"Messing about?" Anna asked,

Dawes spoke up. "Just the usual – breaking fences, making fires, leaving empty bottles of booze all over the place. But the truth is, not much happens up here. It's very peaceful and clean and tidy. Fact is, when you called and said someone had found a body up here I thought to myself, have they found another witch?"

Jacob locked his eyes on him. "I'm sorry?"

"Ignore him, it's rubbish," Talbot said.

Dawes gave a bland smile. "Just over there," he said, quieter now. "There are four witches buried up here among these trees and I was wondering if you'd found the fifth. A giant beech tree marks each of the four graves, see. Some say they haunt the place."

Anna narrowed her eyes. "What are you talking about?"

"Local legend," he said darkly. "They're all buried right here in Four Sisters."

Jacob turned to him. "Four Sisters?"

"That's what this coppice is called, for the obvious reason."

"Well, now there's a fifth grave," Jacob said, looking over the man's shoulder. "I see you brought a vehicle with a winch bumper."

Talbot lowered his eyes from the sky and nodded. "That's what the sergeant here requested."

"And you also brought a chainsaw?"

The man nodded. "How wide's the trunk? If it's too big then I'll have to go and get more equipment."

Jacob pulled his gloved hands from his pockets and measured out an estimate. "Diameter about this size."

"That's just a baby," he said. "We'll have him out with chains, no problem."

"Good, then let's get to work."

CHAPTER 4

I t didn't take Neil Talbot and Adam Dawes long to drive the Land Rover up to the tree, and after a few minutes of work, they had secured the winch's anchor chain around the slender trunk. Talbot climbed back into the cab of his mud-encrusted four-wheel-drive and fired up the engine. A cloud of blue diesel smoke billowed up out of the vertical exhaust and drifted into the bare branches above.

Anna called the uniformed officers over and when Talbot activated the winch it tore the trunk out of the ground with remarkable ease. When the job was done and the tree was on its side, they worked together to guide the fallen trunk up out of the stump hole and away from the grave. Years of darkness were now exposed to the light, and roots wrenched from the soils and leafmould. Working slowly, they got it clear without causing too much damage to the crime scene but part of the skeleton had snagged inside the root system and one of the arms twisted up out of the hole.

"Woah!" Jacob called out. "That's enough!"

Anna signalled to Talbot who killed the engine and silence fell over the woods once again. As she walked over to the hole, Jacob pulled up his collar and stamped his feet in the snow in a bid to warm himself up. For a while, neither of them knew what to say.

"All right," he began. "Have uniform get some barrier tape up around this part of the woods, and make sure it's far enough out that we don't get any rubberneckers on their Christmas walk."

"Guv."

While Talbot and Dawes talked quietly by the Land Rover, she walked over to the policemen who had helped pull the tree out of the stump hole and gave them their orders. Jacob looked at their cold faces, and then down the ridge at the metal detectorists who were still standing by their SUV. Joined now by an ambulance, it was an atmosphere of curiosity and confusion, lit by the strobing of the blue LED emergency lights.

When Anna returned, the two of them walked over to the grave and got their first real look at the crime scene. Lying crumpled in a heap in the base of the rounded, root-strewn stump hole was a rag-covered skeleton, its mud-streaked skull staring back at them in the frozen silence. A few flakes of snow drifted down through the branches and began to lay on the bones.

"What do you think, Anna?"

"There's the ring that set the detector off," she said.

Jacob said nothing.

She continued. "And female, from the clothes."

He nodded.

"Maybe we might get lucky with the clothes," she said quietly. "And there's always DNA."

"Plus the tree," he muttered. "Have Talbot cut that thing in half and age it."

"She could have been in there long before the tree started to grow, guv."

"I know that but do it all the same. She might have gone into this grave well before the tree started growing, but she certainly didn't get into it afterwards. Look at the way she was tangled into the roots."

"Agreed."

Leaning on one of the trunk's roots for support, Jacob leaned over the edge of the hole and peered at the remains from another angle. "Take a look at the back of the skull."

Anna gasped. "Root damage?"

"I don't think so," he managed. "Looks like she sustained a serious head injury, and it could possibly be the cause of death."

"Poor soul."

He craned his neck and looked at the surrounding trees, taking in the isolation. "I'm not getting a good feeling about this at all. A skull with damage like that would rule out accidental death or suicide."

"So we're looking at a murder?"

He gave a sullen nod and brought his attention back around to the remains in the hole. "I'd think so, but we'll wait till we get confirmation from the quacks."

As the chainsaw revved and bit into the beech, Jacob turned to Anna. "When he's finished, interview both of our friends from the Forestry Commission. They likely spend more time up here than anyone else so get what you can from them."

"Even if it's just more nonsense about how these woods are full of dead witches?"

He sighed and shook his head. "Full of dead witches my arse…"

The loud, rasping roar of Talbot's chainsaw filled the woods as the cutting teeth ripped through the bark and began slicing down into the trunk's heartwood. Jacob watched the concentration on the ranger's unshaven face, obscured from behind the scratched visor of his safety helmet, as he slid the saw chain through the trunk and finally reached the bottom.

Cutting the two-stroke engine, he studied the cut tree and wandered over to them. "All done."

"How old is it?"

Talbot scratched his chin as he thought the matter over, glancing once again from the growth rings on the freshly cut trunk back up to the expectant faces of the police officers standing in front of him. "Through a quick count o' them rings, I'd say it's around a quarter of a century old. Not easy to be entirely accurate, mind you."

A quarter of a century, minimum, Jacob thought grimly.

"How busy does it get up here?" Anna asked.

"Depends on the time of year, of course," he said. "You get people walking all over these woods. They're supposed to stick to the paths but they go blundering wherever they want, especially those fools who come up here because they think it's haunted by them witches. They have no respect at all for nature."

Her phone rang and she stepped away to take the call.

"We have both of your details," Jacob said suddenly. "We'll be in touch, so don't go anywhere."

"Where would I go?" Talbot said. "These woods are my life… come on, Adam."

They unhooked the anchor chain from the felled trunk and padded back over to the Land Rover where they began to reset the winch.

Anna got off the phone and returned to the grave. "The good news or the bad news?"

"Surprise me."

"It's already in the news."

"How?"

"Five emergency vehicles driving through a quiet village and parking up in one place attract attention, guv. Local rag got hold of it and it looks like they've been talking to one of the uniforms."

Jacob clenched his jaw. "Bloody hellfire. And what's the good news?"

"CSI are on their way up."

"About time," he said.

"They got here as fast as they could."

"I know… twenty-five years old, at least, Anna," he muttered, shaking his head. "And the location of the grave alone makes this a suspicious death as far as I'm concerned, never mind the state of the skull."

"Also agreed."

He saw once again the lonely grave and the frozen woods beyond, brittle with frost. "When the CSI is finished we need to get the remains and what's left of the personal belongings down to the lab for a post-mortem. And I want the clothes analysed and DNA taken from the remains."

Anna met his eyes and they shared a knowing glance. "Okay."

He pushed his hands in his pockets and gave a sigh heavy with thought. "Something very nasty happened here a long time ago, and I'm not going to stop until I find out what."

*

Sophie Anderson changed down into third gear and took the bend at high speed. The engine growled in response as she hit the straight and pushed back down on the accelerator. The drive from Salisbury up to the woods was usually safe and quiet and today was no exception. Snow-dusted chalk plains stretched out on either side of her as she powered the Audi A5 coupé north along the deserted B road, but she had no idea what she would find at the end of her journey.

The news on the radio repeated what she had seen on the morning television news – a body had been found in Grovely Wood and police were working on the assumption it was murder. She had offered to help with the last two murders in the county, and each time the Senior Investigating Officer in charge of the cases had rejected her. She prayed that this time she would be allowed to help. Her career depended on it.

The news reports were vague, but that was to be expected this early in a criminal investigation. She suspected the police already knew a lot more than they had let on to the press anyway, but the few details that had been released were intriguing. The death was already being described as a historical case, but it was the word *witches* that had grabbed her attention.

Into fifth and out onto the long straight over the downs. The weather was worse up here than in her new hometown of Salisbury. She switched on her main beams and the fog lamp and returned to the radio to try and catch another report but all the stations had moved out of the news cycle. As she made her way up the main road, her mind spilt over with possibilities concerning the grisly discovery.

Drawing closer to the woods, her headlights lit up the high-visibility Battenburg markings stuck on the side of the emergency vehicles gathered at the eastern end of the ridge. Several police cars and an ambulance. That would be going straight to the police morgue, she thought. She scanned the area for the SIO's car. What would he drive? When she saw the rust heap parked up behind one of the police cars, she knew she'd found her man.

Pulling up at the side of the road, a young constable stooped down until his face was almost inside her car. "Can

I help you, madam?"

"I'm trying to find Detective Inspector Jacob."

He furrowed his brow, eyes scanning the interior of the brand new car before returning to meet her gaze. "If you mean Detective *Chief* Inspector Jacob, then he's up on the ridge in the woods, but the entire area is off-limits to the public. Are you here on police business?"

Sophie felt her neck muscles tense. "No."

"In that case, no one goes past this point, madam." He extended his hand and turned his face into a serious frown to emphasise his point. Flicking his head to indicate the man up in the woods he said, "Orders from the top."

She held his eye and lowered her voice. "I think I might be able to help, that's all."

The policeman furrowed his brow and gave the top brass up on the ridge another thoughtful glance before retuning his attention to her. "And why is that, madam? Do you have any details concerning the remains?"

Sophie drew in a deep breath and sighed. "Not specifically, no. I work in the field of criminal psychology."

"That's very interesting, madam, but my orders are to let no one past this point."

Sophie tried not to let the frustration show on her face. She looked out over the fields and watched a light snowfall drift across the landscape, settling on the mud. The wind was growing in strength and she could see some more policemen struggling up a winding track on their way to the woods.

"Please, will you at least tell him I'm here?"

Before he could reply, his radio squawked. "Mike Delta 479, are you receiving?"

He smiled at her and reached for the radio receiver fitted to the lapel of his tunic. "If you'll excuse me for a moment, madam."

"Well..."

Turning away from her, he tucked his chin down towards the radio. "Mike Delta 479 receiving loud and clear dispatch."

She sighed and rolled her eyes. Pushing back into the soft, warm seat, she turned up the heater to compensate for the open window. When he finished on the radio, he turned to her with a smile.

"Yes?" she asked.

"If you want to speak with the Chief Inspector you'll have to wait down here."

And that was that.

*

In the dull, morning light Jacob watched one of the CSI team members carefully laying several plastic duckboards across the frozen mud to the gaping stump hole. Further out, another was creating an outer perimeter around the hole with a length of crime scene tape.

A woman in a white paper forensic suit and nitrile gloves slammed the rear doors of a police CSI van and approached him at a brisk pace.

"You must be Jacob." Before he could speak, she went on. "They told me to look for a man with a face like thunder and it looks like you might be the chap."

"And you are?"

She looked slightly put out. "Mia Francis. Senior CSI."

Jacob flicked Mazurek a glance and suppressed a smile.

"Of course you are."

"Good morning Anna," she said, ignoring him. "And how are we today?"

"Cold and tired."

"Jolly good. I thought you were flying away somewhere warm?"

"I was."

"Oh dear, I just got back from the Med two days ago," she said. "And how is old Morgan bearing up?"

Jacob had heard that Mia Francis and the old Welsh inspector had become close friends. As unlikely as it seemed, the two of them had an interest in rugby and real ale and were known to get pretty raucous at local derbies. Looking at the lean, petite woman in front of him he found it hard to picture her on the terraces with a pint of mild in her hand.

"He's well," Anna said. "He says you owe him a pint."

"That was weeks ago," Mia said, taking in a sharp breath of the cold air. "Good to know he never changes. Anyway, shall we get down to it? I don't know about you but I have a very large Boxing Day dinner planned and I'd rather be doing that than this."

"Of course."

She followed Jacob and Anna over to the stump hole and peered inside for a few seconds. "It's obvious even to the layman that the body is a very old one, so I hope you don't expect miracles."

"No expectation of miracles," Jacob said.

The ranger had already told him that the woods were a popular place with the public for walking and cycling. Twenty-five years of people and dogs trampling all over the place would have left its toll, and part of that price would be the destruction of any evidence left at the scene by the killer.

Stepping carefully into the hole, Mia continued calmly talking them through her findings. "The skeleton is female and as far as I can see there is no tissue on the bones at all. Again, not surprising considering the location and age of the body."

"No."

"Looks like the remnants of some kind of nylon bag under here but it's badly decomposed."

"Anything in it?"

"Appears to be but it's under the remains."

"That's where the story starts," Jacob said. "Get it back to the lab and go through it with a toothcomb. Any other observations?"

"From my preliminary investigation I would say that my team are unlikely to find anything just lying around in the debris on the forest floor but I've ordered a standard fingertip search as protocol dictates. The remains have been out here so long I doubt the murder weapon is just waiting to be found, either. I've looked at the variation in vegetation in the area but can find no difference between the grave site and anywhere else. It's my opinion that this body was deliberately buried in a shallow grave rather than simply rolling into a ditch and being covered with soil and leaves."

"Right."

"It's the eye holes that freak me out," Anna said.

"Orbits," Mia said with a sigh. "They're called orbits, Sergeant."

Jacob caught Anna's eye, but neither dared say a word.

"I can't find any disturbance in the surrounding soil and that's hardly surprising given the age of the grave, but the surface of the area seems to be smooth enough to use ground-penetrating radar to see if there are any more buried out here."

Anna sighed. "We'll know more when pathology has gone over it, I suppose."

There was no doubt that the remains would have to be properly examined and that meant contacting Ethan Spargo, the Home Office pathologist for Wiltshire. With a reputation for his cutting wit and dry humour, Jacob had heard a great deal about him but never met him.

Mia nodded. "The skeletal nature of the remains means you'll also need a forensic anthropologist to take a look.

Henry Vane should be available, and he's very good."

"I know Henry from Oxford," Jacob said. "Unfortunately."

He watched Talbot and Dawes packing away their equipment into the back of the Forestry Commission Land Rover. Climbing into the cab, they slammed their doors and sent a cloud of startled rooks flying into the air above the woods.

"Twenty-five years in this place, alone in a shallow grave," he said quietly.

The foresters' 4x4 pulled away and drove slowly down the track towards the B road.

"Where does Vane live these days?" Jacob asked.

"Same as Ethan – just outside of Salisbury," Mia said. "Beautiful home. I was there for his annual summer garden party."

"How nice," Anna said. "I never got an invite."

Mia cocked an eyebrow. "What a shame."

"Nor me," Jacob returned. "But I'll get over it, and in the meantime get the remains down to the mortuary there as fast as possible."

Mia twisted the corner of her mouth up. "Ethan's going to moan forever and a day about having to drive anywhere in this weather, especially at this time of year."

"Too bad," Jacob said.

Mia pulled her mask from the top of her head and started to peel off her nitrile gloves. "Fancy lying out here in these woods all these years, being on your own like this, gone and forgotten."

"She's not forgotten anymore," Jacob said. "And neither is the bastard who killed her. His luck has just run out."

CHAPTER 5

He turned from the busy efficiency of the CSI team and walked to the edge of the woods. The downs were beautiful at any time of year, but last night's frosting of snow had lent an extra majesty to them. Now, he watched as a young couple walked hand-in-hand along a bridleway half a mile or so to the south.

Dressed in matching anoraks with hoods pulled up tight around their faces, they marched through the snow until reaching the crime scene tape. After a short conversation with one of the uniformed police officers, they turned around and marched right back down again, disappearing behind a copse of trees near the main road. It was then he saw the woman in the red hat and scarf. She was shielding herself from the weather in the cover of the ambulance, her face obscured by a black umbrella, but whoever it was, it looked like she was giving PC Smith a hard time.

Jacob turned and wandered back down the other track until reaching the small collection of police vehicles parked up on either side of the road. Standing among them were Philip Croft and the other detectorists, huddled around the back of their SUV.

"Mr Croft?"

The man in the middle nodded sullenly. "Yes."

"I'm Detective Chief Inspector Jacob. We met earlier."

"I remember," Philip said quietly.

"Can I have a word?"

With their faces partially obscured by new Christmas scarves and bobble hats, the three of them glanced at one another before Philip spoke. He looked shocked and cold and with dry, colourless eyes. "Of course," he managed. "Absolutely."

Jacob put his warrant card back in his coat and gave them a quick, professional smile. "It was you who found the remains, wasn't it, Mr Croft?"

Philip paled and took a step back. "Yes, it was me."

"But we weren't far behind him," the other man.

"And you are?"

"I'm Stephen Cornwell, and this is my wife Denise."

A few awkward smiles followed.

"I couldn't believe it when I heard Phil cry out," Denise said. "I thought he'd seen a ghost."

"You can say that again," said her husband. "Phil's not one to make a fuss so for a moment I wondered just what on earth had happened."

Somewhere above their heads, hidden in the boughs of a birch, a redwing sang out for its mate, its sharp call lighting the dark moment below.

"Have you been up here before?"

"To walk, yes," Philip said. "But not with the detector, at least not around Four Sisters. This is brand new. I only got it yesterday. It was a present from my kids."

"What about you two?"

"We've detected up here before, yes." Stephen Cornwell and his wife caught each other's eye for a moment. "We've been trying to get Phil into it for a long time, and the first trip out – look what happens."

"You say you've brought your metal detectors up to Grovely before?"

"Yes, several times," Stephen said. "But it's a big place – the second largest woodland area in the county. We've never got around to searching Four Sisters. It's a virgin site – at least it is for us."

"When you discovered the remains you phoned the police immediately, is that right?"

Philip nodded. "I didn't touch a thing, except for when I reached out for the ring. Oh, God."

"All right, thank you all. I know it's been difficult for you but we have all your details and we can get in touch if we need to."

"Is that likely?" Stephen said.

Jacob slipped his notebook away. "You never can tell."

*

Anna Mazurek watched Jacob walk back up to the woods. Snow was settling on the shoulders of his black peacoat by the time he'd reached the top of the field, hands pushed down into his pockets and the lower part of his face now hidden even more by a thick black scarf.

The icy wind whipped his hair but he never flinched as

he trudged on up the hill. She had remembered him from her first days in the police as a defiant man, although his enemies used the word stubborn, so seeing him back so soon after the fire hadn't surprised her. He'd spent his career working hard to stop crime and violence and protect innocent people. Hiding away even after such a profound personal tragedy wasn't in his nature.

She balled her gloved hands into fists in a bid to warm them. He was halfway up the hill now and Mia Francis and her CSI team were conducting an ever-expanding fingertip search, the radius gradually moving further away from the shallow grave.

Just a week past midwinter and the shortest day, and even approaching midday the light was weak. What little of it broke through the clouds was further blocked by the dense woodland. It had a frail and spent feel to it and made her wish to be anywhere else but here. She'd been in places like this before, but usually during the summer when families walked and children played. When photographers took pictures of bluebell carpets and dogs played in an undergrowth twisted with pignut and foxglove.

It was a very different world today.

She thought back to what the ranger had said about the dead witches, and the young people coming up here to drink and make bonfires at night. Is that what had happened to their victim? She shuddered as she thought of the last few minutes of her life. Had she died here in the trees or was she murdered somewhere else and dumped here?

Jacob had made it to the woods and was now walking over to the hollow.

"Anything?" she asked.

He shook his head. "He was up here with a new Christmas toy and he stumbled onto the remains when the detector located the ring. We've got their details, but not sure there's anything more there that can help us. I want you to organise some uniforms to do a house to house within a three-mile radius. That might shake things up."

"Guv."

"And who's that having it out with Smith down on the other road? I saw her earlier."

Anna turned away from the huddle of emergency vehicles and the detectorists and looked down to the other road further along to the south. "No idea. Probably irked that the woods are shut and her Boxing Day walk has been cancelled."

"She seems very persistent. I think I'll go and have a chat."

*

"All right, Smith. I'll take it from here."

"Thank you, sir."

"Are you Detective Chief Inspector Jacob?" The woman in the red hat stepped closer and held out her hand.

"I am, yes. And you are?"

With one hand holding the umbrella, she fumbled in her bag for a business card. "My name is Dr Sophie Anderson. I'm a forensic psychologist and criminal profiler."

He took the card and read her details. "I've heard of you. You were involved in the Keeley Murders, is that right?"

She looked momentarily to the ground, searching in the snowy stillness for time to think of a response. "I was part of the team that caught him, yes."

"Nasty case."

"Yes, it was."

"But what are you doing here?"

"I'm here to help."

His smile faded. "I don't understand."

"I heard what happened on the news and I knew straight away that I could help. I've researched and written a great deal about both serial killers and occult deaths."

"Woah, no one has said anything about that."

"Reports on the internet mentioned a possible occult dimension to the murder."

Jacob sighed and handed the card back. "Then reports on the internet are wrong, or at the very least wildly premature. We know next to nothing about what happened here and nothing has been formally communicated to the press. Any reports you might have read are based on nothing but pure speculation," he said, shooting a dark look at PC Smith. "The investigation is barely off the ground."

"But you're aware of the history of these woods?"

Another sigh. "If you're talking about the witches, then yes I have been made aware of that history. But I fail to see any reason at the moment to link those murders, if indeed they ever happened, with the discovery of these remains."

Anna Mazurek reached the bottom of the hill. "Guv."

"This is Dr Sophie Anderson," he said with the trace of a smile returning to his face. "She wants to help us catch the killer."

Sophie said, "I developed an interest in criminal psychology when I was finishing my master's degree, so I wrote a PhD in it. I've been working in America."

Her words were met by silence. Jacob spoke next. "America?"

"Trained by the FBI." She handed her card to Anna.

"Dr Sophie Anderson," she read out. "Forensic psychologist and criminal profiler."

"I'm impressed by your credentials," Jacob said. "But…"

"But you don't want me to help?"

"I can see why you're such a good psychologist," Anna said. "You're good at picking up on what people are thinking."

The two women exchanged a glance as frosty as the surrounding fields.

"It's not that," Jacob said. "It's just that we have people who do this for us. People on our payroll who we know and trust." He saw the look on her face and backtracked. "Not that I don't trust you, but it's more complicated than that. There are all sorts of things to consider, like your potential access to confidential information off-limits to the public, your Disclosure and Barring Service check, hell – even insurance to be in our headquarters building."

He held the card up and handed it back to her.

"Well, that last one's just silly," Sophie said, waving her card away. "No, you keep it. My number's on there and something tells me you'll be needing it."

"Cocky," Anna said. "Nice."

"Confident in my abilities," Sophie said. "Not cocky."

Jacob blew out a breath and scratched the side of his head as he pocketed the business card.

"Will you at least consider it? I'll work for free and you look exhausted. I think I can help."

"All right, I'll speak with my boss. That's all I can do and I can't promise – wait, I look exhausted?"

She shrugged. "Just saying."

After a pause, he found the words he needed. "Thank you for your time, Dr Anderson."

Jacob watched Sophie climb back into her car, a new Audi coupé liberally covered in mud and filth from the recent cross-country drive.

"What do you think Kent will say?" he asked.

Anna snorted a dismissive laugh. "No way."

"I like her," Jacob said. "She risked her life to get Keeley behind bars."

"I know. I remember the stories in the papers, but there's still no way Kent's going there."

Jacob tracked the progress of Sophie's car as it climbed the hill and then turned around a bend, disappearing behind a line of trees. "Still, I like her."

CHAPTER 6

In the corner office of the HQ building in Devizes, a man sat at his desk and stared thoughtfully at his computer screen. Seeing his old friend leaning on the doorjamb, he shook his head and smiled. Deadpan, he said in a strong Welsh accent, "They'll let anyone into the police these days."

"Bill."

Detective Inspector William Morgan leapt to his feet with his usual high-energy and walked over to the door. The two men clasped hands and Jacob was once again reminded of his former colleague's strength. Twenty years in the Royal Marines Commandos had instilled a powerful ethic of fitness and exercise that he was maintaining with vigour.

"When they said you were coming back, Jacob, I thought about retiring."

Jacob gave his best withering look. "You haven't changed."

"This leopard is far too old for any of that nonsense. Coffee?"

He accepted the offer of a cup of coffee and took a seat beside the desk while Morgan switched on a black plastic kettle and dropped some instant coffee into two chipped mugs. Handing the steaming brew to him a moment later,

Jacob peered down inside the mug with a frown.

"Thanks."

"And you look like shit."

"Thanks again. When I left the message on your answerphone I wondered if you'd get it or not."

"Not much else going on in my life these days."

Jacob took a sip of the coffee and decided not to tell his friend how bad it tasted. He'd met Bill Morgan in his first weeks on the force when he was a uniformed police constable. The tough, no-nonsense Welshman was fifteen years older and had already made it to sergeant by that time, although both men transferred into the CID in the same year. He'd always considered him to be the salt of the earth – a solid old-fashioned policeman and a top-drawer detective, if a little rough around the edges.

On the surface, Morgan was blunt and his physical strength made him an intimidating presence but Jacob had got to know the real man over the years before he had left to work in the Met. A fairer and more loyal man he had never met or worked with before or since and they had shared many ups and downs than most colleagues over the years. Despite his junior rank, he valued his opinion more than anyone else on the force.

"How's life post-Leanne?" Jacob asked.

"Getting there."

There wasn't a man or woman in the station who didn't know about Morgan's wife and how she had walked out on him after declaring a long-running affair with another man.

Some had thought he would collapse like a house of cards but Jacob knew him better than that. He'd circled his wagons and rededicated himself to his fitness training. Despite developing a new, cynical attitude to life, he was the same man he'd always been.

"Talking of which – how many men does it take to screw in a lightbulb?" Morgan's voice was tinged with bitterness.

"I don't know."

"No one knows," came the weary Welsh accent. "They never get to keep the house."

Jacob narrowed his eyes and cocked his head. "Is that funny?"

"Not right now it bloody isn't." The cynical smile faded from his lips as he jabbed a sausage finger at Jacob. "Enough about me, What about you? You're all right now?"

Both men knew what he was referring to, and both men wanted to keep it brief.

"Same as you – getting there. I'm ready to lead the team again if that's what you're talking about."

A long silence.

"I heard about the remains."

Jacob's mind was taken back to the woods. The shallow grave, snow as soft and white as ermine and the barking deer. "We think they've been there for around twenty-five years."

"Bloody hell, I was on the beat back then. CSI have any

luck?"

"There was a bag buried with the remains, but it's very badly decomposed. Nylon. Mia told Anna it takes forty years to rot away completely so we got a break on that one. Anyway, everything's gone over to the mortuary for the PM."

Jacob watched his friend push back in his chair and sighed. Wiltshire Police was divided into four sectors, each headed by an inspector but Morgan was part of the senior management team based here in the county police's headquarters. He'd hoped for a few days off over Christmas but had come straight in after the call about the remains.

"Listen, thanks for coming in, Bill."

Morgan sipped his coffee and seemed to enjoy it. "No problem. It's better than being at home now the place is empty."

Jacob paused a beat. "Have you got anything else on at the moment?"

"Cashpoint thefts. There's a lot of it about at the moment and we picked up two just last night in a joint operation with Thames Valley. Conspiracy to burgle and perverting the course of justice. Needless to say, the lawyers are already working around the clock to get them both off."

Jacob spoke without hesitation. "As I said on the answerphone, I want you on the team looking into the remains."

Morgan weighed the words in his usual measured way. "A quarter of a century, you say?"

Jacob said nothing but gave a simple nod.

"Beats ATM thefts," the Welshman said. "What was this about bringing a private consultant in?"

"A criminal psychologist," Jacob said.

"Have you run it past Kent?"

"Not yet."

"Well, good luck with that."

"Is he difficult?"

"You'll find out. Bastard came in when he heard about your discovery this morning. He's upstairs now, as we speak."

"You should be in that office, Bill."

"Yeah, right."

"We both know that you'd be Chief Super by now if you only stopped and took the time to butter people up."

"Career advice from the man who turned down the chance to be a superintendent at Thames Valley."

Jacob shrugged. "Didn't like the office space, but I hear Kent's an ambitious man."

"He has a lean and hungry look," Morgan said.

Jacob recognised the Shakespeare quotation but ignored it. "Sounds like trouble."

Morgan gave a conciliatory sigh. "I don't know. He's not all that bad."

"Rumour has it that he doesn't want me here," Jacob said. "Says I'm not fit for work."

"When you say rumour, you mean Anna Mazurek?"

He nodded.

"But the Chief Constable has every faith in you, Jacob. He doesn't suffer fools gladly and he wouldn't have approved your return to work if he didn't think you were ready for it. That's what counts. Hey – talk of the devil."

Jacob twisted in his chair to see Detective Chief Superintendent Marcus Kent looming in the doorway. "Welcome back to the force, DCI Jacob."

"Thank you, sir."

"My office. Now."

When Kent was safely out of earshot, Morgan tossed his pen on the desk, pushed back into his chair and crossed his chunky arms behind his head. "Off to the lion's den," he said with a smile.

"So they say."

When he reached the door, Morgan spoke again. "And Jacob."

"Yeah?"

"It's good to have you back."

*

"It's *not* good to have you back," Marcus Kent purred, "if you're not ready to be back."

"I'm ready."

"Please, sit." He made a generous sweeping gesture towards a plastic chair situated opposite his expansive hardwood desk.

"Thank you, sir."

Jacob sat down and tried to make himself comfortable in the cheap seat. He noted that the CID chief's seat was a plush leather captain's chair, nicely softened by his extensive use of it. His boss was tall, lean with a thick thatch of neatly-combed grey hair framing a tanned face, which at this time of year suggested a sunbed or an exotic holiday. He wore fashionable browline glasses and had an aura of expensive aftershave.

Kent leaned back in the seat and casually pulled a manila folder from the top of his in-tray. Flipping the cover open, he began to study the first page of the report. "That's not *exactly* what Dr Lovelace says, is it now?"

"What, sir?"

"About you being ready."

"I've read the report, sir. It concludes that I'm ready to return to work."

Kent sucked his teeth and shifted in his seat. "Yes, that is the *conclusion*, but it's the observations along the way that bothers me."

Jacob knew where this was going. He'd heard about Marcus Kent. A ruthlessly ambitious man who took no enemies, his chief concern was avoiding blowback on any department he was heading. He'd worked in the force rising to DCI before Jacob joined, and left to take a promotion in Cumbria Police before returning home a year ago. He guarded the integrity of his career fiercely. If one of his senior officers had a public meltdown, his judgement would come under the sort of scrutiny a man with an eye on the top job could well do without.

"I wouldn't be here if I didn't feel up to it, sir."

Kent leaned forward and rested the heels of his hands on top of the report. Steepling his fingers, he gave a long, concerned sigh. "That's all well and good, but if your judgement is impaired by the terrible tragedy you endured, then your own views aren't reliable."

"My judgement is sound," he said flatly.

Only now, did the man opposite him start to relax. He leaned back in his chair and crossed his arms casually behind his head, rocking himself gently in the sumptuous swivel chair. "Terrible business, Jacob. My condolences. Losing a loved one in a fire like that. I can't imagine…"

"No."

"Getting Kyle Marsden put away for life was a damned solid result," he said. "A minimum of forty years."

"But his brother got away with it."

"Oxford CID found no evidence to link Kurt Marsden to the crime and you know it. You have to move on."

Jacob ran a hand over his face. "Jess died because Marsden was trying to kill *me*, sir. She died in the fire because she was sleeping at my house. I was supposed to die that night, not her."

"I understand that, but it's in the past. Marsden's locked up for life and you have to put it behind you or it will consume you and have an impact on me and my team. I can't risk any loose cannons on my deck, you understand?"

Jacob nodded but said nothing.

After a pregnant pause, Kent spoke again. "We've never worked together before because I only recently returned here to take this position, but I make it a point to know all about everyone under my command. My impression of you is that you're a maverick, Jacob. You get results but you're no friend of the rule book. This is unfortunate because I like rules and I expect my officers to follow them to the letter, like a military operation."

"Yes, sir."

Kent winced. He looked almost in pain. "You say that in here, but breaking the rules is in your nature. You can't change human nature, Jacob."

"No, sir."

Kent dropped Jacob's file in his top drawer and pulled another towards him. It was thin and smooth with no creases but both men knew that wouldn't last for long. "Anyway, to the case. Nasty business this morning."

"Yes, sir."

"It's already all over the news for some reason."

"A uniformed constable spoke with a journalist on the scene, sir. He's been reprimanded."

"Good, because I don't like the way this is being reported. They're saying the remains belonged to someone who was killed in some sort of depraved ritual. Nonsense like this attracts the press like bees to a honeypot and the next thing you know you've got them crawling all over the place. Not to mention all the weirdos."

"There's nothing to suggest any sort of ritual. It's press speculation."

Kent shifted forward, his steely eye fixed on him like a laser. "Well, if it turns out to be a bloody ritual we'll have the nation's press down here in a heartbeat. The scrutiny will be intense." He leant over the desk and once again steepled his fingers, a frown darkening his face. "You *are* up to this, aren't you?"

Jacob opened his jaw to reply, but Kent cut him off.

"Because if you're not then say so now. I know you requested a transfer home again, back to somewhere quieter and familiar, but this isn't Narnia, Jacob. We have our fair share of murders here too."

"As I've already said, sir – I'm fine."

"You'd better be." He peered over the top of his glasses at the papers on his desk. "I've read your initial summary and so far everything looks in order. I see Mia Francis and Ethan Spargo are already involved, thank God, but what's all this nonsense about a consultant?"

"Her name's Dr Sophie Anderson, sir. She was instrumental in the arrest and conviction of Alistair Keeley."

"I know that," he snapped, and started to read the briefing in front of him. "First Class Honours in Psychology from Imperial College in London and a Doctorate in Clinical Psychology from the University of Oxford. Has experience working in the United States with the FBI as a forensic psychologist and criminal profiler."

"Exactly, sir."

Kent flicked the folder shut and removed his browline glasses. "All very impressive."

"That's what I thought."

"But the answer's no."

Jacob wondered if he'd heard his senior officer correctly. "Sir?"

"There are many of us in the force who think this psychological profiling is a load of mumbo jumbo, but I'm not one of them. It's a clever and useful science, but she's simply not required on a case like this."

"She's offering to help free of charge, sir."

Kent glared at him. "The answer is still no. What sort of publicity would it attract if we hired a civilian consultant with her case experience to work with us within a day of the body being discovered? Think things through, man. The local papers will have a field day talking about serial killers."

"I hardly think…"

"So just get on with the case, Chief Inspector and don't let me down. The CC might think you're the source of heavenly goodness but I'm a much tougher nut to crack. I'll be watching you closely. One screw up and you're out. You can count on it."

Jacob felt a wave of anger rising. "Yes, sir."

"I'm presuming you've got Morgan and Mazurek on the team?"

"Yes, sir, and Inspector Morgan recommends Matt Holloway as well."

Kent gave an appreciative nod. "I want Laura Innes on it too. She's new to CID and she needs the experience."

"Sir."

"Good, and in the meantime, I've arranged a small press gathering for you to set the record straight and end these rumours."

"What, now?"

Kent glared at him. "Yes, now. They'll be outside the station in five minutes. I want you to create an atmosphere of cool, calm police work, understand?"

"Sir."

A knock on the door broke the tense silence.

"Come!"

A uniformed PC stuck her head around the door. "It's your next appointment, sir. Shall I send them in?"

"Yes, the Chief Inspector was just leaving, weren't you, Jacob?"

He calmly rose from his chair and gave Marcus Kent a relaxed smile. "I'll report when I have something, sir."

*

Day into night.

And light into dark. He stared out of the window and slowed his breathing. Once again after all these years, the bloated feeling of being sated rose grotesquely somewhere deep inside him. He watched the sun slowly sinking towards the ancient downs far to the west, its blood-red light bleeding into a low line of trees on the horizon. A moment of stillness, and then the dark plains consumed the dying sun like a hungry snake swallowing a bird's egg.

He liked the imagery, but not the insomnia. He'd been awake now for what seemed like forever and his eyes felt like hollow coalpits. It struck like a thief in the night, stealing his sanity and leaving him bereft of hope. These sleepless curses could sometimes stretch for days. Five was his record, and he never wanted to go there again.

The disorientation came first. Not knowing where he was. Then the paranoia and the hallucinations. The dancing shadows and the shifting walls. The cries of the dead outside his window. If only he could sleep, it would all go away again. How long had it been this time? He reckoned three nights, but it was so hard to count. This was definitely the third sunset since he had slept. Or was it the fourth? Best to stop thinking about it and keep to the business at hand. The grim business of twenty-six years ago, he thought with a shudder.

So they had found her at last.

He raised the rim of a whisky bottle to his dry lips and tipped the spirit back into his mouth. It burned its way inside him but soon delivered its gentle sedation, depressing his central nervous system and smoothing out the wrinkles of his life.

There would be more wrinkles now they had found her.

More problems to iron out.

He didn't like problems.

He watched the news now, studying the lead detective as he sauntered out of the station and approached the television cameras. There was an air of the hunter about him. Keen, sharp eyes and a brooding look he didn't like one bit. Something about the way he looked at the journalists and TV reporters made him think of a bird of prey. For so long now, the girl up at Four Sisters had been their little secret, but now this man, this Jacob, was going to tell the world about her. He was going to throw light on the darkest night of their lives and when he did – how the cockroaches would scuttle away in all directions.

Another hefty slug of the Scotch.

The fire crackled and spat.

Local news today, national tomorrow. That was how these things always worked, especially with a man like this DCI on the case. Soon the entire country would be following Jacob as he hunted down the killer. He listened carefully as he updated the world on the case. Words like *investigation* and *suspects* and *witnesses* stung his ears like acid. He described the new enquiry as a cold case.

He watched the salamander climbing up the glass tank beside the television set. Round and round it went, never losing the will to escape, but never getting out.

If only you knew just how cold, Chief Inspector.

This detective was tenacious and intelligent. Jacob the muckraker, raking up the kind of history that was better left in the past. If he wasn't careful, this could go in the wrong direction. The long, twisted arms of the law needed to choke the right neck and not his, and that meant acting fast.

CHAPTER 7

An hour after Kent's grilling and almost dark now, Jacob stood in the car park outside Salisbury General Hospital and wondered what was awaiting him inside. As much as he hated coming to these places, he gave serious thought to whether or not he preferred this or speaking to the press.

His thoughts were interrupted by the familiar sound of Anna Mazurek flicking her Zippo lighter to life and firing up another cigarette. The smell of burning tobacco drifted on the cold air and took him back to being a teenager, as it often did.

"You're not going to pack those in, are you?" he asked.

"If I need a smoke, guv, then it's before I go into this place." She jutted her chin at the rear door of the hospital. "One before going in, and one on the way out. That's my rule. Calms the nerves."

"Well, you'd better put it out because we're late."

"I'll warn you now," she said. "He thinks he's funny. He's not."

With the cigarette crushed under her shoe, Jacob led the way inside and they soon found themselves walking through sombre white-painted corridors on their way to the mortuary. After following the signs along another short corridor, they finally reached their destination. There was a small, round window in the door and now he peered through it at the neat line of stainless steel autopsy tables lined up in the middle of the room.

"The Chief Inspector, I presume," Spargo said, peering over his shoulder. "Not stalking me, I hope?"

Jacob nearly jumped out of his skin and turned to see the Home Office Pathologist looming over him in a pristine white laboratory coat and freshly starched shirt. For a moment, his eyes were drawn to the novelty Father Christmas bow tie.

"Bloody hell! You nearly gave me a heart attack."

Spargo looked at his watch and then over at Anna. "Not today thank you – we're far too busy. Hello Anna."

She returned the friendly nod. "Ethan."

Early fifties, average height and sharp, glinting eyes, Ethan Spargo was the principal police surgeon for the county, and Jacob noted with dismay that despite his age he seemed to have an unfortunate hair gel habit. His dark brown hair was naturally tight and curly, but the gel had some success in smoothing it back flat on his head. It was clear he still worked out too – his body was lean and when he moved it was with an athletic bounce usually found in people half his age.

"Who's been smoking?" he asked, sniffing the air in front of the two detectives.

Anna raised her hand. "Guilty as charged, Your Honour."

"Well, pack it in you stupid sod or you'll be in here

next."

They shared a grim laugh and then Spargo pushed through the double doors. They entered a world neither of them wanted to be in. Smooth squares of stainless steel covered one of the walls, concealing behind them dozens of mortuary drawers filled with corpses. Anna's heels clipped on the cold white tiles beneath their feet, and a harsh, surgical light glared down from a row of strip lights on the ceiling.

"Welcome to my world," Ethan said.

"Gee," said Anna. "*Thanks.*"

"And it's nice to see you, too," said the senior pathologist, pulling a disposable mortuary sheet away from the skeletal remains. "Happy Christmas."

Jacob winced and pulled his notepad out. "What can you tell us?"

"Here's the dirt," Spargo began, squinting down at his notes. "Caucasian and aged somewhere between the late teens and early twenties."

"Can't you be any more precise?" Jacob said. "That's a big range."

Spargo lifted his head from his notes and raised his eyebrows as he peered at Jacob over the rims of his tortoiseshell glasses. "No."

"Thanks."

"You're welcome. I can, however, be much more precise about her height. She was five foot seven inches tall in old money, or what some people insist on calling one hundred and seventy centimetres high."

Jacob and Anna exchanged an amused glance as Spargo grumbled about the metric system for a few moments. When he returned to his notes his shoulders visibly slumped.

"Her clothes were pretty comprehensively decomposed with nothing much left to speak of but some fibre analysis indicates a substantial jumper and a heavy woollen coat."

"So she was killed in the winter," Anna said.

"She's fast, Jacob," Spargo said. "But aren't you supposed to throw her a biscuit when she gets something right?"

Anna raised an eyebrow. "Bugger off, Ethan."

Jacob suppressed a smile. "We saw a head injury back in the woods. Any way to confirm if this was how she was killed?"

He gave a professional nod. "Yes, it was a violent, fatal head injury."

Anna furrowed her brow. "But isn't it possible she fell and banged her head?"

Spargo answered without hesitation. "In most cases, and for the purposes of your question, there are two main head injuries – the coup and contrecoup. A coup injury is found on the same side of the head that sustained the impact, while a contrecoup injury will be on the opposite side of the head."

"And you can use that to determine if she fell or she was struck?"

He frowned. "Not in this case. These injuries relate primarily to brain injury, and after so long in the ground, there is no brain, but all hope is not lost." He leaned forward over the dead body and calmly pointed to the back of the skull with the top of his pen. "Here, as you saw in the grave, we can see severe trauma on the right parietal bone and another smaller trauma to the left frontal bone and also some damage to the left zygomatic bone."

Jacob caught Anna's eye and knew they were thinking the same thing.

"In English, please Ethan," he said.

He sighed and gave them both a withering look. "She was struck from behind, most likely by a right-handed person holding a heavy object such as a rock and then she fell forward."

He stepped away from the body, set his pen down on the desk and acted out his words in slow motion. "Struck here, like this." He raised his right hand to the back of his skull and then acted as if he were falling over. "She went forward, almost certainly unconscious after a blow of this severity, and then sustained the damage to the front of her head when she hit the ground."

"And that killed her?"

"It should have, yes," Spargo said coolly.

"Should?"

"She was stabbed too."

Jacob's eyes flicked up. "Stabbed?"

Spargo gave a sad sigh and nodded his head. "I'm afraid

so, and with incredible violence. There are precisely seventeen knife marks on her ribcage and ten on her pelvis. The attack was frenzied. No doubt about it. She may have been choked or strangled too. Possibly in the act of holding her down while he stabbed her in the abdomen area after the impact on the skull."

"Jesus Christ in a hotdog bun," Anna said. "This shit never gets any easier to listen to."

"No," Spargo said. "It doesn't."

"It's murder, then?" Jacob asked.

Again, Spargo gave a brief, professional nod. "Absolutely."

Jacob rubbed his neck. "The CSI team mentioned some personal belongings in the grave."

"Yes, they're here." Spargo pulled an evidence bag from a stainless steel shelf behind him and placed it on the gurney beside the remains. "In addition to the shreds of clothing, there were several other objects in this bag which as you know was found in the grave alongside the remains, as well as the ring that the detectorist found. It's not a wedding band but a simple solitaire with a diamond in a bezel setting. Gold, no tarnish of course. Not worth a great deal but not cheap."

"Engagement ring?"

"Possibly."

"And the bag?"

"A badly deteriorated nylon bag with some personal belongings, and here's where it gets interesting, so do pay attention."

"I'm all ears," Anna said.

"First, a purse with some loose change. The notes are threadbare now, but the coins are metal and therefore relatively unharmed. Most date from the 1980s and the newest was minted in 1992 and after cleaning it up it has hardly any scratches on it so I'd say it was new when she got it."

"Getting closer to a date," Jacob said.

"Next, what's left of a 1980s Sony Walkman, inside which was a cassette of *The Immaculate Collection* by Madonna. Tape eroded but the labelling on the cassette is legible enough. I've checked on this and it was released in November 1990."

Anna caught Jacob's eye. "So she went into ground between November 1990 and December 1992."

Jacob frowned, "Unless these things were planted on her to provide a false date. Anything else?"

"Yes. A barely legible antique pewter-covered copy of Sir Walter Scott's *Letters on Demonology and Witchcraft.*"

Jacob and Anna exchanged an anxious glance. He had dismissed the young forester's talk of witches back in the woodland earlier today but this changed things. He understood why the press was already running with the angle, and now the numbers were starting to add up to something much uglier than he had previously thought.

"Say that again, please Ethan," he asked.

Spargo rolled his eyes. "Sir Walter Scott's *Letters on*

Demonology and Witchcraft."

"That's what I thought you said."

"At least there's nothing wrong with your hearing, Jacob."

Anna pointed at the blackened, rotten book. "What exactly is that about?"

"I'll go out on a limb here, Sergeant," Spargo said. "And say it's a book about demons and witches."

She sighed. "You're not funny, Ethan. You do know that?"

"Not exactly light reading for a young woman," Jacob said, quietly.

Spargo slid the book back into the bag. "Not exactly light reading for anyone."

Jacob blew out a long, frustrated sigh and drummed his fingers on the side of his trousers.

Anna noticed his discomfort. "Guv?"

"Witches again. First, we have old tales of four witches' graves in the woods and now we have a cold case turn up dead in the same place with a book about witches in her bag. I'm starting to get a very bad feeling about this case."

"Only just starting to?" she said. "I got that the minute I stepped into the woods."

"What about Henry's report?" Jacob asked.

"All done and dusted." Spargo handed him a file. "This is the full forensic osteology report here, alongside my own, although dental records are still outstanding. There's nothing in there to contradict anything I've just told you.

71

Henry's the best but he wasn't very pleased to get dragged away from his family today. Anyway, it's all in there – age, sex, medical condition at the time of death, previous traumas to the bones, even an ancestry report based on her DNA. Consider it a Christmas present from everyone here on the team."

Jacob gave him a wry look and took the report.

After a long pause, Anna broke the silence. "Who would do something like this? An angry lover?"

As he removed his nitrile gloves and squirted some liquid soap into his hands, Spargo weighed up her words. "Quite possibly. Love, after all, is a kind of warfare, Sergeant."

"It is in *my* life, anyway," she said with a short laugh.

Jacob buttoned up his peacoat. "Thanks for this," he said. "I'll read it back at the office."

CHAPTER 8

Jacob watched Chief Constable Bernard Portman as he made his way from another location on-site across to the HQ building, neck down to keep his face out of the wind. Leaning over the staircase rail, he followed his path inside the building and then up towards the canteen. He hesitated for a moment and then turned back to the vending machine. After buying a chocolate bar and a can of drink, he headed for the stairs. He was going back to his office and by the look of things trying to keep a low profile.

Jacob hurried along the corridor and beat the boss to it.

"Sir."

Portman looked surprised to see him and slipped the chocolate bar into his trousers pocket. "Ah, Jacob. Can I help you?"

"Have you got a second, sir?"

He made a big show of looking at his watch. "Not really, no. It might have slipped your mind but it's Boxing Day and my wife wasn't very happy when I told her I was coming in today in light of your discovery. I've been briefed by Chief Superintendent Kent and now I'm trying to get away."

"It's important."

A weary sigh. "Go on then."

"It's two things. We now think the victim was killed in

the early nineties, which was before my time here, but you were here then, weren't you?"

"I was – a humble superintendent."

"Do you remember anything relating to missing persons and Grovely Wood?"

He shook his head. "We have countless disappearances every year, of course, but Grovely never came up." Checking his watch, he said. "You said there were two things?"

"It's about Dr Sophie Anderson."

He sighed again. "I'm not going to countermand the Chief Superintendent's orders, Jacob. If he says this profiler is unnecessary to the case, then I'm happy to take his word for it. Marcus Kent is a good policeman with a solid record. You know that."

"If you'll just let me discuss it with you."

The Chief Constable pushed the magnetic key card into his lock and opened the door. "Knowing Marcus the way I do, I'm more than certain he would have not only given the matter a good deal of thought but also made his decision very clear to you."

"He has."

Portman turned to him. "You've always been a bloody obstinate bastard, Jacob. Why can't you ever accept an order?"

"With all due respect, sir, Chief Superintendent Kent is wrong on this. Dr Anderson has dealt with occult murders in the US. She has experience in this."

74

"Occult? I thought that was speculation."

"Maybe, but there was a book on witchcraft among the remains."

Portman thought it through. "No, it's too early to make a leap like that."

"But sir…"

"You're not hearing me. You know how much I respect you, but… You're a bloody skilled detective – maybe the best I've ever known but trying to go over the Chief Super's head like this just isn't on."

Jacob felt the frustration rising in him. Truth was, he had very little to lose. His career had been hanging by a thread even before his bereavement leave and lately, he had given the idea of walking away increasingly more thought. When it came down to it, he may as well just tell the old man what he thought, raw and unvarnished.

"She's very sharp, sir. I followed the Keeley case intensely and she was central in bringing him to justice. She risked her life to catch the bastard, and I really think she could help us if she just had access to the files."

"And we both know that's impossible, Jacob. No matter how many baubles have been hung all over her by some university, she remains a civilian. I'm with Marcus on this. At this time, I don't want her swimming around in the middle of what could easily become one of the county's worst murder cases."

"You have the authority to make her an official consultant, helping us with the case. Then it's all legal and above board."

Portman sensed his shoulders tensing up – exactly what his doctor had told him should be avoided at all costs. The tension crept into his neck and started to work its way around to his temples. All his worst headaches started this way, and he had a feeling this one was going to be very nasty.

"Do you have any idea how long it would take to run all the proper checks on her? The DBS alone takes days. The fact of the matter is that by coming to me in this way you have gone over the Chief Superintendent's head. You've done this in the hope I will overrule him and sign off on the paperwork to get this *Dr Anderson* on the team. Now, you have been told otherwise."

"I think this is a mistake."

"Noted, now if you'll excuse me, I'm going to eat something, get my briefcase and then go home. My son is visiting from Sydney," he said, stepping inside his office and slamming the door.

Jacob sighed.

That went well.

With a headache starting to form behind his eyes, he left Portman to his late lunch and padded off down the corridor. He had a team briefing to give and he was already late.

*

Jacob sipped his coffee, peered through the glass window in the internal door and took a deep breath. Maybe Amelia had been wrong and he just wasn't ready for all this again. Out in the field, he could work alone, have time to think, but giving briefings to a room full of police officers was different.

Any lapse in concentration would make them lose faith in him, stop respecting him as a leader, and he only had to close his eyes for a moment and visions of Jess rose in his mind, trapped in the blaze. If that happened under the scrutiny of a briefing room full of colleagues things could go wrong very quickly.

When he finally walked in, he held on to his foam coffee cup like a lifejacket, raising it to his lips to obscure his face for a moment as he took a long, slow sip. All of the men and women he had ordered to the briefing were here, waiting with notebooks, expectant and keen to learn from the seasoned Oxford detective they had all heard so much about.

He recognised most of the faces – Mazurek, Morgan, plus Detective Constables Matt Holloway and Laura Innes as well as a handful of the uniformed officers who had helped to establish the crime scene and search the woods. Setting the cup on the desk at the front of the Murder Room, he fought the demons down and cleared his throat.

"Settle down," he said.

The start of a murder enquiry was always tense, but today the atmosphere was made worse by the threadbare tinsel hanging here and there and the sorry excuse for a Christmas tree on top of one of the filing cabinets.

He waited until the incident room was quiet, which thanks to the look on his face was much quicker today than usual. "Okay, thanks for being here everyone," he said, knowing none of them had any choice whether they wanted to attend or not. A cold case murder investigation meant missing a briefing was not an option.

Now, he stepped closer to the small gathering and lowered his voice.

"Some of you know me from my early days here before I transferred to the Met, and the rest of you I'll get to know as we work together. For now, just know that from this second, I'm focused solely on catching the person responsible for the murder of this young woman. I'm sure you all know what I went through, but I want to reassure you that it's in the past and I've moved on."

A murmur of support rippled around the small room, and he decided to change the subject as fast as possible. It was important to keep the team focussed on the investigation and not on his personal life.

"And I know you all know each other, except for a new addition." His eyes fell on a young woman with red hair sitting at the back of the room. "I'd like to introduce DC Laura Innes. She's just joined us from uniform and has a strong interest in detective work. The gods upstairs have attached her to the team for the duration of this investigation to get her some experience and see how she likes the miserable life we all lead here."

Some laughter as everyone turned to her and waved hello.

"Now to business. I've already been briefed by the Home Office pathologist and read both his report and the report made by Dr Henry Vane, a leading forensic anthropologist and osteologist. You'll find copies of these reports in your briefing files, but I'll summarise them here so you get a broad idea of what's happening."

A shuffle of paperwork as everyone got ready to take notes. He turned to the whiteboard behind him and wrote OPERATION GROVELY in large black letters.

"First, the basics. Earlier this morning a metal detectorist found the skeletal remains of a young female out in Grovely Wood. For those who aren't familiar with the area, this woodland is located in the Cranborne Chase Area of Outstanding Natural Beauty in the south of the county, not far from Stonehenge. It's perched on a chalk ridge dividing the West Wiltshire Downs to the north and the Dorset Downs to the south. Her body was in a shallow grave just over a foot deep in the soil, but a beech tree had grown on top of it."

"Happy Christmas, indeed," said one of the uniforms at the back.

Jacob ignored the remark. "The area where the remains were found is a coppice called Four Sisters in the northern part of the wood."

"So where do we start?" Morgan asked.

"First the bad news. We don't have a lot to go on. As you will read in your reports, a Forestry Commission Ranger was able to ascertain the age of the tree, dating it to around twenty-five years old. This only told us that the remains were at least a quarter of a century old, placing the year of death around 1993. However, the CSI team search threw up several other clues, including some personal objects. Those, in conjunction with a post-mortem and a forensic osteology assessment of the skeletal decomposition, mean we can place the time of death between November 1990 and December 1992."

Matt Holloway waved his hand to get everyone's attention. "Was the tree planted deliberately to hide the body, sir?"

"That's something we need to look into. It's possible, but so is a simple accident of nature."

"If so, that's one lucky killer," Holloway said. "For a coincidence like that to help him so much."

"Like any good detective, I don't believe in coincidences," Jacob said. "But it's a big piece of woodland so not unreasonable to conclude the seed fell naturally."

"So are we thinking this is murder?" said Holloway.

"Yes," Jacob said flatly. "And for several reasons. First, the pathology report makes it very clear that the victim's skull was smashed from behind, and second, she was subjected to a frenzied knife attack. Third, we're talking about one of the largest woodland areas in southern Wiltshire, so it's an ideal place to bury a body and keep it concealed for a very long time, possibly forever. All of these things point to a violent murder and a deliberate intent to conceal the crime."

"What about local house-to-house enquiries?" Morgan asked.

Jacob looked at Anna. "Any news?"

"We're still doing them, but it's not an easy or quick job given the nature of the location. There are several small villages and hamlets around the woods, not to mention various isolated residences and farms. We got to work straight away and we're almost finished."

"Good work, when you're done give the witness statements to DC Holloway and he can go through them and report anything significant to me."

"Guv."

"What do we know about the bloke who found her?" Holloway asked.

"His name is Philip Croft. Thirty-five. He's a local man who works as a secondary school teacher in Salisbury. He'd been given a new metal detector for Christmas and he was out in the woods to play with his new toy. He wasn't alone, but part of a small group of detectorists who work the local area looking mostly for ancient relics."

The freshly-minted Detective Constable Innes said, "Like Roman coins and so on?"

"Exactly, only this time they found a lot more than they'd bargained for."

"Any of them ever search the area before?" Anna asked.

Jacob shook his head. "No, or so they say. One of Croft's group, a Stephen Cornwell, told me it's what they call a virgin site. According to him, it was the first time any of them had ever taken their detectors up to that specific location."

"Any of them suspects?" Innes asked.

"There are three in the group, and they've all given their details to us," Jacob said. "I'm sure you'll enjoy asking them some more questions so we can cross-reference their answers to what they told me and check for inconsistencies, but don't hold your breath. She was murdered nearly thirty years ago when Croft was nine so I'm not holding out too much hope in that direction."

"Thanks, sir!"

"So as of this time, house-to-house enquiries are still ongoing, we have CSI and pathology reports in and we know the approximate year she was murdered. Identifying the remains is critical to the investigation, and I'm putting Bill Morgan on that."

"Oh, happy days are here again," Morgan sang, raising a chortle. "The skies above are clear again."

"You can work with Holloway," Jacob added. "Get onto the UK Missing Persons Unit and start searching through all mispers who disappeared from November 1990 to December 1992. Keep it local to start with and work your way out through the postcodes in a radius. The pathology report in your hands says you're looking for a Caucasian female between the ages of 19 and 23."

"Got it, sir," Morgan said. "Leave it with me."

"Be aware that pathology is also running dental checks through the system and may come up with an ID that way sooner."

"Righto."

Jacob hesitated now, reluctant to bring the subject up but knew he had no choice. "The other lead we have is a possible connection to the occult."

The room's ambience changed in a hurry. Pens were set down and eyes fixed on the lonely DCI standing in front of the murder board.

"The occult?" Morgan said. "You *have* to be kidding?"

"I know what it sounds like, but it's a possibility we have to look into. For a start, the location where the remains were found might have some sort of occult or Wiccan significance."

Holloway shifted in his seat. "Wiccan? You mean like baskets?"

A subdued laugh. "Very good, Holloway," Morgan said.

"What's so special about the location, sir?" Innes asked.

"The ranger's assistant mentioned some sort of legend about the woods concerning the ghosts of witches. He also said sometimes people with an interest in that sort of thing go up there."

Someone at the back of the room gave a poor ghost impersonation and caused another uncomfortable laugh among the team.

"Surely we're not basing part of the investigation on a

stupid legend, sir?" Holloway said.

"Not at all," Jacob said flatly. "Among the personal belongings the CSI team found was an antique pewter-covered book. It has badly deteriorated but we've managed to identify the text." Another pause. "The book was Sir Walter Scott's *Letters on Demonology and Witchcraft*."

"Bloody hell," Holloway said.

Morgan shifted uncomfortably in his seat. "Well, exactly."

A ripple of laughs.

"Still sounds like a waste of time to me," Holloway said.

"Nevertheless," Jacob said, bringing the room back to order, "it's evidence found on the remains and, stacked up against the legend of the witches in the very same woods, we have to take it seriously." He turned to the young redhead at the back. "Innes, I want you to look into this legend and get me everything you can on it. That means more than just Wikipedia, all right?"

"Of course, sir."

"What a load of crap," Anna said.

"And thank you Sergeant Mazurek for volunteering to help Innes."

Anna groaned. "You're shitting me?"

"No."

"But it's just a load of mumbo jumbo."

"Let's hope so. Any other questions?"

"What about the consultant?" Anna asked.

A sea of confused faces turned to her.

Jacob explained. "While at the crime scene this morning, Sergeant Mazurek and I were approached by Dr Sophie Anderson. Some of you will recognise her name if you followed the Ferryman killings that occurred last year in London. Dr Anderson played a key role in bringing this so-called *Ferryman*, also known as Alistair Keeley, to justice. She lives locally and she heard about the discovery on the internet. She drove up and asked if she could help. It's that simple."

"And what do we think about that?" Morgan asked.

"It doesn't matter what we think about it," Jacob said. "All that matters to us is that Chief Superintendent Kent thinks it's a lousy idea and doesn't want her anywhere near the case."

"But she was very good when it came to catching Keeley," Innes said. "She lured Keeley out by pretending to be a victim and nearly died."

"Yes, she was very brave," Jacob said, his tone indicating the subject was closed. "But it's not happening, and if there are no more questions then this briefing is over. You all know what you're doing and it goes without saying that the Chief Super wants this brought to a close as fast as possible. We all know cold cases can be tough, but you're a good, solid team and you'll have all the resources you need. Let's get on with it."

As chair-legs scraped on the floor and people started talking, Innes turned to Jacob.

"What's the good news?" Innes asked.

"I'm sorry?"

Everyone had stopped and was now looking at him, waiting for an answer.

"When we walked in and you opened the briefing, you said, 'first the bad news'. I just wondered what the good news was?"

Jacob gave a wry smile. "I'm the SIO."

Everyone gave a final laugh as the team filed out of the room.

Everyone except Jacob.

CHAPTER 9

For the first time in as long as he could remember, Bill Morgan was more than happy to be in the office over the Christmas holidays. This time of year usually meant presents, drinks, and more turkey and sausages and puddings than he could shake a stick at, but this year was different.

When Leanne had walked out on him less than six months ago it felt like his world had collapsed. The house was dark and cold when he returned after work. Meals had gone from properly cooked dinners to cartons of takeaway food picked up on the way home. He didn't know how, but somehow the bed had doubled in size. He'd concealed how his crumpled marriage had made him feel from his friends and work colleagues with his usual efficiency but inside he still felt the rawness.

Over time he had grown into a new routine. His many years in the Royal Marines had taught him how to be self-sufficient and look after himself. After a short period of depression, also carefully hidden from the world, he'd had a sharp word in the mirror and picked himself up by his bootstraps. But the house was still too quiet and spending extra time at work was no longer the pain it had once been.

His thoughts were interrupted by the sound of DC Holloway sighing from the other side of the frosted acrylic desk divider.

"All good, Holloway?"

"I'm loving it, sir."

"Good stuff. I can't think of a better way to spend Boxing Day afternoon, can you?"

Holloway didn't sound convinced. "If you say so, sir."

Morgan stood up and watched the young man's eyes crawling over the data on his laptop screen.

"Not losing your mind are you?"

"No, sir. At least, I don't think so. This is the list of missing persons you asked me to research."

Morgan sipped his coffee and wandered around the double desk. "Let's have a gander then."

"Because of the long time frame, the original list was thousands of names, as you would expect, but when I restricted the search parameters to the local area as you suggested things got more manageable. These are all women in the Chief Inspector's cohort who went missing from the immediate local area during the specified time."

Morgan ran his eyes down the list, taking hold of the laptop and clicking on names. "Good work."

"Thank you, sir."

"What have we got here, I wonder?" Each name he clicked on opened another window, a file of a cold case unsolved for years. Another face looking back at him from beyond the grave, waiting for justice to be served. With thousands of missing women across the time frame, he had made the early decision to start with local cases and slowly move out, but the truth was she could have come from anywhere, not only in the country but the world.

He pointed a chunky, nicotine-stained finger at the screen. "I remember that one… and that one there. All those hours of searching, manhunts, in some cases dogs and everything, and yet look at this list. Dozens still missing and probably never to be found."

"They say a lot of them just don't want to be found."

"I don't know what to think, frankly," he said with a heavy sigh. "Everyone on that list is someone's loved one, Holloway. Someone's wife, girlfriend, mother, daughter or sister. Each one of those names is like the tip of an iceberg concealing masses of grief and loss under the surface."

"Yes, sir."

"All right then, email them over to me and I'll be a second pair of eyes. In the meantime, let's hope the bods over in pathology can make an ID through a dental record match because if not, we've got a bloody huge amount of work to do here."

*

As night covered the landscape, Sophie weaved her Audi through an endless maze of narrow country lanes and prayed her GPS satnav hadn't malfunctioned in the terrible weather. When she finally reached the Old Watermill, she breathed a sigh of relief and pulled off the main road. Slowing to a crawl, she drove along the gravel drive and braked, bringing the car to a stop just as another light snowfall began to drift out of the sky.

No, he wasn't expecting her. No, he probably didn't want to see her. Yes, it was worth another try.

Knocking on the door, she straightened herself up to her full height and quickly tidied her hair.

When it swung open, she was surprised to see Jacob in casual clothes. Jeans with a slight rip in one knee and a tea towel over his shoulder.

"Dr Anderson?"

He looked just about as surprised as she had visualised in her head. "Sorry to call like this, but I was wondering if you'd spoken with your boss about getting me on the case?"

"Wait, you drove out here to ask me that?"

"You weren't answering your phone."

"It's Boxing Day."

"Yes, but…"

He narrowed his eyes. "Didn't you say you lived in Salisbury?"

"That's right."

"That's a long drive," he said coolly. "Nearly half the county."

"I'm keen to be part of the investigation."

"Some would say stubborn."

"Others would say tenacious."

Jacob sighed. "You'd better come in."

After she had taken off her boots, she followed him

along a narrow exposed-brick corridor until they reached a sunken lounge. Messy, stacks of boxes and books and a viola with no strings on it was carelessly dumped on one of the chairs. Not one Christmas decoration. Through French windows, she saw the rear aspect of the property lit by the soft amber glow of LED lights. She glimpsed a river winding through a large meadow and what looked like a walled kitchen garden, albeit it in a certain amount of disrepair, now frozen and silent in the late December gloom.

Jacob stooped over to pull his jacket off a leather armchair and then he smashed his head on one of the exposed beams as he stood back up to his full height. He cursed loudly and rubbed his head. "Damn it," he said. "Not too many six-foot people around when this was built."

"No, I don't suppose there were."

"Please, take a seat here by the fire."

"Thank you. Hell of a place."

"Is it?"

"It looked big on Google Earth when I checked the address but not *this* big."

"It's too big," he said casually. "And away from the fire, it's cold too. I'd forgotten just how cold – especially the original part of the house, but then that's eight hundred years old."

"Still... it's a beautiful home."

Ignoring the compliment, he fixed his eyes on her, the

ghost of a smile on his face. "Have you eaten?"

*

He pulled a bottle of chilled white wine from the mostly empty fridge and uncorked it. Searching through the cupboards, he eventually admitted defeat and grabbed two china mugs from beside the kettle. "Sorry, not had a chance to sort the place out yet." He was embarrassed as he poured the Chablis out into the mugs and made a big show about giving himself the one with the chip on it. "Hope that's all right?"

"Please don't worry about it," she said.

"I've been renting in Oxford for the last year and I only moved in a few days ago. It's my parents' place but they live abroad now so they're letting me crash here while I get organised." He looked down at the floor for a second. "Pretty embarrassing at my age. Anyway, that's why it's, well… *minimal*."

"That's very generous of them."

"They have their flaws, too," he said with a smile.

"Don't we all?" she asked, taking a sip. "Tastes lovely by the way."

"Which is probably more than I can say about dinner."

She laughed. "Why, what are we having?"

He shrugged and pointed at the fridge. "Whatever's in there."

After another sip of the wine, he opened the fridge door

and rummaged around in search of something good to eat. It was still stocked from his short trip to the supermarket on Christmas Eve, and after a few moments of careful consideration, he decided to go Italian – pancetta, shallots, mushrooms, fresh basil and garlic.

"You go and relax while I get this going."

He opened a fresh pack of linguine and started boiling a pan of water on the hob. Peering through the door he saw Sophie settling into the big leather sofa, a mug of wine in hand. Anyone else would be relaxing but he could tell from the look on her face she was busy working on the case even now.

He left her to her thoughts as he cooked dinner and then brought the two full plates into the living room. Wandering over to the nook by the fire, he handed her one of the plates.

She sat forward and set her wine down while he put some more logs in the burner. "It's pretty cosy in here," she said.

"One of the nice things about an old place like this is the thickness of the walls. Keeps the stormy weather out where it should be and us nice and warm."

On cue, a gust of wind howled outside as he settled in an old leather wingback chair beside the fire.

"Look, before we go any further I have to tell you that I spoke with my boss and he turned down your proposal. It was a very firm no, as well."

She felt disappointed but was determined not to show

it. "Okay, well – thanks for asking."

"If it's any consolation, he's a difficult bastard and never gives an inch to anyone. With him, if it's a no, it's a no."

She laughed. "That makes me feel a bit better. Sort of."

"Good."

"I would have liked to help though."

"I knew you'd be disappointed. Tell me, what made you come back from America?"

She paused before answering. "I want to say it was the right choice for my career, but the truth is I missed my family and friends."

He lifted some of the pasta and bacon off the plate and took a sip of wine before speaking. "Fair enough. Did moving back damage your career?"

"Not really, well…"

Already he could see a change had come over her.

"Keeley?" he said, quietly.

"Yes," she ran her hands over her face. "Most of them you can forget, or at least put out of your mind, but not the Ferryman. He's as close to pure evil as I think you can come and still be human."

"As I said to you this morning out at the woods, I read about your involvement in that case with great interest. You worked with Dr Theo Miles, is that right?"

"Yes. He's probably the best forensic psychologist in the world and it was amazing to be able to work with him, but I was more of a researcher and not heavily involved."

"A second fiddle type of thing?"

She took some wine. "More like third chair trombone, really."

"But you were on the case – you risked your life."

"Yes, and it changed me. It left a scar on me."

"I understand. This job can do that. It *will* do that."

"What about you?" she asked quietly.

"What about me?"

"I saw on the news today that you were new to the area."

"That's not right," he said. "I was born here and brought up here. I even started my career in the police here. It's home, but I moved to London and then Oxford for my career, taking up a DCI post in Thames Valley CID."

"Why did you move back?"

He set down his fork. "I'd rather not talk about if it's all right with you."

"Of course," she said, finishing her meal. "I'm sorry."

"No need."

"No, I've come here uninvited and started asking personal questions. I should go."

Outside, the wind howled. "You're not going anywhere in this," he said, setting his plate down on the side table. "Besides, you've had two mugs of wine. There are seven bedrooms to choose from, but if it makes the choice any easier only two of them are made up – the spare room is in the old part of the house."

"Sounds perfect," she said.

*

Jacob woke from his sleep covered in sweat and his heart pounding in his chest like a jackhammer. He smelt smoke and when his eyes flicked open he saw it gathering on the ceiling of his bedroom. Hot, grey and noxious, it rolled and billowed into every corner and started to crawl down the walls.

Tumbling from his bed, he knew he had to get Sophie out of the house at all costs but the bedsheets were tangled around his ankles. He kicked and screamed but there was no escape. The smoke burned his throat and stung his eyes, and now he saw the tell-tale orange glow of flames as they crawled under the door and started to lick up the walls. Paint peeled and blistered and wallpaper ignited.

"Sophie!"

No reply.

"There's a fire! You have to get out and save yourself!"

He screamed when he woke, jerking upright in bed like a jack in the box with his heart going a mile a minute.

He wasn't in Oxford but the Old Watermill.

It had all been just another nightmare.

There was no smoke or fire.

There was no Jess.

*

A few miles away, the man turned the late-night news off and returned his gaze to the fire. Things were going from bad to worse and he felt control slipping away from him like smoke. They'd found the witchcraft book on the remains and were now considering the possibility of some kind of ritual murder more seriously.

He stared into the glowing embers of his fire and watched the flames licking over the sides of the blackened logs. Once part of a mighty tree, they would soon be no more than a heap of ash. What a little fire could do, he mused.

Lifting the Scotch bottle to his lips and gulping a good double shot, he lowered it back down between his legs and wiped his mouth with the back of his hand. His eyes danced over the bookshelf above the plasma screen as he took in all the titles. Aristotle, Herodotus, Sophocles and more modern offerings – Shakespeare, Hegel, Dostoyevsky, Camus. He liked intelligent books. He was an intelligent man, but the question on his mind was how intelligent was the new Detective Chief Inspector?

They would find out soon enough.

The fermented grain mash burned its way inside him. The tension in his shoulders and neck started to unwind and his breathing began to slow. It felt like the perfect sedation, and he greedily took another swig from the bottle. The spirit's malty vapour drifted up to his nostrils as he once again wiped the excess from his lips.

Yes, they would find out soon enough.

CHAPTER 10

Thursday, 27ᵗʰ December

Kieran Messenger had been watching the woods for an hour from the cab of his Hilux. Working alongside Adam Dawes as one of the ranger's two forester assistants, he knew them like the back of his hand. Now as dawn light began to break over the hills to the east, he watched the one they had once called Artio clambering back up the hill towards a track leading into the woodland.

He'd been unable to focus on anything since Adam had told him about what had happened yesterday, and since then he'd compulsively watched the TV news. Not much happened around here at the best of times, so when a skeleton was found buried in his woods he sat up and took notice.

Especially when it presented such an opportunity.

He'd wasted no time that morning, hurriedly getting dressed and leaving the house before sunrise so he didn't miss his chance. Artio came up here most days, and today was no exception. He had considered waiting a little longer to make his move, but the fear of leaving it too long worked on his mind and forced him to act.

You'll only get one shot at this.

This way he could give Lorna everything she wanted, everything he had ever promised. If he played his cards right things might change for the two of them. They might even be able to move out of that dump and find somewhere nice to bring up the baby. All he had to do was keep his nerve.

Artio reached the top of the track and stepped into the woods.

What was that being carried in the bag?

He fought to control his nerves. Leg pumping up and down in the footwell and fingers tapping on the steering wheel. He switched the radio off and a deathly silence filled the cab like poison. Alone with the thought of what he was about to do, he started a low, tuneless whistle as he tracked the progress of his prey deeper into the woods.

"Maybe this is a bad idea, Kip," he said to himself.

With Artio turning away from the main path and walking away from him, he gently clicked open the pickup door and swung his legs out into the cold air. Boots squashing down into the mud, he pushed the door into the frame but stopped short of clicking it shut.

No sense in announcing yourself.

He followed his victim along the path for several minutes, unheard and unseen. Artio had slipped out of sight for a moment, but when Kieran turned a corner on the track he saw his quarry once again, walking off the path and into a thicket. When he stepped on a branch and broke it loudly in two, Artio turned sharply and gasped.

"What the hell are you doing here, Kieran?"

*

Kieran Messenger paused before replying, nervously slicking the fingers on his right hand.

"I might ask the same of you."

"My quad broke down and I walked home to get my tools."

"What's in the bag?" Kieran asked.

"Are you following me?"

He took a step closer. "I just wondered if we could have a chat, *Artio*."

"No one's called me that for years, so don't."

"Why not? Don't you like it?"

"No."

"But you *did* use that name a long time ago, didn't you?"

"Well, I don't use it anymore."

"No." Kieran took another step closer.

Artio unzipped the bag. "I asked you what you're doing up here?"

"Nothing much – just out for a walk."

"At this time?"

Kieran took a deep breath and glanced over to the eastern part of the woods. "I was thinking about the body they found over in Four Sisters."

"Oh, yes?"

"Yes."

"What about it?"

"Horrible stuff, dying out in a place like this and then getting buried in an unmarked grave so no one ever knows where you are. No funeral. No loved ones visiting you, leaving flowers on your grave. Nasty."

"Yes, it is."

"And then I started thinking about all those rumours about that weird little club you were in."

"What are you talking about?"

"That secret society you were in. Don't you remember? It was a long time ago, I know, but…"

"I was never in any secret society, Kieran. I don't know what you're talking about and you're starting to bother me. I'm going to have to ask you to leave me alone."

"Or what? You'll call the police?" Kieran snorted dismissively. "I don't think so, mate. I'm the only one who'll be calling the Old Bill around here. And the thing is, I might have to mention your little Grove to the police and see what they make of it. It might be relevant to their enquiries, don't you think?"

Artio was silent.

"That copper running the show seems pretty sharp to me, too. Reminds me a bit of a bird of prey, the way he circles around and then gets down to business. A no-nonsense sort of bloke. I don't reckon he'd mess about if he got hold of a lead like that, do you?"

Artio swallowed. "So what do you want?"

"I was thinking we could come to some kind of

arrangement."

"You're blackmailing me?"

"Maybe a quarter mill."

"What?" Artio felt the rage rise from deep within. After everything they had been through and now this – this creature was trying to profit from it.

"Call it what you like, mate, but if you don't pay what I want, I *will* shop you to the law."

A red mist descended and there was nothing that could be done about it. Kieran saw it coming, but a moment too late to save his life. Artio had snatched the first thing that came to hand from the bag and was now bringing the weapon down on the top of Kieran's head. The sound of the skull shattering echoed in the frozen woods like a gunshot and then it was all over.

The fractured dawn light covered the murder scene like a cloak as the killer stared at the body with unconcealed horror, heart pounding like a fist and head dizzy with adrenaline. Then, to the west, a branch snapped and the killer's head jerked up to see a familiar face staring through the gloom. The man took off into the trees like a frightened hare and Artio whispered a pathetic curse.

Another loose end to tie up.

*

The HQ briefing room was packed with police officers, each of them staring at Jacob and waiting for him to lead them into the next phase of the investigation. He clapped his hands and brought everyone to attention. "All right settle down. We've had a big break in the case today and we need to get on."

He turned and drew a large black circle around the photo of a young woman on the white murder board behind him. "Emma Russell, a student from a village just outside of Salisbury. I'm sorry to report it was Emma's remains that were found in the wood yesterday morning."

"I remember that case," Morgan said. "I was a PC, still in uniform. They searched all over Salisbury and Oxford for her but she was never found. In the end, they concluded she'd gone to Italy."

"It was a famous case but well before my time," Jacob said. "She grew up in the area and did very well in school. Her father is Ian Russell, one of the top men in a major investment bank in London at the time and now retired, and her mother is Chiara Russell, originally from Tuscany. Emma went to Oxford to study medicine. Twenty-three years of age, she was in her final year of the clinical stage of her medical degree."

"Clinical stage, sir?" Holloway asked.

"I don't know about other institutions, but in Oxford, a medicine degree is divided into two distinct sections," Jacob replied. "They have a period of pre-clinical study for three years in the city and then there are three years clinical study, usually at a hospital and not necessarily in Oxford."

Holloway gave an appreciative nod. "How do you know

all this?"

Jacob paused a beat. Some in here already knew, others might not. "My fiancée was a doctor, and she studied at Oxford before moving to the Royal London Hospital."

A respectful hush descended over the room, and only one person could break it.

"This is a big lead for us," Jacob continued. "And we all have Morgan and Holloway to thank for it. They didn't stop working last night until they got what they were looking for. I'll let Bill explain."

Morgan stepped up. "In the end, we got her thanks to a DNA match, but the ID has now also been confirmed by dental records."

"DNA, sir? Innes asked. "Criminal record?"

Morgan shook his head. "Not at all. She wasn't on a police database, naturally, but we were able to use the names that Holloway and I tracked down on the missing persons' register last night to find the name of a medical student who had gone missing in 1992."

"Nice work," Anna said.

Morgan smiled. "She was almost finished with her studies and had moved back home at the time of her death, but during her degree, she'd been part of what was at the time cutting-edge DNA research, and luckily for us, there was some of her DNA on record at the John Radcliffe hospital. We had a sample sent over to our pathology bods and they confirmed that the two records were a perfect match."

Jacob took over. "She was reported missing in October 1992 by her parents and also some of her friends at university and the actual university authority itself. Last seen leaving a pub called the Fox & Hounds in Salisbury at eight in the evening, alone. Thames Valley Police and Wiltshire Police looked into it at the time in a joint operation but never had any luck in tracing her. She was officially registered as a missing person due to a lack of evidence pointing to murder."

He turned to Morgan. "I want you to order the case files for the original investigation from archives and start to go through them with Holloway. If you can remember the original case you're the best person to go through those files."

"No problem, boss."

He looked over to Anna and DC Innes who were both sitting suspiciously close to the radiator running below the long window at the side of the room.

"Now, how's the witch-hunting getting on?"

"I think it's over, sir," Anna said. "As in I'm not sure we can dig any deeper if you'll excuse the pun."

"Go on."

Anna stepped up. "The basic legend concerns some young women called the Handsel sisters."

"The Handsel sisters?"

"A very sad story," she began. "There were four of them, and they moved from Denmark to Wiltshire nearly three hundred years ago back in 1737. They settled in the

Wilton area right next door to Grovely Wood, but unfortunately for them, their arrival in the village coincided with the deaths of 137 people from smallpox."

"Very unfortunate," Morgan said. "What happened next?"

"So many deaths at one time in such a small village was serious business, and the villagers concluded that the sisters were witches. They accused the women of being in league with the devil and sentenced them to death."

"My God."

"Exactly. A few days later they dragged them into Grovely Wood, beat them to death and buried them out in the woods. Local legend says they were each buried beneath a beech tree some distance from one another so they couldn't conspire with each other after death and plot revenge on the living."

"And has anyone ever found these graves?" Holloway asked.

"Some claim to know which trees mark the graves," Innes said. "They're very large beech trees and obviously very old, but as far as I know no one's ever dug down beneath them."

"The point is," Anna said. "Emma Russell's body was also found beneath a beech tree in the same place – Four Sisters coppice."

"But that doesn't necessarily indicate someone planted one on her grave," Morgan said quietly. "There are thousands of beeches in Grovely and that means millions of seeds floating around every year. Could just be a coincidence."

Jacob sighed. "I don't believe in coincidences. Whoever killed that woman planted a beech tree over her grave for some other reason than merely to hide the body, which was probably the same reason the villagers put the bodies of the women they killed under beech trees."

Morgan frowned. "Still doesn't mean there was any witchcraft involved. As you say, the tree could have simply been a practical measure to cover the body."

Jacob shook his head. "I think there's more to it, Bill. Anyone smart enough to plant a beech tree on a grave knows it's not going to provide any real cover for years, decades even. There must have been some other significance to planting the tree on her grave."

"You mean a load of bloody voodoo nonsense?" Morgan said.

"That's what we've got to find out."

"We found a lot of stories of the wood being haunted," Anna continued. "Not just the Handsel sisters but also another story of a poacher or possibly a woodsman who was caught stealing and hanged. A lot of people come to the wood to ghost-hunt or talk with the dead. I know it's ridiculous but there it is."

"I don't know," Morgan said. "I've been in those woods at night and they're pretty spooky."

Anna raised a disbelieving eyebrow and fixed her gaze on the Welshman. "You're not being serious?"

"But three hundred years ago?" Morgan said, changing the subject. "How can there be a link to the death of this girl thirty years ago? Please tell me we're not talking about some satanic nutjobs."

"No, I don't think so," Anna said. "This has nothing to do with that."

"Oh, go on then," Morgan said. "Tell me why."

"According to the research we did last night, none of this points to what we know as satanism at all. What we're seeing here predates all of that by thousands of years. This is far more ancient and far darker than anything to do with modern ideas of heaven and hell, God or Satan. This stuff is right out of the ancient world."

"But you were talking about witches," Holloway said. "Necromancy... I thought these were relatively new ideas. Salem witch trials and so on."

Anna shook her head. "Not according to what I was reading last night. Witchcraft, vampires, you name it – all of these things go right back to the very beginning of human civilisation. I found references to these things from ancient Egypt and even Mesopotamia, and certainly, they are well documented in texts and poems from the Classical world – both ancient Greece and Rome."

"Bloody stuff gives me the creeps," Morgan said.

Anna gave him a look of vaguely patronising sympathy. "It was just how the ancients tried to explain the world. The fact we associate witches with the last few hundred years is simply because our cultural history focuses on those eras, and also the rise of popular publishing during that time as well."

"Cultural history?" Morgan said. "You sound like one of those nimrods up at the uni."

"It's amazing what being able to read can achieve, sir. You should give it a try."

Her famous wink made Morgan laugh, and then she continued. "The truth is, people from every country in the world have told stories about witches for thousands and thousands of years."

"Could this be a coincidence though?" he said. "Three hundred years ago they kill these women for being witches and now a body turns up in the same woods, under another bloody beech tree!"

Jacob was reluctant to accept the link. "We're way too early to be drawing parallels, Bill."

The Welshman shrugged. "If you say so, boss. Just putting it out there."

Jacob turned to Innes. "You said you looked into the book we found with the remains?"

She nodded. "Yes, sir. I did some basic research and found there's not much to it. The book was written by Sir Walter Scott who was a Scottish baronet born in 1771, and he's most famous for his historical novels, even though he was also a judge."

"Tell me more about this book though."

"He wrote it in 1830, sir. Its central premise is that society even at that time still believed heavily in things like ghosts and devil worship and witches."

"Go on."

"From what I can gather from the internet, the book is considered to be critical reading for people with an interest in the darker side of life."

"You mean the occult?" Morgan said.

"Not just that, sir. It provides a lot of historical information about the witch trials in Europe. I'm still reading it and it's pretty unsettling stuff, particularly the bits about the witch hunts and trials and also sections on torture. Scott himself was very sceptical about it all and considered most of it to be nothing but ridiculous, silly superstition."

Jacob sighed. "And it was in a twenty-three-year-old medical student's bag on the night she died in a wood haunted by witches."

"So what next?" Morgan asked.

"Next, Sergeant Mazurek and I have a very unpleasant house call to make."

CHAPTER 11

"When she went missing our world ended." Jacob listened as Chiara Russell struggled with the words, even after so many years. When they had knocked on the heavy oak door of their large country house, mid-morning, she had appeared with a tumbler of vodka in her hand, and a vacant stare over their shoulders into the snowy garden beyond.

She knows he had thought. *She knows why we're here.*

"Tell me, Mr Jacob. Are you absolutely certain?"

He gave a short, businesslike nod. "I'm sorry, but yes. When your daughter was at Oxford studying for her medical degree she took part in a DNA trial."

"That's right," she said, interrupting him, trying to delay the hammer blow. "It was a very cutting-edge subject during the late eighties-early nineties and Emma was very proud to be part of it."

"We isolated various names on our missing persons' database and went through them, researching their backgrounds very carefully one by one until we reached Emma's. When we saw the Oxford connection we contacted the university and they surprised us by telling us they had her DNA on file as part of the research she had been doing."

He paused a beat, reluctant to deliver the final cut.

Aware of a ticking carriage clock somewhere behind, and Chiara's eyes burning into him, he continued. "Unfortunately, that sample was a perfect match for the DNA sample our pathologist extracted from the remains found in Grovely Wood yesterday morning. I'm very sorry for your loss."

Chiara Russell said nothing but raised the vodka glass to her lips and downed a good inch of the spirit without flinching. The ease with which it went down, the burst veins on her cheeks sloppily covered by blush and cheek foundation, the slight slurring of her words all painted a terrible picture of what this crime had done to her life.

"I see," she said at last.

He watched her composure slip. She had steeled herself for this moment every day for the last twenty-six years but not even the expectation of the darkest news, long-held in her heart, could hold back the reaction Jacob now saw as she began to sob violently.

Anna moved to her and put an arm around her shoulder. "I'm very sorry, Mrs Russell. You've suffered a terrible loss."

"Twice," she said sharply, wriggling free of Anna's arm. "Back then and again today."

She rose from the chair and tottered over to the drinks' cabinet. It had been decorated with tinsel and nestling in between some bottles was a plastic dancing Santa, mercifully switched off. "Are you certain you won't join me?"

Jacob raised his hand. "Not for me, thanks."

"Nor me, but thank you," Anna said respectfully.

She slopped another good inch into the cut-glass tumbler and returned to her seat. "We have an en tout cas tennis court at the rear," she said out of nowhere. "Darling Emma used to play on it all through the summer months."

The words hung in the air for a few seconds until the sound of the ticking clock returned to break the tense silence.

"I'm sorry," Jacob said, "but I'm going to need to ask you some questions."

"Ask away," she slurred, "but I fail to see what I can add after so many years. I was forty-one when she went missing. I'm sixty-seven now. It was all so long ago." Her words drifted away into the cosy lights of the Christmas tree towering nearly twenty feet beside the fire. It seemed the Russells' considerable wealth had not taken the slightest edge off their grief.

"Did your daughter have an interest in the occult at all?"

She turned to him, suddenly lucid. "In the occult? Certainly not."

"You're certain?"

"She was a clever girl, a kind girl with a promising career ahead of her. She wouldn't waste time on drivel like that."

As Chiara buried her face into the tumbler, Jacob and Anna exchanged a glance.

"Is it possible she had an interest in it but simply kept it from you?" he asked.

113

"It's possible," she said sadly. "She was in her twenties when she went missing. I didn't keep her on a leash. She was in her final year at university and getting ready to start her career in hospitals."

"Did she have close friends at university?" Anna asked.

"A few, I suppose," she said.

"Can you remember their names?"

"It was twenty-six years ago."

"That's all right," Jacob said. "We can contact the university and see if anyone there remembers."

"What about more locally?" Anna asked. "Who were her closest friends growing up?"

She sighed. "Her last group of friends when she was a teenager?"

"That's a start."

"I gave all this information to the police when she went missing."

"We have the file," Jacob said. "I read it very carefully and saw the names of her friends on the list you provided. They all had alibis for the night she went missing, but it's worth asking again because sometimes people forget things or make mistakes." His eyes flicked to the vodka glass. "You were under a lot of stress when you gave that list."

"I can think of no new names to give you," she said quietly. "I expect I've forgotten most of the ones I gave the first time around. It was a long time ago and it's been a hard twenty-six years."

"Just give it some thought," Jacob said. "I know it's

painful having to revisit such a terrible time in your life, but anything new you can give us might help us catch who was responsible for this crime. You would be surprised how even the tiniest detail can lead to an arrest."

"Leave it with me," she said. "I can't promise anything, but if I…"

Her response was cut short by the sound of a car swerving into the sweeping gravel drive. Jacob peered out of the drawing-room window to see the impressive view of the mill race as it snaked up to an old windmill by the front gate. Now, a shiny black Jaguar was screeching to a halt beside the house.

He watched a solid, angry man climbing out of the car and slam the door shut hard behind him. He stormed into the house and moments later entered the green oak frame drawing room where they had been talking. Throwing his car keys down on an antique card table beneath one of the windows, he padded over to the police.

Jacob rose to his feet to greet the man. "I'm Detective Chief Inspector…"

"I know who you are and why you're here," he snapped.

"I'm sorry?"

"It's Emma, isn't it?"

"I'm afraid so, Mr Russell. Yesterday morning the remains of a body were found not far from here in Grovely Wood, and…"

"I'm aware of that. I read the news."

Jacob felt the man's pain radiating across the room. "It's

my duty to inform you that after a successful DNA match we have been able to identify the remains. I'm very sorry to tell you that they belong to your daughter, Emma Russell."

The man's face was steel. Tight jaw, fixed, sharp eyes. "I see," he said, and then without hesitation, "What happened to my little girl, Chief Inspector?"

"We believe she was murdered, Mr Russell. I'm sorry."

"Murdered?" he said coldly.

"Yes."

"So what's the game plan?" he barked. "I want this moved along fast. I know the Chief Constable. If things don't start happening then you'll hear about it from him, not me."

"We've only just opened the investigation, sir," Jacob said. "And we take every murder case very seriously – including cold cases."

"You'd bloody well better," he said, raising his voice to a shout and making his wife jump in her chair.

"Historical cases are taken every bit as seriously as present ones, sir," Jacob replied patiently. "But, I do have to warn you that historical cases present a special challenge due to the lack of trace evidence and the difficulty of finding reliable witnesses, among other things."

Ian Russell waved a shaking finger in his face. "No excuses, Jacob. I want Emma's killer caught and I want him caught now."

"We're going as fast as we can, sir. I assure you."

116

"You'd better be quick, man," he said, face reddening. "Because if I catch the bastard before you do I will kill him where he stands and bugger the consequences."

Jacob raised his palms. "Please, Mr Russell, I urge you to be careful what you say. I am a police officer and I must take these threats seriously."

Russell wasn't backing down an inch. "It's no threat, Chief Inspector. It's a promise, and I'll happily swing for the bastard."

*

Ian Russell watched Jacob as he walked across the gravel drive and swung open the door of a vintage car that had seen better days. Turning to his wife, he said, "Go and put some coffee on and try and sober up, for God's sake."

Without putting up an argument, Chiara Russell heaved herself out of her chair and swayed out of the room on her way down to the kitchen at the rear of the house.

When she was safely out of earshot he snatched up his phone, hit the speed dial and listened to the ring tone. Outside, the Chief Inspector had fired up the old car and was buckling up his seatbelt.

"Mr Russell," the low voice said. "I wasn't expecting you to call me so soon."

"We need to talk," Russell said. Outside, Jacob was turning his car in the circular driveway and heading towards the double electronic gates. "And in a hurry."

117

"You just spoke to Jacob?"

"Yes."

"Name the time and place and I'll be there."

"I do hope you're not going to let me down."

"Just make sure you bring the money."

*

"That was not good," Anna said.

"It never is." Jacob steered the Alvis out of the property's driveway and pulled onto the narrow lane. "And it never gets any easier. It's the bit I hate the most about this job."

"You think she'll remember any of the conversation we just had with her by morning, guv?"

He gave her a withering glance and returned his eyes to the road. "It's understandable though. If you think about what she's been through, I mean. Her life pretty much ended a quarter of a century ago when she was forty-one."

"She wasn't too happy about the occult stuff."

"No, but who would be?"

"And the husband's going to be trouble too. Especially if he knows the CC."

"He's just been confronted with the news he's been dreading for twenty-six years. Listen, I want you to get hold of Emma's uni friends and speak with them again. They were all alibied, but you never know your luck."

"Will do, and another...look out guv!"

Jacob saw it now. A woman had emerged from the woods at the side of the road and was desperately trying to flag them down with one hand, while her other was holding a brown dog on a leather lead.

He changed down into a lower gear, using engine braking to reduce the risk of skidding on black ice and steered the old car over to the side of the road. Pulling up, he switched off the engine and hit the hazard lights.

Climbing out of the car, they both ran over to her.

"I'm a police officer," Jacob said. "Just relax and tell me what your name is."

"I'm Jennifer," she said. "Jennifer Redfern."

"All right, Jennifer, tell me what's happened."

She strained for air, the sharp gasps punctuating her words like steel rivets as she spoke. "I found him just now on the other side of the woods."

He knew from long experience that the young woman was on the verge of a panic attack and softened his voice as he steered her over to his car and made his reply. "It's okay, just take it easy and have a seat." Guiding her down into the passenger seat, he said, "Now, you said you found someone?"

Her face contorted once again, her eyes reddening and welling up with tears. "Yes, Kieran."

"Someone you know?"

She wiped the tears away and gave a hurried nod. "I was out jogging in the woods with Louie when I saw him."

The dog flicked his head up when he heard his name.

"What do you mean saw him?" Jacob asked. "You saw him out walking in the woods?"

She shook her head and tried to steady her trembling hands. When she spoke, her voice was fragile like glass and no more than a ghostly whisper. "No, he was *dead*."

CHAPTER 12

J acob and Anna exchanged a glance and he saw that the seasoned detective sergeant looked almost as shocked as Jennifer Redfern. It was common enough for people to react in this way when they heard news like this but he was the senior officer and had to control the situation fast.

"Are you sure of this?" he asked.

No reply.

He crouched down so they were face to face. "Jennifer, I need you to answer me. Are you certain Kieran was dead?"

"I think so... I don't know! I'm not a doctor or anything and I didn't get close. It was something about the way his body was just lying there in all the snow and leaves."

"Where was this, Jennifer?" he asked, his voice still low and soft. "As specific as you can, please."

"I was only speaking to him a few days ago. We met in the supermarket. He said life was going all right for once."

Fixing his eyes on the shocked woman, he said, "I need the location where you saw him, Jennifer."

"On the north ridge, just off the main track where I jog. I can take you there easily enough." Her voice started to trail away. "It's not that far from here..."

His mind raced to put things in order. "All right, how old is Kieran and what's his surname?"

"Forty," she sobbed. "Kieran Messenger."

He turned to Anna. "Get onto HQ and get things moving."

"Guv."

Anna reached for her mobile and walked around the back of the car. "This is DS Mazurek out near the Russell house. We've had a report of another body on the north ridge of the woods. Name is Kieran Messenger, forty years old. Send an ambulance up here right away and get hold of CSI as fast as you like."

When she cut the call she caught Jacob's eye. He'd been comforting the young woman but it was clear he had made the same assessment that she had made. The chances of Kieran Messenger simply being unconscious seemed very slim indeed but they had to give him every chance.

She slipped the phone back into her pocket and crouched down beside them at the side of the car.

"Are you sure you can remember where you saw him?"

"Yes."

The dog barked, keen to get on with the walk.

"Then you need to take us there right away," Jacob said. "It's very cold and if he's had an accident and he's still alive it won't be long before hypothermia sets in. If he's unconscious he could be in real trouble."

*

With the witness in the back seat, Jacob pulled the car off

the B-road and braked to take a sharp turn which lead to a narrow lane twisting further north towards the woods. They followed the lane for a few hundred yards until they reached a dead end and parked on the side of the old Roman Road cutting the woods in two.

Climbing out of the car, he took a deep breath of the fresh air and scanned the dense trees surrounding them. Craning his head inside the cab, he spoke quietly to the sobbing woman in the back seat. "Where am I going, Jennifer?"

"He's just over there," she said. "In between those two big trees, just off the path."

"Thanks."

He caught Anna's eye. "Keep an eye on her while I check it out, and join me when the backup arrives."

She checked her watch. "They shouldn't be too long now."

He stepped through the dead bracken and made his way deeper into the tangled woodland. Rounding a thicket of vines dangling down from the lower limbs of an oak tree, he stopped dead in his tracks when he saw the corpse of a middle-aged man.

Kieran Messenger's dead body lay cold and sightless in a small clearing not far from one of the many footpaths running through the western end of Grovely Wood. Back of the skull caved in and he had already lost an eye to the crows. He had to refrain from throwing up as he took the hideous scene in for the first time. After breaking the news of a murdered person to their loved ones, this was the worst part of the job. He slid a mint into his mouth to block some of the smell of the bloody rotting corpse and started to think about what he was seeing.

This area of the woods was less remote than where they had found Emma Russell. It was slightly more elevated and offered a beautiful view across snowy fields to Great Ridge Wood to the west. Popular with ramblers, dog walkers and joggers, today the place was made still and silent by winter's frozen hand.

Jacob's eyes crawled back over the frozen ground to the corpse. He was no medical expert but he'd seen enough corpses in his time to know this man had been dead for several hours. Evidence of autolysis was clear enough and the blood around his headwound was totally dry and smooth in the earth, like black acrylic.

What had possessed him to come all the way out here so early in the morning? The clearing might suggest a meeting place, but exactly who met before dawn on the coldest December in living memory, and why, was still an unanswered question.

He made a quick search of the scene but aside from what he presumed was the man's pickup truck he found nothing. Sitting on a fallen tree trunk he stared at the dead body, his mind lost in thought as the minutes ticked by. This was no coincidence, he considered grimly. Somehow this was tied in to the murder of Emma Russell.

Alone with the dead for over half an hour, every

thought he had brought him back to Four Sisters and the witches and yet this was happening now, not hundreds of years ago.

He heard rustling behind and turned to see Anna Mazurek walking through the woods. She was walking beside DC Laura Innes and they were in deep conversation. When they reached the hollow and took in the corpse, Innes gasped and turned away.

"Bloody hell," Anna said.

"My thoughts exactly," Jacob said. "How's Jennifer Redfern?"

"Still shell-shocked and seeing *that* I'm not bloody surprised."

"Who's with her?"

"Two PCs, a third is putting some tape on any paths leading here."

"Good. CSI?"

"Mia Francis is en route. ETA in around twenty minutes."

"All right."

"This is not a good development, guv." When Anna spoke, her breath condensed in the air in front of her. She pushed up her scarf to cover her mouth and nose from the cold. "I'm starting to think Inspector Morgan is right and that these woods are cursed."

"There's no curse," Jacob said, quietly. "Not on the woods, anyway."

"If you say so."

"I do say so, he said shortly. "I want you to make a quick search of the area, Anna. I've already looked but a second pair of eyes can only help. Go out in a short radius and see if anything catches your eye. Emma might have died here a quarter of a century ago but this murder was today. The killer might have got sloppy."

"Got it."

She walked off, and Innes took a step back, shaking her head as she went. "I didn't realize there would be so much blood."

Jacob turned and fixed his eyes on her. "You've not seen a violent murder before?"

"No, sir. Not like this."

He nodded once. "It looks like it was a frenzied attack, for sure, but I've seen worse," he said, darkly. "Much worse."

*

Ten minutes later, they heard Anna as she made her way back to them from the other side of the clearing, crunching frozen leaves and snapping fallen branches. "Nothing obvious that I can see," she said, breath billowing out from her mouth and nose. "Fresh snow around in most places, and as we didn't have any snowfall last night it's safe to say our killer used this path."

She indicated the footpath behind them. Also used as a bridle path as well as by people on foot, it was a chewed-up mess of squashed frozen mud, footprints and hoof marks, as well as at least two sets of bicycle tracks. Trying to find a set of the killer's prints in this mess would be almost impossible and they all knew it.

Jacob shoved his hands in his pockets. "Unfortunately, it looks like the tradition of the great British Boxing Day walk is faithfully observed around these parts."

"You can say that again," Anna said. "Looks like the Red Army marched through here."

"Greatly reducing the chances of finding the killer's footprints," he said. "Which I know we will all agree is not very bloody helpful."

Their conversation was broken up by the arrival of Mia Francis and her CSI team.

"Good morning, Chief Inspector," she said with mock cheer. "If this is your idea of some sort of depraved Christmas gift, I urge you to rethink your strategy."

"Thanks for getting here so fast, Mia, but I'm not sure this place is going to give much up."

"I'll be the judge of that," she said. "You'd be amazed what turns up when you look closely enough. It's Locard's Exchange Principle."

"Locard's what?" he asked.

"Edmond Locard, Chief Inspector. He was a pioneer of forensic science and the inspiration for the Sherlock Holmes character. His guiding principle was that the perpetrator of a crime will always bring something to the crime scene and leave with something from the crime scene. Both things can be useful when building a case based on forensic evidence."

He opened his mouth to respond, but she cut him off. "Now, do be a dear and let the dog see the rabbit, yes?"

Suitably admonished, he moved aside and let her team approach the body. Within moments they were setting up a professional crime scene and getting down to work. He watched the efficient operation with respect, but couldn't stop his eyes from wandering over to the gruesome remains of yet another victim. Morgan was wrong about the curse, but with the discovery of this second body in the same woods he was now convinced that something evil was at work in this place.

He walked up the path back to his car and greeted the uniformed constables who were keeping a close eye on Jennifer Redfern. She was still sitting in the back of his car with her dog, but someone had managed to supply her with a cup of steaming tea.

She looked up at him with expectant eyes. "Was I right about him being dead?"

"I'm afraid so, yes. I know he was a friend of yours and I'm very sorry for your loss."

"It wasn't an accident, was it?"

"I haven't been briefed by my CSI team yet, but to my eye, no, it's not looking like an accident."

"Oh my God. I jog through here every day."

"Again, I'm sorry."

Jacob pulled himself out of the car and wandered over

to one of the uniformed constables. "Have you taken all of her details?"

"Yes, sir."

"Good, then make sure she gets home safely."

"Yes, sir."

When he returned to the scene of the crime and joined Anna and Innes, Mia straightened up to her full height and walked over to them.

"So what's the verdict?" Jacob asked.

"He's dead, I'm afraid."

Jacob rolled his eyes. "We'd worked that much out all by ourselves, Mia."

"Still, you never can tell with policemen."

"Thanks."

"The end was delivered courtesy of a very hefty cylindrical object."

Anna frowned. "The original blunt object."

"I'm afraid so."

"Cylindrical?" Jacob asked.

"Metal tubing, most likely."

"Some sort of walking stick?" Anna asked. "Adjustable canes made of aluminium are often used by older people."

"Any prints?"

"Not many. There are some bootprints but they're very poor samples because of all the mud and snow, and we've found nothing in the way of any obvious fibres or anything like that."

"Any idea when this might have happened?"

She shook her head. "Post-mortem will confirm but I'd say early this morning between seven and eight."

Anna sighed. "Another murder."

"Looks that way," Mia said. "No rest for the wicked, isn't that what they say? Oh, and you might like to know we found traces of fentanyl in his pickup truck and there's a set of quad tracks about a hundred meters to the west behind that thick mat of ivy over there."

"Fentanyl?" Jacob said, making a note in his pad. "That switches things up a bit."

"Thought it might."

"And the quad tracks?"

"Yes, over there. It looks like two sets but one has completely driven over the top of the other, so either we're talking about two quads or one quad that has driven back on itself. Either way, you're only getting one set of tracks."

"I didn't check that far out."

"Me neither," Anna said.

Mia rolled her eyes. "Well, they're there, and they're quite fresh too. I'd say within the last twenty-four hours."

"Get casts of them right away."

Mia said, "There's a lot of bike tracks and quad tracks in this part of the world, Jacob."

"I'm only interested in the ones that are close to this body."

"I've already ordered it," she said with a smile and wink.

"Good," he said, turning to Anna. "And I want a Mobile Major Incident Unit up here in a hurry," he said.

"We have cold case remains and now a fresh murder not half a mile from each other in the same woodland. Emma's murderer could be dead for all we know, but whoever killed this man is out there right now, an active killer. Something's going on and these woods are at the heart of it. I want to be at the heart of it, too and a mobile incident unit is the only way."

"On it, guv."

He reached for his mobile phone. "Now I need to make a call."

*

He walked away to an isolated part of the woods and with a glance over his shoulder, he dialled a number.

"Hello, Dr Anderson?"

"Yes."

"It's DCI Jacob."

"After meeting twice before, including sharing a meal, I think it might be Sophie and Tom by now."

"It's Jacob," he said. "Everyone normally calls me Jacob."

"Okay, *Jacob*. How can I help?"

"I want to talk to you, somewhere private."

"Sounds mysterious. Where?"

"I passed a pub on the way here," he said. "The Lamb – do you know it?"

"I do, yes. When?"

He checked his watch. "I've got some things to do first. What about a late lunch around two?"

"I'll be there."

When he returned to the murder scene, he saw DC Holloway had arrived and was complaining loudly about the cold temperature. Behind him, Mia's team were already busy taking a cast of the quad tracks.

Jacob approached his team and put his hands in his pockets. "Glad you could make it, Holloway."

"Wouldn't miss this for the world, sir."

Jacob gave him a look. "All right, quad or no quad, which way did our killer come from?"

"Hard to say."

To the north, he saw an old country house surrounded by woodland. "What's that over there?"

Mia saw it first. "Grovely Manor. It's a famous wellbeing centre run by that actress – what's her name?"

"Lucinda Beecham," Innes said.

"That's the one."

"I've heard of that place," Holloway said. "Read about it in the papers. Anyone else?"

"I don't read the sort of papers you do,' Anna said. "I prefer words to pictures."

Holloway snorted, accepting the dig. "Good one."

"I know it," Jacob said. "It's a private retreat and wellness centre where people go when they want some peace and quiet in their lives."

"Why don't they just go down the end of the garden

like everyone else?" Holloway asked.

"It's more than that," Jacob said. "They offer a sort of sanctuary to people recovering from major trauma in their lives. Deaths of loved ones, recovering from addiction, you name it, and it doesn't come cheap. They have a large celebrity clientele, for one thing."

"Wow," Anna said, her voice dripping with sarcasm.

Jacob narrowed his eyes, squinting at the white landscape. "And what's that place just in front of it?"

Anna followed his pointing arm to a small cottage surrounded by a separate piece of woodland that almost joined up with Grovely Wood. A column of smoke was twisting up out of the chimney stack and dissipating in the chilly air.

"I have no idea," she said.

When their eyes turned to her, Innes gave an apologetic shrug. "Nor me."

"Mia?"

"What?"

"Any idea who lives there?" he asked. "Several windows are looking out onto this section of the woods."

She sighed. "How the hell should I know?"

Jacob nodded. "Fair point."

"Only one way to find out, guv," Anna said.

After considering the situation, he turned to Holloway. "I want you to organise another house to house but this time in a radius of five miles. That's going to include several small villages and lots of isolated farms so make sure you don't leave anyone out."

"Sir."

"In the meantime, Sergeant Mazurek and DC Innes are with me. We're going to have a chat with whoever's sitting in front of the fireplace down in that cottage."

CHAPTER 13

They went on foot using a bridlepath that tracked down the side of a field and by the time they were halfway to the cottage the sky had started to clear leaving a crisp blue in the air above them, stretching to every horizon. Out here on the rolling downs, the skies were big, and on a day like this, they seemed to go on forever. Beneath them, a frozen landscape of sepia mud and washed-out juniper green in the hedges scratched here and there with the gorses and blackthorn that flourished so well in this part of the world.

"I forgot the sky was blue," Innes said.

"Enjoy it," said Anna. "It won't last long. The weather report this morning was talking about some sort of mega-storm on the way. A proper blizzard they reckoned, blowing in from the northeast."

"Good," Jacob said, his voice dripping with sarcasm. "A foot of snow will make the investigation so much easier."

They reached the bottom of the field and had to walk through another small copse before emerging into the daylight once again. They followed the path until they reached a bend, on the other side of which was the cottage they had seen so clearly from the wooded ridge at the top of the hill.

Nearer now, they were able to see the cottage much more clearly. Up close it was shabby and unloved, with a rusted lawnmower and a roll of galvanised fence wire stacked up against one of the garage walls. An old tireless Mazda pickup truck was stacked up on bricks just in front of it. The grass hadn't been cut for at least a year, which was no surprise considering the condition of the lawnmower.

Jacob turned to Anna and lowered his voice. "You go for a wander. Innes and I will go and have a chat with whoever's inside."

"All right, guv," Anna said, pulling out her phone. "I'll see what I can see."

Innes frowned. "Wouldn't taking pictures on private property constitute some sort of illegal search, sir?"

Anna answered. "I'm just going for a walk, DC Innes. Nothing more."

They watched her walk around the side of the house and when she was out of sight Jacob knocked on the door. A moment later it swung open to reveal a tall, well-built man in his thirties with vacant, bloodshot eyes and a face covered in straw-coloured stubble.

He looked at them suspiciously before talking. "Yeah?"

"I'm Detective Chief Inspector Jacob and this is Detective Constable Innes. My colleague and I were wondering if we could have a word with you."

"What about?" he asked, his eyes shifting between their faces. "Because if it's about them remains you found up there I don't know nothing about it."

"No one said you did," Jacob said. "Mr...?"

"Cooper, Dean Cooper."

"Perhaps we could talk inside, Mr Cooper?"

"You ain't supposed to let coppers in, are you?"

Jacob gave an inquisitive smile. "No?"

"Don't let 'em in, Deano!" shouted a woman's voice from over his shoulder.

He turned and yelled back. "Shut up!"

"We don't bite," Innes said.

"Fine but take your shoes off. They're filthy."

After removing their shoes, they followed Cooper across a small hall and instantly found themselves in his front room. Sparsely decorated with laminate flooring and an ashtray beside every chair, the whole room reeked of cigarette smoke. Jacob studied the ceiling for a moment and saw from the nicotine stain which was his favourite chair. It was the one pointed directly at the enormous plasma TV screen bolted to the wall. On a chair in the corner, a large woman with black hair was smoking a cigarette.

"We're the police," Jacob said. "And you are?"

"That's my girlfriend, Rach," Cooper said, answering for her.

Jacob's eyes stayed fixed on the woman. "What's your name?"

"Rachel Ryall."

Cooper cleared his throat. "So what's all this about

then?"

"As you saw from our identification, we're from Wiltshire CID," Jacob said.

"I got that, yeah," he said. "But why are you in my house? Like I just said, I don't know nothing at all about them remains."

"And neither do I," his girlfriend said.

"Earlier this morning there was another incident in the woods not far from this cottage, and I was wondering if you might be able to shed any light on it."

"What sort of incident?"

"A man was murdered."

"They said the remains were of a woman."

"The remains were found yesterday, Mr Cooper," Innes said patiently. "We're talking about a second incident in which a middle-aged man was murdered in the woods, not ten minutes' walk from here."

Dean Cooper tucked a lock of greasy hair behind his ear and sniffed as he watched Jacob look around his front room. He wiped his hands on his jeans and studied the detective. He had stopped to peer out of the sliding door at the end of his lounge and look out at the junk-strewn garden.

Now, Jacob turned his sharp blue eyes on the man in the ACDC sweatshirt. "Well?"

"I don't know nothing about no remains and I don't know nothing about no bloke getting murdered, neither."

"And neither do I," his girlfriend repeated.

"What do you do for a living, Mr Cooper?" Jacob asked.

"What's that got to do with the price of fish?"

"Just curious."

"I'm a farmhand over at Langford Heath," he said flatly, lighting a cigarette and blowing the smoke into the room. "Done it all my life and it's all I know."

"And do you own this house?"

He laughed. "You got to be kidding! On what I earn?"

"So you rent it?"

"It's a tithe cottage if you must know, so I ain't got much rent to pay. Suits us, anyhow."

"Does it belong to Langford Heath Farm?"

"As a matter of fact no," he said, dragging once again on his cigarette. "It belongs to the Grovely Manor Estate."

"Yes, I think I saw that from the hill," Jacob said. "It's a little to the north of here, is that right?"

"The main house is, yes. You're already on its land."

From out of nowhere, Jacob fixed his eyes on the man and said in a calm, understated voice, "Where were you this morning between seven and eight o'clock?"

"At work, just like every other day at that time," he said with a smirk.

"Something funny?"

"Bloody city types," he said. "I said I work on a farm. What else did you think I was doing at that time? Lying about in my fartsack like you bloody lazy bastards?"

"And what about you, Miss Ryall?" Jacob asked.

"I was in bed fast asleep."

"No witnesses?"

"Bloody well better not be," Cooper said, balling his fist. "Or they'd get more than a thick ear, I can tell you."

Rachel Ryall gave a nervous laugh.

"Well," Jacob said, rising from the chair. "Thank you both for your time. I'm sure we'll be in touch if we need your assistance again."

*

Walking away from the property and back up to the copse, Jacob stopped and shoved his hands in his pockets, turning to take another look at the little tithe cottage by the river. Anna had finished looking around the grounds and was walking over to them from a second path.

"Thoughts?"

Anna's eyes peered over the snowy grass and watched the front curtains twitching. "Definitely hiding something. For one thing, I found these."

He looked at her phone and saw a photo of a pile of vehicle registration plates stacked up behind a panel of corrugated tin inside the garage.

"Very interesting," he said. "Run them through the system when we get back."

"Will do, guv."

"He's still watching us now," Innes said.

"I bet he is," said Jacob. "Did you notice the way all the doors were closed?"

Innes nodded. "Yes, sir. Not often someone keeps all their internal doors closed."

"Unless he was trying to keep the heat in that one room," he said. "It's possible he's trying to save money and only has the one radiator on."

Anna leaned forward so she had a clearer view. "And he's still watching us."

"It wouldn't take long to get from here to the woods and have a quick word with Kieran Messenger. He's dodgy. It's only copper's nose, but I know he's dodgy."

"I agree," Anna said, lighting a cigarette. "There's something not right about this place."

"And run a full background check on both of them."

"Will do," Anna said. "What now?"

"We go back to the woods and get the cars. Then, I want you two to go and speak with whoever owns Langford Heath Farm and check out that alibi."

"What about you?"

"I'm going around to this famous retreat. The top floor of their manor house would have a clear view of the part of the wood where the murder took place and I want to know if anyone saw it."

*

The man they called Magalos sat in a darkened room, his face obscured by shadows and smoke. "On the television this morning I saw some news concerning the violent death of a forester near the sacred grove."

The man sitting opposite him nervously wet his lips. "I saw it, too."

"And when I heard about this death, I couldn't help but think that one of us has killed again."

"Someone in the Lucus?"

Magalos closed his eyes and savoured the smoke. "Yes, Dullovius. Someone in the Lucus."

Lucus. Sacred grove. Dullovius hadn't heard that word for a quarter of a century, but then he hadn't spoken with Magalos for all that time, either. Now, his mind whirred with the possibility. If someone in the Grove really was killing again it meant trouble for everyone.

"If someone has broken the oath, then they must be punished. This puts us all in danger."

Magalos dragged on his cigarette. The tip glowed, and illuminated the centre of his face, tinting it flame-red for a few seconds. For a moment, Dullovius thought he was looking at the devil himself.

"But who?"

The older man drummed his fingers on the arm of his chair. "That is for you to find out, Dullovius."

"He or she, that is the question."

Magalos dragged on the cigarette. "A question you will answer."

"And what then?"

A long, pregnant pause and another long inhalation of the smoke. The dull bronze pendulum in the grandfather clock's wooden belly gently punctuated the awkward silence as Dullovius awaited the reply.

"You know what."

CHAPTER 14

Jacob drove through slushy piles of black snow as he made the short journey out to the Grovely Manor Wellness Retreat. The lack of traffic in this isolated place often meant he was able to go well over eighty miles an hour on some of the straights, but the weather conditions demanded a more measured approach.

After a short drive, he signalled left. The wellbeing centre had been in the news in the past for its treatment of various famous actors and musicians as well as providing a venue for creative writing courses, but when he pulled off onto its private approach road there wasn't even a sign, just a tasteful wrought iron gate, unlocked and open.

He cruised into the property, blowing up a cloud of fallen oak and chestnut leaves behind the car as he followed the twisting drive around to the main building. The day was still clearing, with patches of blue in the sky to the west, and he wondered if all this talk of the New Year's Eve storm was the usual panic over nothing.

He turned the final bend on the private drive and reached the retreat. The main house was a mid-nineteenth century Grade II listed former vicarage set on twelve acres of formal gardens and ancient woodland. The period property was finished off with a large outdoor heated swimming pool and gymnasium.

Jacob killed the engine and emerged into an icy wind. He pulled his collar up and closed the car door as he scanned the large house for the main entrance. Classy yet homely, it was a study of freshly painted sash windows and crumbling Victorian brickwork covered in trellises ready for when May brought the wisteria into bloom. He looked up at the impressive building for a moment and noted how quiet this place was.

A middle-aged man with ruddy cheeks approached from an archway formed in a line of pleached hornbeams. Behind him, Jacob saw what looked like an impressive formal garden, largely shut down for the winter months. He wore a mud-streaked body warmer and a tweed flat cap and was holding a pair of oiled shears. The man narrowed his eyes as he studied the imposing stranger standing in front of the house.

"I'm not sure we're expecting any new guests today," he said.

Jacob returned a polite smile to the man and produced his warrant card. "I'm not here to check-in. I'm trying to find the owner, Lucinda Beecham."

Somewhere beyond the garden in a frost-bitten field, a hefty Hereford cow was lowing. Jacob turned and saw its breath pluming into the air above its head.

"She's in the house."

"Thanks." Jacob indicated over the man's shoulder. "Is that a formal garden through there?"

"It is. Laid mostly to lawn but some rose beds and a

small fountain."

"The box hedge parterre is very impressive."

The gardener raised an eyebrow. "You know gardens?"

Before he could reply, they heard a woman's voice calling from the portico entrance across the other side of the gravel drive.

"Who is it, Ted?"

"Police."

The woman's brow furrowed as she walked over to them. She was slim and in her forties with her hair up in a low knotted ponytail. A pair of cat-eye tortoiseshell glasses was perched on a slim, aquiline nose and she wore skinny jeans and a bronze jumper covered by a flour-speckled blue and white striped apron.

"The police?"

Jacob recognised her face from her acting work but followed the usual protocol and produced his warrant card a second time. "Are you Lucinda Beecham?"

"I am, yes."

"I'm Detective Chief Inspector Jacob from Wiltshire CID. I was hoping to have a few words with you."

"Gosh, I wasn't going *that* fast, was I?"

"I'm sorry?"

"I came home a bit sharpish last night in the Merc."

Jacob gave the ghost of a smile. "It's not about a speeding fine, no. But I would like five minutes of your time if you have it."

"Goodness, what for?"

He slipped the black ID wallet back into his pocket and smiled. "Just some routine questions. Is there somewhere we can speak privately?"

She exchanged a quick look with Ted.

"I know when I'm not wanted," the gardener said and padded back through the hornbeam arch on his way into the formal gardens.

She wiped floury hands on the apron. "Please come in. The kitchen's a tip because I'm just making lunch for everyone, so we'll go in here."

He followed her into a reception room and took a seat on one of three cream leather sofas forming a horseshoe around an impressive fireplace. It had been lit some time ago and now a good blaze was in the firebox.

She turned to him. "I've just made a fresh pot of coffee, would you like some?"

"Thank you."

A pocket of sap exploded inside one of the logs and sent a shower of sparks pluming up into the chimney.

"Applewood?" Jacob asked as she poured the coffee.

Lucinda looked surprised. "I'm impressed."

Jacob said nothing. He took a sip of the coffee and set his cup down on the table beside his seat.

"It's a very impressive home – I take it you *do* live here?"

She nodded and drank some coffee. "We've recently finished a very extensive renovation programme. High-spec roll top baths, silk Isfahan rugs, Farrow & Ball paper… the works. I even replaced the butler's sink in the kitchen."

"I saw that as we walked through," he said. "I thought they were called Belfast sinks."

She shifted in her chair and sipped more coffee. "Technically it's a *butler's* sink."

"You learn something every day."

"We have a very special place here," she said quietly. "As you've already seen, the grounds are absolutely perfect for a retreat and the feeling of peace and isolation is entirely genuine – the house is totally surrounded by substantial woodland." She paused and drank some coffee. "But I'm sure you didn't come here to talk about sinks."

"No," he said quietly. "It's concerning the incidents up in the woods not far from here."

"I'd heard about them," she said. "Some remains yesterday and then another man killed last night."

"We believe he was murdered this morning."

"How awful. What was his name?"

"I'm afraid we haven't spoken with his next of kin yet so that's classified."

"Of course – but so close to the retreat," she said. "It's frightening."

He took some more coffee and lowered his voice. "You have paying guests here, is that right?"

"Yes, most come for a few days and others for weeks or even months. We offer whatever they need."

"Do your guests stay at the house?"

"Some do, but others prefer our luxury lodges out in

the woods. It's a wild and wonderful place and perfect to escape from the modern world. We have oak, ash, chestnut, redwood and banks of ferns. In the summer wild orchids line the paths between the lodges and the main house. It's divine."

"But is it self-catering?"

She smiled. "Food and drink are provided here at the main house. Guests wander over from their lodges at set mealtimes if they want to eat here, or they're welcome to bring their own food and eat privately in the lodges. We're a local family and always try and buy locally and seasonally and only the very highest quality."

"But you don't just offer a retreat – you also run residential courses, is that right?"

"Yes. We offer one-on-one tutorials on creative writing, painting and a number of other things in various venues around the estate, including a beautiful summerhouse down by the lake."

"I can see. Maybe a few days here might be good for me."

She laughed. "We're all booked up months in advance – sorry." She looked across at the tall man's sharp blue eyes when a loud snapping sound in the fire made her jump. "Silly," she said. "It's just the sap again."

He smiled. "Tell me more about the business."

"We like to keep our guest list quite small at any one time. It keeps things more exclusive and our maximum capacity here is six guests in the lodge retreats."

"What about the residential courses?"

"We offer creative writing and painting courses here but only during the summer. At this time of year, the business is focussed exclusively on our guests in the lodges."

And how many of the six lodges are being used at the moment?"

"Three."

"And what are the guests' names?"

She twisted her mouth and took another sip of coffee. "Is it strictly necessary that I give you their names?"

"Not at this time, but it would help me."

She hesitated. "You do understand that some of the people who come to Grovely Manor are very famous, household names?"

"So I've heard."

"There's Bryony Moran, the romance writer. She's in Lodge 1. We have Simon Wickham, a Harley Street consultant in Lodge 5 and Richard Everett, the TV presenter in Lodge 6. I'm not telling you why any of them are here as I don't see why it should be relevant."

"It might be, but we'll cross that bridge when we come to it. Tell me, when they've checked into the retreat can they just come and go or are they supposed to stay on-site?"

"It's not a prison, Chief Inspector. They can do as they please, but most stay on-site for the duration of their stays. These are serious people, often very wealthy and famous and they don't come to a place like this unless they're serious about getting away from the world."

"And what about staff members?"

"You've already met Ted, and there are a few others. It's a skeleton crew. With only six lodges there's not very much work to do until the summer when I often hire additional staff on a more casual basis."

"I'll need all of their names and addresses."

"Of course. I'll write you a list now."

Jacob watched Ted pushing a wheelbarrow full of logs through the garden while she wrote the shortlist. When she handed it to him, he looked down at the five names. "Anyone else?"

She shook her head.

"Did you see or hear anything unusual up in the woods this morning between seven and eight?"

She frowned and shook her head. "No, sorry."

"It's just that if anyone was on the top floor of your house they would have a very direct view of the track where the murder happened."

"There wouldn't have been anyone up there this morning, sorry again."

"Where were you at that time?"

She stopped to think. "Well, I took breakfast over to Richard in Lodge 6 at seven. He's an old friend of mine from my TV days, and he arrived out of nowhere after a blazing row with his wife earlier this morning. I think he's left her for good this time."

"I see, and you were there for a whole hour?"

"I'm sorry?"

"You took him breakfast at seven, but stayed till eight?"

"As a matter of fact, I stayed until closer to nine. I often spend time chatting to the guests, but only if they want to, of course. As I said, Richard and I go back a long way."

Jacob got up to leave. "Thanks for your time, Miss Beecham. I have to say that I'm a fan of some of your television work."

She looked embarrassed. "That's kind, but it's a part of my life that's over now."

"Any particular reason?"

She sighed. "It's a very different life from what it looks like. I much prefer being back here at home, helping people."

Jacob set his coffee cup down and slipped his notebook away. "Thank you for your time."

*

Anna Mazurek pulled up in the farmyard and cut the engine. The property was typical of every other farm she had ever visited in the area, with a well-kept main house and a jumble of mud-covered corrugated outbuildings dotted here and there, slowly turning to rust.

Before she or Innes had got out of the car, a stocky man with a tweed walking hat walked across the yard.

"Here we go," Anna said, opening her door.

"This is private land," he said loudly.

"Mr Freeth?"

"Aye, that's me. Who are you?"

She showed her ID. "I'm Detective Sergeant Mazurek and this is DC Innes."

"Sergeant *who?*"

"*Mazurek,*" she said slowly.

He raised his eyebrows. "Coppers, eh?"

An astute observation, she thought.

"Could we have a word, sir?"

"If it's about those idiots lamping on my land I showed 'em the shotgun and they ain't been back since." He jabbed a fat sausage finger at them. "No thanks to you useless buggers, who I called three times and who did sod all."

Anna and Innes exchanged a glance.

"This is about something quite different."

"Ah, I see," he said, crowing. "So now you want *my* help!"

"We're trying to confirm the whereabouts of one of your workers this morning."

"Who's that then?"

"Dean Cooper."

He smiled. "Oh yes? What's old Deano been up to then?"

"Can you confirm if he was at work this morning?"

"He was at work on time as usual."

"And what's his job?"

"He's a farm labourer," he said, slowing his words. "He labours on my farm."

Anna held in her frustration. "And was he here the whole time?"

"You might find this hard to believe, but in the farming community we don't hold hands when we work so he wasn't in my line of sight for every minute."

"What *did* he do today?" Innes asked.

"Why?"

"Because a man was murdered earlier this morning and we're trying to rule people out of our enquiries."

"Murdered?" he asked. "Bloody hell."

"So what was he doing?"

"Er... the usual stuff. I had him repairing the gearbox in the bale processor and after that, I sent him out on one of the quads to check the fencing."

Anna and Innes caught each other's eye. The senior officer said, "When exactly was that?"

He sighed, clearly running out of patience. "Between seven and eight, Your Honour."

Anna's response was calm and collected.

"Do you mind if we take a look at the quad Mr Cooper took out this morning?"

He hesitated, thinking it through. "Not at all, it's right there in the shed."

They followed his pointing arm and saw the quad parked up in between a stack of tarpaulin-covered hay bales and a pile of brand new, untouched hay tarps. "Be my guest."

Wandering over, Anna pulled out her phone and started

snapping pictures of the quad and close-ups of all the tyres. "This should get Mia started," she muttered.

They strolled back over to the farmer and smiled.

"Thanks for your time, Mr Freeth."

As they walked over to the car, he called out to them with a cheery wave.

"Make sure to keep in touch."

CHAPTER 15

As Jacob stepped into the office and closed the door behind him, the look on Marcus Kent's stony face telegraphed the imminent conversation that was rapidly racing towards him. Judging by the colour on the Chief Super's cheeks, he had obviously been fuming for some time and when he finally smacked his phone receiver down in the plastic cradle and looked over at Jacob, he saw just how tight the man's jaw was clenched.

"Another bloody murder in the same woods?"

"Unfortunately yes, sir."

"How could this have happened?"

"It was a blow to the back of the head," said Jacob, unable to resist the temptation.

"Not the cause of death, man! What I meant was how the bloody hell did you let another brutal murder happen on our patch just one day after the discovery of the remains?"

"There's a link."

"You think?"

"Well…"

"Victim details."

"Kieran Messenger. Forty years old. Local man. He worked as a forester alongside Adam Dawes for the

Forestry Commission under the ranger Neil Talbot."

"Next of kin?"

"His wife, Lorna Messenger. Pregnant."

"Christ all bloody mighty."

"I'm going around there this afternoon."

Kent cursed loudly as he tossed his pen on the desk, rose from his chair and padded over to the window. "It's all over the internet now, predictably," he said in a concerned tone. "And I've just had the Chief Constable on the phone. Some of the American news networks are running it too. They've picked up on the whole witch ghost thing. Soon the whole bloody world will be watching us. They're calling it the Witch-Hunt Murders, for pity's sake. One internet site is claiming they were both killed by the ghosts of the women murdered for being witches. This is getting out of control."

Jacob said nothing.

"Did you hear what I just said?"

"Yes, sir."

"So what's your next move?"

"We think a local man who lives very close to the murder scene may have some knowledge of what happened. We talked with him this morning and his alibi is very shaky. Out fixing fencing on a nearby farm on a quad and could have easily made it to the murder scene, where we found quad tracks, and back to work in time."

Kent's jaw opened in disbelief. "That's it? That's all you've got, two days into what is now a double murder enquiry?"

"I've also re-opened the original case files from the Russell disappearance. Something's not right about it."

"What do you mean?" he asked sharply.

"I don't know yet. It's just instinct, but something about the original investigation is bothering me."

"You'll have more than your bloody instinct bothering you if I don't start seeing results." He raised his hand and separated his finger and thumb by a quarter of an inch. "I am that close to officially questioning your competence to be SIO on this case."

"To questioning officially, sir."

"What?"

"You split your infinitive."

Kent fixed his steel-grey eyes on him. "I hope you understand the sensitive nature of this case, Jacob."

Jacob narrowed his eyes. "All murder enquiries are sensitive, sir."

"Yes, but let's not play games. The SIO on this case must understand that not all murders are equal, do I make myself clear?"

Jacob was shocked by the man's bluntness. "If you're suggesting that…"

"I'm suggesting nothing. I'm ordering you to get me some bloody progress, and in a hurry. Ian Russell ran one of the biggest investment banks in the country and is an extremely rich and influential man. Word is he's in line not only for a knighthood but also to be the next Governor of the Bank of England."

"The Messenger murder is more important now, sir. We have an active killer on our hands."

"And how do you know they're not connected?"

"They may be, and that's what we are trying to establish, but in the meantime, I have to prioritise the Messenger case."

"I want a result for Ian Russell, Jacob, however, you do it."

"I'll do what I always do and give it my best, sir."

After a short pause, Kent's eyes narrowed and a grim frown appeared on his face. "For now, I'm leaving this in your hands, but don't take your eye off the ball. If there's a link between these two murders that's one thing, but don't rule out the possibility of a rogue nutter living out some insane copycat fantasy. Keep everything in mind. As I said, the eyes of the world are on us, and more specifically *me*, Jacob. We can't afford any screw-ups on this one, and you can be damned sure of one thing – any blowback on this and I'll make sure it all goes in your direction, understand?"

"Yes, sir."

He understood only too well.

*

Kent watched Jacob walk down the corridor outside his office, then he stepped over to the door, shut it quietly and moved back over to his desk. Lifting the receiver, he dialled a number and waited patiently for someone to answer.

"Dr Lovelace?"

"Yes."

"This is Chief Superintendent Marcus Kent at Wiltshire CID."

"Good morning, Marcus."

"I want to talk to you about DCI Jacob."

"I thought you might. What about him?"

He heard a note of worry in her voice. "I have my concerns about his competence to be back at work."

"Why?"

"He's uncommunicative, difficult and frankly I'm worried about his judgement."

"In what way?"

"Reasons I can't go into during an active investigation, but don't take it personally."

"If you're questioning my assessment of him then yes, I do take that personally."

"I'm not questioning your judgement but I feel being SIO on a high-pressure case is taking too much of a toll on him and I'd like you to see him."

She paused. "If you feel that strongly about it then you can have him assessed again by another psychologist. But in my professional opinion, he has processed what happened in the fire and he's fit for work."

"Amelia, please... there's no need to be so defensive. I'm merely trying to explain to you that he seems very uptight and I'm worried about him. I think he should be re-evaluated. Frankly, I'm amazed he ever got through initial psych screening."

She sighed heavily. "If that's what you want then you can order it as his superior officer."

"I do. I feel we need to make sure he's fit for the job. Will you please talk to him?"

He waited a long time for her response and when it came she sounded uncertain. "I'll organise another session with him, but I don't think he needs another full assessment."

"Just talk to him," he said. "We all want what's best for him, after all."

*

Jacob shifted into second and slowed for the bend. The road was dangerous, and a notorious stretch for black ice, plus he'd spent half the day driving up and down the county. If he had an accident it would only add to his woes; the last thing he needed now was Marcus Kent questioning his driving skills along with everything else.

Powering out of the bend, he changed into third and then fourth as he accelerated for the straight. In his mind, he kept going over the conversation he'd just had with Kent. Doubting his ability, almost questioning his mind… He realised with shock he was gripping the steering wheel so hard he'd squeezed most of the blood from his knuckles.

I want results…

Jacob saw the turn-off he took to drive home but made a snap decision to turn around and head back in the opposite direction. It was nothing but intuition, but this case was no ordinary murder investigation and he was sure of it. Witches and ghosts in the woods, two deaths a quarter of a century apart, books on demonology. Something far more wicked than simple murder was stalking his patch and he knew he needed all the help he could get.

"If it's results you want then it's results you'll get," he muttered and activated his hands-free phone kit.

"Sophie?"

"Hi, Jacob."

"Can we bring our meeting in the pub forward?"

A short pause. "Sure, when do you want to meet?"

"Yesterday."

Another pause. "I'll be there in twenty minutes."

*

Back at the station in Devizes, Anna was standing outside and smoking a cigarette when her phone rang in her pocket. She looked at the screen and felt her neck muscles tense as she read the name listed on the caller ID. Everyone at the station knew about her ex-husband and his long career of crime but none of them knew the full details.

She had been young when they married and for a while, it looked like he might just drag her down with him. But she had fought hard to get away from him. She joined the police and worked her way into the CID and up to the rank of sergeant. It had taken a long time to escape from the long shadow of Declan Taylor and she sure as hell wasn't going to let him ruin it all for her now.

She had spent over a decade rubbing him out of her life but she always knew his release from prison was going to be a problem for her. He was a dangerous man and he was capable of some serious cruelty. He would work his way back into her life until she had no option but to offer help and money all over again.

She agonised over whether or not to tell Jacob about it. Could he help? Probably, and she knew she could trust him too but she didn't want to change the way he thought about her. He respected her and valued her judgement. If she told him the whole truth about Declan it would rock him to his core and she just couldn't risk it.

Slipping the phone back in her pocket, she finished her cigarette and walked back inside the station.

CHAPTER 16

The sun was trying to break through a low cloud on the horizon when Jacob pushed open the heavy oak door and stepped down into the public bar of The Lamb. Located well off the beaten track, most of its clientele during the warmer months were tourists either staying in one of its rooms upstairs or using the campsite over the road, but this time of year most of the patrons were families celebrating Christmas. Today, a small group of people were standing around a roaring fire with pints in their hands while Christmas carols played through a concealed speaker above their heads.

He shuffled through the drinkers gathered around the tinsel-covered bar and ordered a pint of beer and a glass of white wine. Picking up both glasses, he took an inch off the beer and then scanned the busy pub for Sophie. He knew she was here because he'd seen her Audi in the car park, but there was no sign of her in the public bar so he weaved his way around the back to the snug.

He saw her sitting on a window bench seat on her own. She was tapping the foot of a glass full of white wine with one hand and scrolling through something on her phone with the other. As he approached her his shadow fell on the table and she looked up and gave him a startled smile.

"I got you some wine," he said with an embarrassed

smile. "In a glass this time."

"Thanks, but no thanks," she said. "I'm driving, so one's enough."

"Yes... may I?"

She moved her bag and he sat down opposite her. The window behind gave an impressive view of the downs rolling away to the west, coloured amber in the low winter sun.

"You look exhausted," she said, taking a slow sip of her wine.

He was halfway through a sip of his own when she said it, and it occurred to him that this was the second time in two days she had told him he looked tired. It felt good that she was expressing concern for him, but on the other hand, he made a mental note to get more sleep. He knew from the press reports of the Ferryman murders that she was several years younger than he was, but he looked much older than that, and it wasn't doing his ego any favours.

"It's just been a tough few days, preparing to go back to work and then finding the body up in the woods. Not a great start to a new life that was supposed to be less stressful."

He lowered his pint glass and set it on the little cardboard coaster. He noticed that Sophie was smiling. "What's so funny?"

"Just the way you're so precise."

"Eh?"

"The way you put the beer glass down, exactly in the

centre of the mat like that."

He paused a beat, unsure how to reply, and then changed the subject. "About the consultant work you offered to do."

"I thought you said your boss said no?"

"He did, but I want you on the case." He lifted the beer to his lips.

"But I thought you said if Kent said no then it's a no?"

The shadow of a smile appeared on his lips, but he suppressed it and pretended to be absorbed in his beer. "Did I?"

"Yes, you did. We were by the fire in your watermill at the time. I remember it well."

Behind them, he heard the pub fire crackling and spitting. "That's nice."

"Well?"

"Well, what?"

She looked like she might be fighting an urge to slap him. "Is a no a no?"

"No."

"Jacob!"

"I overruled him, so you're on the case."

Her protest was already on her lips when she realised he had agreed to her request to work on the case. She watched him looking back at her, and it occurred to her she should probably give some kind of response, or even show some gratitude. Instead, she said, "But what about Kent?"

"He's my problem, not yours."

"Won't you get into trouble if he finds out you've gone behind his back? I don't want to be responsible for you getting suspended or something."

"Listen," he said, "I'm running this case, and I'm making the decision to bring you into it. You know your stuff, and after the Ferryman murders, you need a new chance. Leave Marcus Kent to me."

She looked at him, sitting in front of her with his hands around the beer glass as the wind beat at the windows. A rare break in the clouds allowed a shaft of sunlight to shine through the window and dance on the vintage copper table. It flashed on the empty flower vase and then the clouds swallowed it back up, once again leaving only the small table lamp to light the moment. "Thank you, Jacob. I mean it."

"Forget about it. It looks like we could help each other, so let's just get on with it."

"I'm presuming the second murder made you call me?"

"Yes."

"And you're thinking this all has something to do with the occult?"

"Maybe, that's why I wanted to speak with you. I know you dealt with some occult murders in America and I know Keeley dabbled in that neck of the woods, too."

"The case in Illinois was fairly straightforward occult, but Keeley was more Greek underworld mythology, but there are similarities, yes."

"If you ask me it's all a load of crap."

"But the woods do have a strong legend about the witches' murders."

"It only shows us that a real historical event occurred, but that doesn't mean we should be inferring anything concerning this case."

"I'm not so sure."

"You're a shrink, of course, you're not sure."

She stopped drinking halfway through a sip and turned to him, half a smile on her face. "And what is that supposed to mean?"

"It means you're trained to look at things a certain way."

"So are you."

"Yes, but a very different way."

"So you don't think it could be relevant?" she asked.

He paused and finished the last of his beer before blowing out a slow, uncertain breath. "That's why I want you here. It's why I want you on the team. If these are occult murders then I think we need your experience."

"And I can help, I know I can. For a start, I just think it's too much of a coincidence," she said. "An area of ancient woodland containing the bodies of four women murdered for being witches, and now two more bodies turn up in the same place."

"But not from the same era. The witches were murdered nearly three hundred years ago. Emma was murdered less than thirty years ago and Kieran Messenger was killed this morning."

"Still, something about it's not right. I don't like it when

I can't see a pattern, and these things bother me."

Jacob finished his beer and set the glass on the table. He had read her CV online and knew better than to doubt either her professional judgement or her instinct.

"How do you want to proceed?" he asked her.

She answered without hesitation. "If I could see anything from the original case files, like notes or better still interview videos and so on, that would be helpful."

Jacob knew handing information to a civilian like this was a line he couldn't uncross, but he'd already decided to trust her. "I can email over some of the scanned documents this afternoon, but the CDs will have to wait. Can I bring them over to your place tonight?"

"Sure – that would be a great start."

After a pause, he said, "You've gone very quiet."

"Sorry," she said quietly. "I'm just thinking about those witches in the woods."

*

"I've ordered a full investigation into the death of Kieran."

Jacob spoke firmly but quietly, desperately aware of Lorna Messenger's fragile and shocked state. "It's early days, but at this time we think his murder may have been drug-related."

Lorna Messenger looked at him, her red eyes confused and angry. "Drugs? Kieran ain't taken no drugs for bloody years. What makes you think that?"

"I can't go into specifics at this stage, Mrs Messenger, but we found traces of fentanyl in his pickup truck."

She stared up with shock etched deeply on her face. She looked much older than her age as she ran her hands over her pregnant stomach. "No way, not my Kieran."

"As I say, it's early days and we'll do everything we can to make sure we find out what happened and to bring whoever was responsible for this terrible crime to justice."

She snorted dismissively. "Yeah, right."

Jacob understood her reaction. "Does he have any other family?"

She shook her head. "At least not worth knowing, no… His father left home when he was a baby and he walked out on his mother as soon as he was sixteen. She took up with a bloke who used to knock him around when he was drunk, which was most of the time. He ain't spoken to her for years."

Jacob nodded. "I understand."

"So it's just me."

He watched as she reached out for the tissues with a trembling hand. He doubted she had much faith in the police to find her husband's killer. "As I say, we're already actively investigating his death and as soon as I have any news I will bring it to you personally."

Out of nowhere, she gathered the courage to ask what was on everyone's mind. "Has it got anything to do with the girl they found up there a couple of days ago?"

He knew this question would come. "At the moment,

given the very long period of time between the two murders, I'm not happy to say there's a direct link but it's something we're discussing as the investigation goes forward."

"They're talking about bloody witches in the papers. It's not that, is it?"

"Well…"

"I hate all that occult rubbish, witchcraft, druids. Kieran thought it was a load of crap as well. He worked in those woods morning, noon and night and he never heard or saw nothing but the birds."

He saw something more than birds, Jacob thought.

"Again, this is nothing but speculation and idle gossip. We're still gathering the facts concerning the murder of Emma Russell, and there's very little pointing to anything of that nature."

It was a lie, but a necessary one. The book on witchcraft and demonology they had found in Emma's canvas bag was evidence suggesting a possible link to witchcraft. In combination with the location where she was found and the disturbing tale of the Handsel sisters, he had privately conceded the occult may have played a part in not only her death but perhaps also Kieran's. He also knew the value of keeping a lid on public panic.

"Legend has it they murdered women up there once," she said, darkly. "Accused them of being witches and beat them to death. Buried them under the trees."

Speak of the devil and he doth appear.

"That was a very long time ago, Mrs Messenger."

"Still, you never know with these weirdos."

No, he thought. *You really don't.*

CHAPTER 17

Jacob watched the Mobile Major Incident Unit pull off the lane and make its way up the narrow track leading to the woodland. The MIU was a hefty Iveco Eurocargo truck containing mobile office space in the rear which enabled detectives to set up a command in the field. Now, the driver was struggling to navigate the large truck through a series of iced-over potholes before pulling up on the gravel turning circle at the entrance to the woods.

As well as the office space, the inside of the MIU provided everything else they needed to run a command and control centre from out here at the scene of the crimes and would save a lot of driving back and forth to the nearest police station in Salisbury. At nearly thirty miles there and back on narrow lanes no-one fancied having to make that journey throughout the investigation, and HQ in Devizes was even further away. The MIU was a solid solution Jacob had used before on previous cases out in the Oxfordshire sticks and he was glad Kent had approved its use so fast.

When the engine went silent, the passenger door in the cab opened to reveal the smiling face of Innes. She swung her legs around and slipped down to the ground. "Afternoon, sir."

A stocky man in a police tunic climbed out of the

driver's side and joined them. "Sir."

"Sergeant Oliver," Jacob gave a nod. "You made good time."

"Which is a miracle considering some of the roads, sir."

Jacob called his small team over and they gathered around the entrance to the MIU. Anna Mazurek, Bill Morgan, Matt Holloway, Laura Innes and Mia Francis, were all waiting for his lead. He didn't want to tell them yet about his decision to bring Sophie Anderson onto the team. He had already emailed her some of the files relating to the case and wanted to see what she could do before telling them about her.

"So this is Home Sweet Home," he said.

Mia frowned. "Lucky us."

Morgan clapped his hands together. "We're going to need something to eat."

"There's a bakery in Wilton, sir," Innes said. "That's not too far from here."

"Sounds like you just volunteered to get the coffees and cakes, DC Innes," he said with a smile.

Jacob stepped inside the police truck, passing a critical eye over everything to ensure all was present and correct. It was the same as the one he had used in Thames Valley, only slightly larger and with more space to use as a briefing room. A satellite dish on the roof provided all the comms they required and there was even a small kitchen area for making tea and coffee.

Poking his head out of the door, he said to the others,

"Seems perfect."

They looked doubtful, and he hid his smile as he placed the files on the desk and waited for them to climb inside and take their seats. When they were all gathered around the table, he stood up in front of them and started the briefing.

"As you can see, after the murder of Kieran Messenger I decided to bring this MIU down here and give us a command unit in the woods for the duration of the investigation. A twenty-six-year-old cold case is one thing, but an active killer is quite another and I felt it was important we can react as fast as possible to new developments. That's not realistic if we have to go back and forth to the headquarters building all the time."

"It's a big county, all right," said Morgan.

"Nearly a million acres," Mia Francis said, sipping some bottled water. "I know because I've counted them."

A ripple of laughter, but Anna folded her arms and raised an eyebrow. "But I'm guessing it's not just about logistics, right?"

The corner of Jacob's mouth turned up. "No," he said flatly. "The installation of the MIU here is also a very visible sign of reassurance to the public. This is a peaceful, rural part of the world with a generally low rate of crime compared to the national average. The discovery of the first body was shocking enough for the locals, but with the Messenger murder we're moving closer to genuine concern."

"And if another dead body turns up there could be panic," she said.

"More than likely," he replied. "Having such an obvious symbol of law enforcement here on site will hopefully convince local residents that everything possible is being done to solve these murders and ensure no further harm comes to anyone."

"And there's another benefit you haven't mentioned yet," Morgan said.

All eyes swivelled to him as a broad smile spread on his square face.

"And that is?" Jacob asked.

The Welshman pointed out of the window. "*That* is a much better view than outside my office back at HQ."

"This is true," Jacob said, "and it's a hell of a lot warmer than being out there."

"Unless that storm they're all talking about blows in, guv." Anna gave the room a doubtful look as a gust of wind gently rocked the truck from side to side. "Not sure it could handle a full-scale blizzard."

"We'll cross that bridge when we come to it," he said. "Now, let's get started on the case in hand."

He picked up a black marker pen and turned to the murder board. "Kieran Messenger," he began, drawing a circle around the victim's photograph. "A forty-year-old forester working for the Forestry Commission. Married with a young wife and a baby on the way. He was brutally murdered earlier this morning just a few hundred yards from here."

He wrote *0700 – 0800* on the board and continued. "Thanks to Mia and the CSI team we think he died between these times, but we'll have a confirmation on that after the post-mortem which I've already arranged. I'm requesting a superfast turnaround on the PM because of the timing of the death. There is increasingly less doubt that this murder is not connected in some way to the discovery of the remains yesterday morning."

"I agree," Morgan said. "This is a quiet, safe area. One murder would be shocking enough, but for this to happen it's got to be linked, hasn't it?"

"That's my working assumption," Jacob replied. "Do you have any updates, Mia?"

"Other than the dead man's DNA there was only one other trace at the scene – a tiny sample of skin and dried blood on a piece of barbed wire close to the crime scene. It could be anyone who tried to climb over it. Sorry about that, but we did our best. Sometimes you get more than one type of blood in the splatter or some saliva or even a stray hair, but no such luck on this one. As you will have all seen by now, it was a pretty gory scene and the damage to the victim's skull was substantial. This induced extremely heavy bleeding so there was a lot to go through but we couldn't find another blood sample in that location."

"Great," Anna said wearily.

"Hold your horses. I said there were no other DNA

traces around the body, but we have the small sample from the fence. We also found fentanyl in his pickup truck and a set of quad tracks near the body. Anna and Laura took photos of the quad Dean Cooper had access to for work and I've studied them with computer software and they look like a match, but I'd like to see the actual machine if possible."

"I think we have enough for a warrant to seize the quad," Jacob said. "I'll speak with Kent. And we need to start getting some DNA samples from locals to see if we can get a match with what Mia found on the fence. Anything else?"

Mia nodded. "After searching his flat we found a hidden phone. Luckily, his wife had gone to stay with family so we didn't need to move her out while we worked. Anyway, on the phone was an email message that he had sent to an account requesting a meeting with him at around the time of his death. He'd gone to a lot of effort to delete the message as well."

"I want to know to whom he sent that message."

"The phone is already winging its way down to computer forensics."

"Great work, Mia," Jacob said. "And I want a priority on verifying the quad tracks as soon as I get the warrant."

"I'll brief the team."

"Great – ah! The cavalry arrives."

Innes opened the truck's side door and stepped up inside bringing a rush of cold air with her. In her hands, she carried two large brown paper bags laden with treats from the local bakery, which she started to distribute to the hungry team members.

As they tucked into coffee, cakes and pasties, Jacob tried to rally them, "I know none of us is in any doubt of the significance of the second murder's location, and the intense scrutiny it's going to bring onto our department but we can do this."

"Damn right we can," Anna said.

He brushed the back of his knuckles against the stubble on his chin. He hadn't shaved since yesterday morning and it was starting to bother him. "With the second body found in the woods we're going to need to switch up a gear, and the first thing we do is prioritise finding Kieran Messenger's killer. It's not unreasonable to suggest that Emma Russell's killer could even be dead now, but whoever killed Messenger is very much alive and kicking and highly dangerous."

"Especially when you consider the fentanyl angle," Anna said.

Morgan deftly spun a pencil on his knuckles. "Could be the same person, Guv."

Before Jacob replied, Mazurek spoke up again. "But why kill again now?"

The Welshman shrugged. "Why kill at all?"

"And what's the significance of these woods?" Holloway said. "That's what I want to know. If it *is* the same killer, why go to such lengths to hide one body in the middle of a forest and then, over a quarter of a century later, dump another in such a public setting where it's going to attract so much attention? It doesn't make any sense at all."

"Not yet it doesn't," Jacob said firmly. "But it will when we get to the bottom of it."

"If we do," Anna said.

Jacob gave her a weary look. "No pessimists on my team, thank you very much."

Subdued laughter went around the room.

"As I say, I don't believe in coincidences, and these murders happening in such an isolated place is too much of a coincidence for me. There must be a link and I want to know what it is."

He turned to Morgan. "Anything to report from the work you and Holloway were doing on the archived file of the original case?"

"Not much yet, boss," he said, his face turning sour. "The officer in charge was Detective Inspector Miranda Dunn."

Jacob took a seat around the table. "You look uneasy."

Morgan looked around the small briefing room inside the truck. "Looks like I'm the only one who remembers her then."

"Care to elaborate?"

He looked back at Jacob and sighed. "She retired directly after the Russell case, and not many were sad to see her go. Two pints of trouble in a half-pint pot, as my mam used to say. Always managed to find someone else to blame whenever anything went wrong, and that included juniors on her own team, but when there was a result, she always took the credit. I was glad to see her go. Bloody nightmare."

"And she was leading the investigation into the Russell disappearance?" Jacob asked.

He nodded. "Her last case. She left the force shortly afterwards."

Jacob furrowed his brow. "She'd have been a bit young to retire back then, wouldn't she?"

"Medically retired," Morgan said. "Claimed the trauma of the case was too much for her. Pensioned out and never seen again."

"Anything else strike you from the files yet?"

"Not yet," he said. "All above board – every I dotted and every T crossed."

"Keep looking. I want to know much more about DI Dunn."

"Will do."

He turned to Anna. "Anything on the number plates you found in Cooper's garage?"

"Oh yes," she said with a broad smile. "I can happily report that one of the number plates I found in the pile of junk around the back of his garage has some form."

"At last," Jacob said. "Progress."

"Indeed, the offending article was recently attached to a Ford Transit that was involved in a robbery on a pharmacy warehouse in Swindon."

A mischievous smile appeared on Jacob's face. "Was it indeed?"

She nodded. "I'm working with Mia on some CCTV from the raid to see if we can place Cooper at the scene as well as just the van."

"What was stolen from the warehouse?" Innes asked.

"A list as long as your arm," she said. "Most of it central to the production of fentanyl but also other drugs including methadone, morphine and a number of hospital-grade anaesthetics."

The team exchanged a grim look.

"It's that word again," Jacob said. "Fentanyl."

Morgan shook his head. "And very nasty stuff, too."

Holloway shifted uncomfortably in his seat. "I'll say. Fifty times more powerful than heroin."

"Right," Jacob said. "It's so dangerous most dealers won't touch it because the number of fatal overdoses is so high it draws too much attention to them. Nice work, Anna – keep me updated. It wouldn't be the biggest surprise in the world if all of this were somehow about drugs. Now we have a possible link between Cooper and Messenger through fentanyl, at least."

He blew out a breath and rose out of his chair. "So we've got some ideas, and right now we need all the ideas we can get. If these deaths are linked then it changes things. What might have been a straightforward murder now looks more complex. We could be looking at some kind of drugs vendetta, revenge or even a serial killer who has become active again after a quarter of a century."

"Sounds like we're back to square one," Innes said.

Anna laughed. "Not really sure we ever got to square two, to be honest."

Morgan sniffed hard and swallowed another bite of his pasty. "If it's the same man, the bastard's running rings around us."

Jacob looked over at his old friend. He looked tired. Purple bags under bloodshot eyes and deep creases in his tanned cheeks. Years of commando work in the Royal Marines had taken their toll on his features the way water erodes granite, and yet he was still the man he trusted most to have his back.

"You think I don't know that, Bill?"

The flawlessly dressed inspector shrugged his shoulders, the crisp starched shirt crinkling slightly on the razor-sharp crease. He raised his palms in defence as the team turned their eyes on him and awaited a response. "I know... I know, but it's just so damned frustrating." His thick Welsh accent descended into a low grumble. "Every time we take a step forward we end up taking two back again. It's like he's watching everything we do."

Anna glanced over her shoulder at the window and shuddered. "Maybe he is. Maybe he has us under surveillance now."

"Let's not get silly," Jacob said with a reassuring smile. "I know some of us apparently believe these woods are haunted with dead witches but there's no need for us to get *too* spooked. We're tired and we could all use a good night's sleep. Everyone go home and try and decompress for a few hours. That's an order."

CHAPTER 18

As DC Laura Innes swung into the station on her way home she smiled at her prospects. She was on the up and she knew it. She had graduated with distinction from Hendon Police College and had spent her two years of probation in Surrey Police. Impressing her senior officers a great deal during her tutored patrol phase, she had been earmarked for a fast-track career and she intended to grab it with both hands.

Her return to Wiltshire had been a setback, but nothing was more important to her than family and her mother needed her. She wasn't going to let it slow her progress through the ranks and she would do whatever it took to climb the ladder as fast as possible. She was very clear on that.

She checked her watch and smiled. Still enough time to grab her iPod and get home before it got too late. She liked to jog in the mornings but she'd left it in her desk and all her best running music was on it, so now she made her way to her office, still smiling like the cat that got the cream.

Marcus Kent's decision to move her onto Jacob's team was a surprise. She was good, and to be assigned to a high-profile cold case murder enquiry was a dream come true for a brand new DC with relatively limited experience.

Speak of the devil, she thought.

"Innes."

"Sir."

It was Kent, and he had cornered her in between the office and the cafeteria. "I was wondering if you could spare a few moments before you go home?"

Innes looked up and down the corridor. It was empty except for the two of them, although she could hear one of the kitchen staff stacking a dishwasher back in the cafeteria behind her. Now, his tall thin frame loomed over her and blocked the ceiling light.

"Of course, sir."

He gave a quick smile. "Excellent. How are you getting on in the new team?"

"All going well so far, sir."

"You're enjoying your life out of uniform?"

She nodded. "Yes, sir, and I'd like to thank you for the opportunity."

"And what's life like, working for Jacob?"

She shrugged. "Fine. Is there a problem, sir?"

"There are concerns, DC Innes. Concerns about professionalism."

Her mouth fell open. "I've not done anything wrong, sir. I swear."

"Not with you, Innes, but with Chief Inspector Jacob."

A wave of relief flooded over her and her heart started to slow down to its normal rate. "I don't understand."

A crocodile smile appeared in the centre of his five o'clock shadow. "You don't have to understand, Innes.

Not at all, but it might be useful if I was able to follow the Chief Inspector's progress a little more closely if you see what I mean."

She saw instantly. "You want me to report on him?"

A casual nod. "It's regrettable, but if there are any problems then I need to know about them as soon as possible. Any corners cut, any 'T's left uncrossed and 'I's left undotted, as it were. He's a good detective but he's a maverick and the last thing we need now is any unwanted nastiness involving the press. This is turning into a high-profile case and the scrutiny will only intensify until the killer is caught and brought to justice."

"I see, sir, but he *is* my superior officer and the SIO on the entire investigation. I'm not sure what I can do to help, and I'm not even sure if it's the…" she hesitated, knowing only too well not only the power the Chief Superintendent wielded over her career but also Kent's formidable reputation for using it without mercy.

"Not sure if it's the right thing to do?"

She felt herself blushing. "Well… yes, sir."

He gave a business-like nod and joined his fingertips together, turning his hand into a sort of cage. "Ask yourself this, Innes. It's unlikely DCI Jacob will be around too much longer, but I will be, and I'll be overseeing your promotion to DS when the time comes. How soon that time comes is very much in the balance. Do you catch my drift?"

"Yes, sir."

"Good, think about it – but not for too long."

She watched him walk away and turn around the corner at the end of the corridor. When he was out of sight, she knew she had a hell of a thing to think about, and she didn't like it one bit.

*

The old dashboard lights of the Alvis lit Jacob's face a warm amber as he drove the vintage car south across the downs to Salisbury. It was a clear night, with a wild grove of stars scattered high above the ancient landscape, and for a moment its awesome beauty almost swept him away from his troubles.

This vast chalk plateau stretched across much of southern Wiltshire and over the borders into Berkshire and Hampshire. Endless acres of ancient downland, shivering with rock-rose and bedstraw and the echoes of a primitive Iron Age past wherever you looked.

He glanced down at the well-worn passenger's seat and made sure he had remembered to bring the bottle of wine. Check – one dusty bottle of Merlot nestling in a case of paulownia wood and wheat straw, courtesy of his father's extensive wine cellar. A year since the fire, and tonight he had started to think that maybe there was a future for him after all. Things had started to perk up after the arrival of a certain criminal profiler in his life, but he was too weary of the world to hold any real hopes.

He checked his mirror, squinting at the headlights.

"You're far too close, idiot," he mumbled and then heard his phone ringing.

"Bill, hi."

"Hello, got a minute?"

His normally thick accent sounded thin and tinny in the speaker. "Sure, what about?"

"About DI Dunn."

"Found something else?"

"No, nothing new, but I couldn't speak in the MIU today."

"What do you mean?"

Morgan sighed. "The archive files seem very thin to me, for such a long enquiry, Jacob."

"Funny you should bring the Russell files up," he said, checking his mirror.

"Why's that?"

"Because you're the second person to mention them to me this evening."

"How so?"

"I had a call from Sophie Anderson earlier. She wants to speak with me about the very same subject."

"How's that, then?"

"I'll tell you later. What have you got?"

"I know how it sounds, but I think that either vital information about the Emma Russell case was left out of the report, or someone's gone back into it since then and stolen information from it. I think that certain someone was Dunn. And guess who her line manager was?"

"Don't tell me."

"The then-DCI Marcus Kent."

Jacob flicked his eyes from the road up to the mirror. The car was still following him. When he looked back to the road, his headlights were lighting up the snowflakes like sparks. "You realise what you're saying?"

"Of course, I realise what I'm saying. That's why I'm only talking about this to you. You're the only one I know I can trust."

"Sounds half-baked to me, Bill. What have you got, really? A file that seems too thin? An unexpected retirement after the case? Not enough to risk your career by throwing murder accusations around the force."

"I'm not accusing anyone on the force of murder. I'm just saying that something about this report isn't right, and maybe someone on the inside knows a bit more about the case than they're letting on."

"Keep digging, but for God's sake keep it to yourself."

"I recommend you do the same with your little trip to Sophie Anderson tonight. If Kent finds out he'll burn you, and he'll enjoy doing it too."

"That's my problem."

"As you wish," Morgan said. "There's one more thing."

"What?"

"In the early part of the manhunt for Emma a local poacher was arrested and interviewed on suspicion of her murder, but he was released without charge. Witnesses saw him talking to her in the pub before she disappeared. He dropped off the radar after that claiming we'd ruined his life with our false accusations."

"Name?"

"Jim Latimer."

"See if you can get him back on the radar, Bill. Definitely worth talking with him once again."

"Will do, boss."

Jacob hung up and signalled to leave the main road. Pulling up outside Sophie's flat, he grabbed the wine and walked up her path. When she came to the door she was wearing casual jeans and a baggy white jumper and looked somehow younger with her hair down. When she saw the wine she smiled.

"You read my mind."

"As long as you don't read mine," he said. "I'm not a big fan of psychologists peering inside my head."

"I promise," she said. "Now, come in! It's freezing out there."

CHAPTER 19

"Thank crunchie for that." Innes swung open her fridge door and scanned for any sign of alcoholic relief. Strictly medicinal, she located a bottle of perfectly chilled pinot gris and instantly liberated it from the confines of the shelf above the salad crisper. It would be rude not to, she said and poured the wine into a glass roughly the size of a small goldfish bowl.

Her tiny, one-bedroom flat was the top floor of an Edwardian house just off the main road in Marlborough, and now she walked along the narrow corridor to the front room, switched on a lamp and drew her curtains to block the winter gloom. If only she could block out the memory of that bastard Marcus Kent, but now at least she knew why he had put her on Jacob's team. He wanted her to be his spy.

Collapsing down on her long, soft sofa, she gave a sigh of relief. It was time to put thoughts of work behind her and relax, but that time ended when she heard a knock at her door. She swore loudly as she swivelled off the couch and opened the bay window to peer down at the front path.

"Who is it?"

"It's me."

She saw Vincent and silently cursed. "What do you want?"

"Can we talk?" The face of her on-again, off-again boyfriend stared up at her from the little tiled path leading from the pavement to her front door. "Any chance of letting me in? It's freezing down here."

"It's not much better up here," she said. "Wait a second."

She found herself sighing as she walked down the narrow stairs to the front door. Vincent Goddard had been quite the catch when she first moved to Marlborough but now she was starting to think again.

He had told her his property development company was worth seven figures and judging by the Lamborghini she had no reason to doubt him, but none of that mattered. It was fun, but if the man behind the money wasn't right then she knew it had no future. Working out whether *he* was right or not was the hard part.

Lately, he'd started hinting at marriage. Instead of being excited at the prospect of becoming Mrs Laura Goddard, wife of a millionaire property tycoon, she found herself getting nervous about it and trying to dodge the subject. Now he was on the doorstep in the cold with a dozen red roses in his hand and she knew what that meant.

She opened the door with trepidation and they kissed and walked back upstairs. Inside the flat, he handed her the roses. "For you."

"Thanks," she said, grateful there was no question attached to them.

"Any cold beers?"

She held up the wine with an apologetic smile. "Just this."

"Fine, I'll grab a glass."

*

Thirty miles south in Salisbury, Jacob followed Sophie through to her kitchen where she opened the wine and poured two glasses. "I've been going through your emails concerning the original Russell case files," she began.

"Anything interesting?"

"Maybe, but it's a bit early to tell."

"You sound hesitant. What have you found?"

"I was analysing some of the statements actually."

"Of the witnesses?"

"Yes, but that's not the interesting bit."

"No?"

"The stuff that really caught my eye were the reports and statements made by the SIO of the case, a DI Miranda Dunn."

Jacob stopped sipping his wine and fixed his eyes on her. "How so?"

She ran her finger along some lines of the scanned document he had emailed her. "The way she writes – I mean the vocabulary she uses and where she uses it strongly implies that she knows more than she has included in the report. My assessment of her statements is that she was hiding something from the investigation."

He gave her an anxious look. "I'm not liking where this is going. First Kent launches a major and unreasonable objection to your being on the team – knowing your success rate – and now I find out that his number two at the time of the original investigation was lying in the reports."

"Not lying, necessarily," she said. "I never said that. We're not interpreting or translating her statement here but carefully analysing what she has said and asking why she chose that particular way to say it. I wouldn't say she is lying exactly, more concealment by omission."

"It adds up to the same thing, Sophie. We're going to have to do some more digging under her. If she knows more about Emma Russell's disappearance then I want to know what it is. It would certainly explain why Bill Morgan says the archived files are so thin."

Sophie closed the folder with a smack and looked him in the eye. "Have you eaten?"

"I thought you'd never ask."

"Good, follow me."

They walked back through into the kitchen where she started to chop up some vegetables and set a pan of water on the hob. "Pasta okay?"

"It seems to be what we eat when we're together," he said. "So why not?"

He poured more wine as she served up the fresh pasta, and they sat at the table together, desperately trying to avoid the subject of work, but without much success.

"Thanks again for giving me this break," she said. "I know you're putting yourself at risk for me."

"Not at all."

"It's just that after the Keeley case I wondered if I'd ever work again."

"You mentioned him earlier today at The Lamb," he said. "What really happened? I only know what I read in the press."

She set down her fork and sat back in her chair. "I posed as one of his students," she said quietly. "I allowed him to get close to me so he would make me one of his victims."

"Risky."

"He nearly strangled me," she said. "With his victims the official cause of death was homicidal ligature asphyxiation, which as you'll know is relatively rare, the usual method being manual strangulation."

"That's right," he said. "Depending on the country, homicide strangulation accounts for between ten and twenty per cent of all murder cases, and three-quarters of victims are women and children. As you might expect, children are the majority of victims of female killers who use strangulation but this is nearly always manual."

"But the Ferryman's victims were all killed with ligature strangulation, and that was one of the main leads we had. Some studies suggest that there's a strong correlation between ligature strangulation and cruel, predator murder patterns, as opposed to manual strangulation, which is more closely associated with an explosive, violent outburst."

"In other words, you could tell Keeley was a sadist who was carefully planning his attacks?"

Sophie gave a confident nod, but suddenly she felt like a rank amateur. It was something about the way he was looking at her. Momentarily when she looked into his eyes, she saw the face of the man on the television news, the senior investigating officer of the so-called Witch-Hunt murders instead of the real man she had started to get to know.

"Yes, and he performed a very strict ritual with his victims. They were all wrapped in a shroud and…" she hesitated. "And those *coins*…"

"I know."

"All the post-mortem reports of his victims were frighteningly similar. Cause of death was always compression of the neck leading to suffocation, and substantial quantities of gamma-hydroxybutyrate in their systems."

"Coma in a bottle?"

She nodded grimly. "That's a slang name for it because of its powerful effect as a depressant drug which slows down brain activity. It rendered his victims helpless to defend themselves while he choked them to death. God, how I hated reading those post-mortem reports. All those horrible words, so surgical and impersonal. Compression. Hypoxia. Soft tissue trauma."

She closed her eyes and massaged her temples.

"Try and forget about it all for tonight," he said. "I brought over the videos of the interviews that you wanted to see but leave them for now. Wait till morning, please."

*

If he goes away, it all goes away.

The man they once called Magalos pushed back in the leather seat of his car and dragged on his cigar. The blue smoke gathered in his mouth and he savoured the taste. These were good cigars, and a different world from his cigarettes, he mulled. New, but better, with a robust earthy flavour – peat, truffles, undergrowth. When he exhaled the spicy fumes it masked an uncertain sigh.

After following Jacob along the back roads since the Old Watermill, he was parked up outside the flat and watching both of them now. The hotshot FBI woman was in there too, and the two of them were sharing a joke over a pan of bubbling water. How nice. Very domestic, but he somehow expected more of DCI Jacob. Wasn't he supposed to be some sort of broken, genius detective? Where was the sad, lonely figure with his hands wrapped around a whisky bottle? Instead, he was laughing with this woman.

Maybe she was where the trouble lay?

Now she was dropping pasta into the pan while he filled two wine glasses.

The newspapers had talked about a high-profile case in which she had tracked down a man from the north and snared him like a hare. That had put an end to his killing spree and made her a celebrity in her field.

Another long, slow drag on the cigar as the car slowly filled up with smoke.

Simply have to stay calm, he mulled. Just stay calm and it will all blow away.

Was taking Jacob out of the picture a possibility? Maybe, but not yet. He was cleverer than the detective but one slip and it would all be over.

The smoke tasted so good, he thought, watching as they sat down and started their meal.

But this must end and it must end now.

*

After she had shown Jacob out and watched his car drive away, Sophie looked at the cardboard box full of old police CDs and wondered exactly what would happen to him if his boss ever found out what he had done. She contemplated making a start now but thought better of it and went upstairs to bed.

But when sleep finally came, it brought a nightmare landscape with it.

The Ferryman was there somewhere. She couldn't see him, but she felt his presence in the darkness and strained to see where she was. Her breathing intensified and her legs felt like lead. She realised she was in the warehouse in London's Docklands. The abandoned meat-packing plant where he had nearly killed her.

Rust on the metal walls and fungus on the wood. Cobwebs hung like vines from broken ceiling beams.

She felt his breath on her neck.

His gloved fingers around her throat.

The sting of his needle in her flesh.

Her mind raced with terror as she twisted around and saw the crumpled shroud he would wrap her body in when she was dead and now he was holding one of his silver coins and trying to push it into her mouth. She screamed as hard as she could and tried to push him away but his animal bulk was too heavy to shift and now he was pulling her head back and sliding the coin over her lips.

"I do this because I love you," he breathed into her ear.

She screamed again and leapt out of her bed, dragging the duvet with her, wrapped tightly in her hands as she strained to see in the darkness of her room. Her heart hammered as she searched for the Ferryman.

But he was nowhere to be seen.

Except for in her mind.

CHAPTER 20

Friday, 28ᵗʰ December

With his morning coffee in hand, Jacob walked through the abandoned kitchen garden but paused when he saw a ghost in his peripheral vision. The ghost was him, as a child, playing in the garden. He was hiding from his younger sister around the back of one of the greenhouses. Back then, the garden was still partly in use, cultivated by a local gardener his parents had employed for many years.

All long gone now, all except for the ghosts. What had been a busy, noisy family home full of fun and laughter, was now a cold, dead house in disrepair surrounded by wild, overgrown grounds. His parents were living out their retirement in Australia and his sister was building an exciting career in New York City. It was just him now. He turned his eyes to the overcast sky and watched the low cloud shifting from east to west.

A rare smile danced on his lips. Last night had been good for him and he was starting to enjoy the company of Dr Sophie Anderson more than he would like to admit, even to himself. With luck, she would be able to make progress with the archived CDs he had given her, and in the meantime, he hoped no one else would go looking for them.

A crow cried out from the canopy of a nearby oak tree and shook him from his thoughts. He saw a song thrush with a snail gripped in its beak, mercilessly smashing it against the side of a broken cold-frame in a bid to crack its shell.

Time to get back to work.

Inside the empty watermill, he made himself another strong coffee from the can he had dug out of the back of the larder and walked through the house to the sitting room. Sipping from the cup, he approached his improvised white murder board and stared at the progress they had made so far.

Not encouraging, but there had to be something he was missing.

He finished the coffee, set the cup down and pulled up a chair. Spinning it around so he could lean his crossed arms on the back, he continued to stare at the board. The frustration grew. He turned and looked at the case files scattered on the desk under the bay window. Leafing through the countless statements they had collected from so many witnesses was even more frustrating. Mia's forensic reports were reassuringly neat and tidy, but none of it was advancing the case very much.

He heard a car pull up outside on the gravel drive. When he got to the hall, Morgan and Anna were already halfway to the front door. "Morning, boss," said the Welsh inspector. He removed an unlit cigar from his mouth, rocked back on his heels and glanced up at the façade of the old mill. "I take it you passed a pleasant night?"

Jacob said nothing. It was good to see friendly faces after such a long, sleepless night. He looked at his watch and then made a big show of sighing. "You're both late."

"You can bugger off," Morgan said, clamping the cold, half-smoked cigar between his teeth. "RTA in town. Took an hour to get out of the place. You're lucky we're here at all."

"If you say so," Jacob said and swung the door wide open. "The work's this way. You do remember work?"

They made their way back to the sitting room and gathered around the murder board. "I couldn't sleep last night..." he said.

"We can see that just from the looking, guv," Anna said.

Jacob raised an eyebrow but continued without comment. "Anyway, I spent the night going through everything we've collected so far on both murders, both Emma Russell and Kieran Messenger and one big gap is Emma's social circle when she was studying for her medical degree at uni. Did you manage to speak with them again?"

Anna nodded. "Only one of them so far, but here's where it gets weird."

Jacob and Morgan looked at one another. "Oh no."

"I managed to track down Emma's best friend at uni, Lavinia Hobbes. She gave me her phone number and we spoke last night. She's a fashion photographer now, living and working in Milan."

Morgan sighed wistfully. "I remember when I had that dream."

Jacob gave him a look. "Thanks for that, Bill."

"Welcome."

"Did she give us anything?"

"She was upset at first and reluctant to talk about it, but when she calmed down she was able to speak quite lucidly about her university days. She says their group of friends used to meet up now and again and drive out to the woods and watch the moon rise."

"Sounds a bit nuts to me," Morgan said, chewing on the cold, unlit Robusto.

"And?" Jacob asked.

"She says they would stop off at an off-licence in Jericho to buy beer and cider and then drive up into Wytham Woods to look for ghouls, but she was very clear that after university it all stopped completely and that they never even kept in touch."

"What was her alibi at the time?"

"Family party, and it still stands."

"What about for Messenger's death this week? Is she alibied?"

"Fashion show in Milan," she said. "At least five hundred people saw her accepting an award."

"Excellent," Morgan sighed.

"How many others in this group of university ghost hunters?" Jacob asked.

"There were five of them, including Emma and Lavinia.

She gave me the others' names. They are..." she referred down to her notepad. "Jake Razey, Bradley Mitchell and Ross Hendry."

"Track them down. I want solid, confirmed alibis for all three or I want them brought in and questioned."

"Guv."

"And Bill, any news on Jim Latimer, our poacher?"

Morgan shook his head. "No sign of him at all. He was of no fixed abode during the original investigation and they had a terrible time tracking him down. Witnesses placed him in the pub on the night of Emma's disappearance, badgering her by all accounts, and he always claimed he saw or heard nothing of her after she left the pub. After he was released no one ever heard from him again."

"Great."

Morgan moved over to the window and looked out at the river. Turning, he said, "So, want to tell us what's going on with Sophie Anderson?"

Jacob had already decided to tell his old friend about it, but he made a snap decision to include Anna as well. "Yesterday after the discovery of Messenger's body I decided to bring Dr Anderson onto the case. She's already provided me with some interesting information regarding the SIO on the original Russell case, and last night I took her some of the interviews and other items from archives. I'm confident she will find something to help us."

"You left police property at her house?" Morgan asked, astonished.

"Yes."

"Christ," Anna said.

"If Kent finds out your feet won't touch the floor."

Jacob glared at him. "Well he's not going to find it, is he?"

Anna said, "Wait, who was the SIO on the original case?"

"DI Miranda Dunn," Jacob said. "You don't know her."

"But I have a feeling I'm about to get to her know."

Jacob's jaw tensed. "If Dunn was involved in any way, then we could be moving from a murder enquiry to conspiracy and cover-up at the highest levels. What I have told you in here stays between the three of us, right?"

"Of course," Morgan said.

"Anna?"

"You know you can trust me."

"Good."

"So what's next, boss?" Morgan asked, helping himself to a piece of toast from the toaster.

Jacob checked his watch. "We need to get down to the MIU and get back on the case. You get going and I'll follow you in the Alvis."

*

By the time Jacob pulled up, there was already a large group of press and TV journalists gathered at the entrance to the wood. The discovery of the cold case remains had triggered a larger than expected reaction in the nation's media, but the brutal murder of Kieran Messenger just one day later had sent them into a frenzy.

Morgan and Anna had already run the gauntlet and survived, but now it was his turn. He slowed his car and sighed. He recognised several of the faces from the main national news programmes – the BBC, ITV and Sky were all waiting impatiently for a word from the man leading what they were still calling the Witch-Hunt Murders. Looking at the reverse gear with something approaching despair, he knew he had no choice but to drive on.

But slowing down to pass them, they banged on the window and called out to him. Winding down the window, he answered a few of their questions.

"Is there any progress in the investigation?"

"The investigation is proceeding in the normal way."

"Are the murders linked?"

"One of the purposes of the investigation is to establish exactly that and we'll know in good time."

Jacob leaned his head out of the window and honked on the horn. "Can you clear the way? It's a very narrow lane and I don't want to break any toes."

"Local legend has it that hundreds of years ago four women were murdered in the woods after being accused of witchcraft and some people are suggesting an occult link to how these people met their deaths," asked an unknown woman from the back. "How seriously are you taking this?"

"No comment," he said.

"Can you comment on stories in the press questioning your ability to lead this investigation?"

"Yes, but you wouldn't be able to print it or play it before the watershed."

Some of the press laughed, others rolled their eyes, but Jacob couldn't have cared less what any of them did. He put his car into first gear and drove slowly up to the woods.

When he parked up, Anna leaned out of the MIU's side door and shook her head. "No point turning your car off, guv," she called out. "Ethan just called. He finished Messenger's PM first thing this morning and he's ready to report."

"Great," Jacob said. "Why the bloody hell couldn't he have told us that earlier?"

"Welcome to Ethan."

He cursed and swung himself back down into the car. Turning the engine back on again, he gave it a hearty rev and reversed out of the parking space in a cloud of dead leaves.

*

The man with the pagan tattoo sucked on his cigarette and watched Jacob on the television. He was chatting with the press at the bottom of the hill and looked like he was having a high old time. Was he enjoying the publicity? Yes, it looked like it. The famous detective was honing his public profile in the way a landscape gardener clipped away at a topiary peacock. A snip here and a clip there and then everything was perfect.

The hot smoke filled his lungs. He held it there for a few seconds until feeling the kick of the nicotine seeping into his system. Exhaling it, he watched the detective navigate his way through his adoring fan club and then drive up the hill to the scene of the crime.

You shouldn't have come back here.

He collapsed into a chair and unscrewed the lid from the whisky bottle. He did it with one hand and when the job was done, he casually flicked the aluminium cap to the floor. The only light was provided by the television set balanced on an old chair in the corner of the room. The news was on, and now he reached for the remote and muted the TV as he stubbed out the cigarette.

The discovery of the second corpse truly was an unfortunate development. A sign from the gods, maybe. A punishment. His mind whirred with panic as he thought about the discovery from every angle. Could it be traced back to him? Could he be traced in any way? Never. He had been too careful, and the others would never dare to speak.

Before he'd taken her life, all those years ago, he'd wondered how it would feel. He had felt some guilt and a little power but after a short time, he felt nothing at all. It surprised him, but it would make things easier from now on. He pulled another cigarette from a crumpled pack on the windowsill and fired it up. Stretching his neck, he breathed the blue smoke out into the room's subdued lighting.

His thoughts were once again distracted by the gentle blue and white strobing of the TV. He turned to see the news was still on and so was the imposing and serious figure of Tom Jacob. The BBC was re-running a clip from the interview at the bottom of the hill. In the background among the trees, he saw the Major Incident Unit in the woods. As he appealed for witnesses, a graphic on the bottom of the screen appeared: GROVELY WOOD MURDER: POLICE NOT RULING OUT RITUAL KILLING.

His mouth formed into something approaching a smile, but his eyes were somewhere else, cold and distant and focussed on something far beyond the television screen in front of him. He would never let Jacob hunt him down, no matter how much blood had to be spilt.

CHAPTER 21

When Ethan Spargo turned and greeted Jacob in the county mortuary, the detective was disappointed to see he had switched the Father Christmas bowtie for one covered in tiny elves and reindeers. He supposed this passed for high-humour down here in the gloomy world of post-mortems and medical reports so fixing his eye on the tie he kept his face deadpan and said, "Ho ho ho."

"You don't think I actually *want* to be in here, do you?"

"Maybe." Jacob thrust his hands into his coat pockets. "Who's to say?"

"I'm to bloody well say," he said. "It's Christmas, for heaven's sake. I do have a family life outside of these stainless steel walls, you know." He paused a beat and chewed his lip for a second. "Sorry, that was insensitive of me."

Jacob waved it away. Over a year since his fiancée's death and people still spoke without thinking, but they never meant anything by it.

"What's the story on this one, Ethan?"

Spargo raised his eyebrows and gave a short sigh. "Nothing out of the ordinary. Right parietal bone completely caved in just as before and with about the same degree of force."

"Same killer?"

He wobbled his head for a moment, a study of indecision. "I wouldn't conclude that, no. The injury is far too common and besides, the first one was probably done with something more rounded like a rock but this one was definitely done with a heavy, cylindrical object."

"A walking stick?"

"I doubt that would be heavy enough, same goes for a camera tripod before you ask."

"Why would I ask that?"

"They're very pretty woods, Jacob. It's not out of the realms of possibility someone was up there with a camera taking some nice snowy pictures for the Christmas album."

"So what then?"

"You're looking more along the lines of a crowbar or a spanner. Something with some serious weight."

Jacob gave a long sigh. "Perfect."

"Problems?"

"I can see how a walking stick or a camera tripod gets to the woods, but if it's a spanner then it was taken up there deliberately. It complicates things."

"That, Jacob, is entirely your problem."

Jacob had to agree, and he took his new problem out of the mortuary with a cheery wave and headed back to the MIU. He and DC Innes had some interviews to get done.

*

Anna Mazurek heard Sophie before she saw her. Someone was calling out her name as she walked along the High Street, and when she turned, the psychologist was waving to her as she crossed the road. Her hair was down and she was wearing a winter jacket, casual jeans and what looked like brand new snow boots.

"Anna, hi."

"Hi."

"What are you doing?"

"I've just been to the bank. There was an unauthorised debit so I just tore them a new one."

Sophie winced. "Oh. I was wondering if you had time for a coffee?"

Anna checked her watch. "Sure."

They walked to a café and ordered two lattes. After a short silence, Anna broke the ice. "I hear you and Jacob have been seeing one another."

"I wouldn't put it quite like that. We're working together on the case."

"You realise he'll probably lose his job if this gets out."

"It's his decision."

"You pressured him… sorry, we seem to be getting off on the wrong foot here. He's had a difficult year and I'm looking out for him, that's all."

"I understand," she said. "And I know something's hurting him, but he won't share it with me."

"That is entirely up to him."

"He started to talk about it but stopped. If I knew then

maybe I could help."

Anna sighed and stirred her coffee while she stared outside at the passing traffic. She saw no harm in telling Sophie what she wanted to know. A simple internet search would have given her the information she needed, but she had chosen not to do that and speak with one of his friends instead. "All right, last year at Christmas there was a fire at his old house in Oxford. It burnt to the ground, and he nearly died."

"I had no idea," she said quietly. "That's terrible."

"It gets worse. His fiancée died in the fire."

"Oh my God."

"Right. He woke in the night, choking on the smoke. He turned to check if Jess was okay but she wasn't in the bed."

"Why not?"

"She'd fallen asleep downstairs on the sofa watching the TV. He searched for her but passed out in the smoke. When he regained consciousness he was outside on an ambulance gurney surrounded by flashing lights and chaos. The fire guys worked hard to contain the blaze and they told him they had managed to get her out of the house but it was too late."

"That's just terrible."

Anna took a sip of her coffee and felt her phone buzz, alerting her to an incoming call. "He blames himself for her death. Says he should have looked harder."

She looked at the phone, silent.

"Are you okay?"

Anna stared down at her phone, unsure what to say. The caller ID on the screen had shocked her so much she had almost forgotten to breathe. "Um, sure," she said. "It's nothing to worry about."

*

Morgan and Holloway ate their lunch in the car on their way out to Tithe Cottage. The Welshman had opted for a crispy bacon and avocado baguette and Holloway was already halfway through a sweet chilli and lime wrap. Above them, the sky was still fairly clear and there had been no serious snowfall for nearly twenty-four hours. The main roads had been salted but some of the B-roads and lanes were still covered in a thick black slush as they weaved their way towards the rural property.

They parked up on the lane and strolled through a small copse on their way to the front door. This part of the Grovely Estate was compact at around ten acres, but its woodland was an incredibly ancient heritage. Before mesolithic hunters had cleared the downs of their ancient forests, it had all looked like this, and this was one of a handful of areas that had been left untouched, an echo from the county's most distant past.

"Nice place," Holloway said.

Morgan grunted.

He gave him a sideways glance. "You think you can

crack him then, sir?"

"Piece of cake, easy bake," Morgan said, clamping the cigar in his mouth and heading off down the track. With a trail of thick smoke billowing out behind him in timed puffs, he reminded Holloway of an old steam train shunting its way up a mountain pass.

"Maniac," he muttered and started up the path to catch up with the older man.

"Come on, lad, no dawdling."

"I cannot believe how *cold* it is this week," Holloway muttered, pushing his scarf up around his neck.

"It's nearly as bad as Wales," Morgan said with a chortle. "But not quite."

Cooper answered the door with a sneer and glanced over at their car through the trees. "Oh look, tinned pork."

"Very good, Mr Cooper," Morgan said. "And it's very nice to see you, too. May we come in?"

"Got a warrant?"

Holloway smiled. "We just want a chat, sir. That is all."

"Without a warrant, you can't come in. That's what I reckon."

Morgan stepped up to him. "You reckon right, but the problem you have is that we can get a warrant to tip this dump over without any trouble at all, and then we'll go through the whole place like a dose of salts, all legal and above board, like. If you let us in right now, it's just a little chat in your front room."

Cooper weighed his words, delivered as they had been

in the inspector's usual gruff and unsympathetic manner.

"Fine, come in."

"Thank you, sir."

They followed him inside where he took off his pullover and tossed it over the bannister. They both knew what he was doing. This way, they could see the heavy metal wifebeater he was wearing and all of his tattoos. First impressions counted, after all. Lighting a roll-up and stretching his neck, he padded down the junk-strewn hall and crashed down among the empty cider cans and crumpled newspapers on the sofa in the front room.

"Your girlfriend not in?"

"She's upstairs," he said. "Rach!"

Rachel Ryall came downstairs and looked at them suspiciously. "What's going on?"

"As you know, we had a very nasty incident up in the woods yesterday morning. A local man named Kieran Messenger was beaten to death in a hollow just off the Roman Road near the Four Sisters coppice, not at all far from where some cold case remains were found the day before."

"And?"

"And we're asking all local people to provide a DNA sample and a blood sample to rule them out of our enquiries."

Cooper shifted nervously in his seat.

"Thought you needed a warrant for that, too?"

Morgan and Holloway exchanged a glance before the

Welshman spoke. "Don't take this the wrong way, sir, but you seem remarkably well informed about criminal law for a farm labourer."

Cooper finished making another roll-up cigarette and fired it up with a cheap plastic lighter. "Nothing wrong with knowing your rights."

"Quite."

A long period of silence followed as the young man smoked.

"We've had a very good response from local people helping us with our enquiries by offering to give their samples, and I was wondering if you had any objections to giving one?" Morgan asked.

"Why should I help you tossers out?"

Morgan smiled. "Look, we can't take a blood or urine sample without your permission, and if you won't give a blood sample then we can force the issue with a warrant. DNA on the other hand can be obtained without a warrant. It just depends on how difficult you want the process to be."

"You can't be thinking either of you two is going to take a DNA sample by force from me." He started laughing loudly. "You can't be far off your pension and he couldn't fight his way out of a wet paper bag."

Morgan scratched behind his ear. "Of course, if we have to come back with a warrant then…"

"Blood and DNA you say?"

Morgan nodded once.

"Fine," he said. "You can have your samples, DNA and blood. I ain't got nothing to do with what happened up there," he said, rolling up his sleeve. "Nothing to hide at all."

"Me neither," Rachel said.

Dean Cooper sucked on his roll-up and watched as the young, clean-cut detective in the smart charcoal suit carefully set the DNA testing kit on the table and started to unpack it. Quick and professional, both samples from Cooper and Rachel were taken in seconds and packed away in evidence bags for analysis when they returned to the station.

"Thank you both."

"No problem, he said. "Now piss off out of my house."

With the sound of the slammed front door still echoing in the trees around the cottage, the young detective constable turned to his senior officer.

"Did you see that satanic t-shirt, sir?"

Morgan nodded. "Ugly."

"And did you see that tattoo when he rolled up his sleeve?" Holloway asked.

"I surely did. Can you remember the dates of the birthdays?"

"I think so – I'll make a note of them on my phone before I forget."

"Good lad."

"You should have shown him your commando dagger tattoo. Might have shut him up."

Morgan shook his head slowly and carefully relit his cigar. "I save that for special occasions, not for turds like him. Come on, let's get back to the MIU for a cuppa."

*

The man in the black Chesterfield coat made his way through the woods as quietly as he could, cigarette hanging off his lip. Since his phone call with Ian Russell yesterday morning he'd been busy making arrangements. The envelope containing the new information had been in his post box this morning, along with half of the money and now the rest was in his hands.

Pushing deeper into the woods he saw some movement up ahead and realised he had reached his destination at last. He was a city slicker and thanked God there was no more snow and leaves to traipse through. Settling down on a fallen trunk he began to study the man who was cleaning his boots out the front of his cottage.

"Guilty bastard," he said under his breath. "Now it's time to pay for what you did all those years ago."

CHAPTER 22

Jacob and Innes walked along the gravel path, winding ever deeper into the woods as they made their way to the lodges to speak with the retreat's guests. The first on their list was the journalist and romance writer Bryony Moran. Her lodge was the closest to the main house but still well inside the private woodland belonging to the retreat, and nestled in a tiny, secret glen.

"Looks like it would be very nice in summer," Innes said.

Jacob sniffed in the cold air and pushed his hands deeper into his pockets. "Winter has its own beauty."

"If you say so, sir."

After another few minutes walking along the winding path, they reached Bryony's lodge and knocked gently on the door.

A woman in her thirties opened the door with a steaming coffee cup in her hand and dishevelled red hair tumbling down over her shoulders. She narrowed her eyes with confusion and glanced around the glen to see if anyone else was lurking nearby. "Can I help?"

"We're with the police," Jacob said calmly, the breath condensing in the air as he spoke. Taking out his ID wallet, he opened it and held it up to her face. "I'm DCI Jacob and this is DC Innes."

"What do you want?"

"Five minutes of your time to discuss a serious incident that occurred near here yesterday morning."

"I'm not aware of any serious incidents," she said grumpily. "But come in out of the cold."

With no offer of a coffee to warm them, she gestured to some soft chairs positioned around an expensive two-sided fireplace in the middle of the room. "Please, make yourselves at home. I do whenever I'm here."

"Is that often?" Innes asked.

"Whenever I need peace and solitude," she said defensively. "I live in a flat in London and the noise is intolerable most of the time. When I'm on the later drafts of a novel I can't handle constant disturbances so I come here."

"How did you discover this place?" Jacob asked.

She hesitated. "I had a problem with alcohol a few years ago and a friend of mine recommended Grovely. She'd used it to help decompress after an ugly divorce and found it helped. They have just the right balance of support while understanding you want to be alone. Indie is a star when you consider all the work she's done in creating this haven."

"Indie?"

"Lucinda," she said. "Lucinda Beecham, the owner."

"Of course," Jacob said, making a note of the shortened version of the name.

She set her coffee cup down neatly on a slate coaster.

"So what was this serious incident?"

Jacob lowered his voice. "A local man was found murdered yesterday morning just a few hundred yards from these lodges, just up in the tree line of the woods on the ridge."

She recoiled with horror, raising her hand to her chest as her eyes widened. "Murdered?"

"I'm afraid so, yes. In the course of my investigation, I'm ruling out everyone who was in the immediate vicinity at the time of the murder."

"I see. What was his name?"

"Kieran Messenger. He was a local man who worked as a forester in the woods where he died."

"How awful. Are you sure it wasn't some kind of accident?"

"Quite sure."

"Oh, dear. When exactly did it happen?"

"Between seven and eight yesterday morning. Can you tell us where you were during that time?"

"In bed, here in the lodge."

"Alone?"

"Well… *yes.*"

"And no one can confirm you were here?"

"Of course not," she said, almost offended. "I just said I was alone."

Innes gave a reassuring smile. "You could have been on the phone."

"I was writing if you must know – on my laptop in bed.

Perhaps my computer would have some sort of log to show what I was doing?"

Jacob shook his head. "Easily manipulated."

"In that case, I don't know what to say," she said, her tone shifting from arrogant to anxious. "I assure you I was in here writing. Does this mean I'm a suspect?"

"We're just asking preliminary questions," he said. "Please don't alarm yourself."

"It's just so *grisly*."

Jacob shifted in his seat. "Would you be happy to give a DNA and blood sample?"

"Of course," she said after a slight pause. "Anything to help."

Jacob closed his notebook and slid it into his pocket. "Thanks."

"Will you be back to take the samples?"

"It will be someone from my team but we may meet again if the investigation leads me back here."

He stood up and Innes followed his lead.

"Thanks very much for your time. It's not uncommon for people to think of something else after we leave, so please don't hesitate to contact me or anyone at the station." He rummaged around in his pocket and pulled out a card. "You'll find all the details on here. We're based in Devizes but we have a mobile command unit just over in the woods."

She took the card and read the details. "I see, of course – yes. I'll be in touch if I think of anything else, I promise."

*

"No alibi," Innes said. "Significant?"

"She has an alibi," Jacob said, "just no one to confirm it."

"You think she had anything to do with it?"

He weighed it up. "Spargo said the impact on the back of the skull was quite hefty. She looked pretty fragile to me."

"Not sufficient upper body strength, you mean?"

"I don't mean just that. I meant mentally fragile. Smashing in the back of someone's skull is not something just anyone can do, or even be driven to in a moment of rage. And remember the post-mortem report said a weapon was used. Some kind of metal bar, so a woman or a man with weak upper body strength would be physically capable of doing what we all saw yesterday up near Four Sisters."

They were walking deeper into the woods, moving south as the landscape began to slope upwards to the ridge beyond. Another a few minutes of mulch and dead bracken and ivy and mud they turned a corner in the dense pine forest and spied two more lodges either end of a fork in the path.

"That's Wickham's to the right and Everett's to the left," Jacob said, turning to the keen, aspiring detective. "We'll split up and save some time – crooked Harley Street surgeon or washed-up druggy TV star?" He looked at her with sharp, cobalt eyes. "I know, I know… the agony of choice."

"He's not washed-up," she said defensively. "I was a big fan when I was younger."

"You still are *younger*," he said. "And that's *exactly* why I don't want you to interview him. You speak with Wickham and I'll talk with Everett."

She looked disappointed. "I was hoping to meet Richard!"

"The very fact you refer to him by his first name is enough for me. Off you go."

He watched as she pushed her hands into her coat pockets and padded away through the chilly air to Wickham's lodge, head tucked down in her scarf and upset not to be meeting one of her favourite television stars. Turning away from the icy wind he made his way carefully through the final stretch of woods before reaching Lodge No. 6. As he drew nearer, an eddy of wind whipped around on the path, lifting a cloud of dead leaves and blasting him with another wave of icy air.

When Everett opened the door, Jacob barely recognised him from his TV work but had to ask the familiar question all the same.

"Mr Richard Everett?"

He scowled at him. "If you're the press I'll ruin this place."

Jacob suppressed a sigh and showed his ID. "Can we

have a word?"

The burnt-out star was gaunt and unshaven. Some silver in the stubble. Stone-washed jeans with a rip in the right knee and a casual black shirt. He leaned against the doorjamb and sighed. "What the hell about? I haven't done drugs for years."

"A man was murdered very close to here yesterday morning and I was hoping I could speak with you about it for a moment or two."

"One moment." He leaned away from the door so Jacob could enter. "Not two."

Everett turned his back on him and wandered off into the lodge, so Jacob followed him inside.

"And shut the door," Everett snapped. "I don't want the cold coming in."

Jacob was already closing it and now stepped into the main room to see Everett was already lounging on a white leather sofa positioned in front of the same two-sided central fire he had seen in Bryony Moran's lodge.

"Sit if you must."

Jacob lingered by the chimney. "I see you have many celebrity friends, sir."

"When you've been in the business as long as I have, that tends to happen. Please have a seat."

Jacob started to take off his gloves as his eyes crawled over the pictures on the chimney. Stars from the worlds of TV and music peered back at him and he counted one or two Hollywood actors as well. All cheesy smiles and hanging off each other's shoulders. In one, Everett was stripped to the waist on a desert island with his arm around one of the most famous actresses in the world, both sporting several tattoos, normally concealed from the outside world beneath their clothes.

"That one was taken in St. Barts," Everett said proudly. "We still keep in touch."

Jacob said nothing but finished taking his gloves off and took a seat. Warming his hands by the fire, he turned to face the celebrity. Seeing his face in the warm light of the fire, he realised just how long ago the nineteen-eighties really were.

Like most people in the country, he knew only too well who Richard Everett was but couldn't have cared less about his fame. He was what some called a C-List celebrity, pulling the mid-morning shift on commercial television. His career had culminated in anchoring the TV equivalent of easy-listening with a succession of female co-hosts, most of whom had left citing his behaviour as the reason for their departures.

"When did you check in to this lodge, Mr Everett?"

"I *arrived* yesterday morning," he said. "It's not a mental hospital."

"What time was that?"

"Around seven."

"Driving down from London?" Jacob asked, pulling out his notepad. "Must have been an early start."

"I wasn't in London. I was at our house in Warminster

with my wife. We had a terrific row over breakfast and she threw me out. Indie and I go way back and she's very kindly letting me stay here until I can find somewhere else."

"Why not just go back to London?"

"All my family live here and I want to spend time with them over Christmas if that's all right with you. Besides, it's the most beautiful place I know. It defuses me, Chief Inspector. Sometimes I spend weeks here, as I plan to this time."

"So you were on the road between when and seven?"

"I left as soon as I could pack my personal belongings into the back of the car," he said, glancing at the photos on the chimney. "So let's say six-thirty and seven. The roads were clear of traffic but there was some black ice and sleet on the downs so it balanced out."

Jacob made a note. "And you got here at exactly seven?"

"That's what I just said. Maybe a minute or two after."

"And what then?"

"Indie and I walked to this lodge and I had breakfast with her, this time in peace. We talked for a couple of hours."

Jacob nodded, made a note. "Are you prepared to give DNA and blood samples?"

"I have nothing to hide, so yes."

"It was heroin, wasn't it?"

Everett looked at him sharply. "I'm sorry?"

"Your drug habit was injecting heroin, as I recall."

The man grinned. "I already told you, I haven't used a syringe for years. I barely even smoke."

The clock ticked.

"Thank you. All right, that will be all for now, sir. Thank you for your time and I do hope the rest of your Christmas is peaceful."

"Thanks, but don't hurry back."

Jacob put his gloves on as he followed him down the hall, passing several suitcases on the way. Here, Everett swung open the door and made a theatrical sweeping gesture to show him out. "Goodbye, Chief Inspector."

Jacob stepped out onto the decking. "It's the heat that escapes."

Everett was confused. "I'm sorry?"

"When you let me in you asked me to close the door to stop the cold coming in, but that's not what happens."

"No?"

"No. It gets colder because the heat goes out, the cold doesn't come in. Goodbye, sir."

Behind him, he heard the door slam. It echoed across the trees and sent a murder of crows flapping up into the brittle sky.

*

Innes didn't have to wait long to get out of the cold. No sooner had she finished knocking on the door of Lodge No. 5 when a short, vaguely rotund man with receding hair and thick, black-framed glasses was standing before her.

"Mr Simon Wickham?"

"I knew you'd get here eventually."

"Expecting me, sir?" Innes said.

"We're not in Antarctica," he said with a frown. "We've been talking about nothing else since the discovery of that poor girl up in the woods on Boxing Day. I presume that is why you are here?"

"Yes, it is. I'm DC Innes," she said brightly, and then fumbled around for her ID wallet. "Here's my warrant card."

He peered through his glasses. "I see."

"We're going house to house, or lodge to lodge in this case, to speak with people concerning the incident in the woods up the hill yesterday."

"Another incident?"

"A man was murdered, sir."

The surgeon took a step back. "God, was he?"

"Have you not heard?"

"No. You'd better come in."

They settled in the lounge, which was identical to all the others. Innes kept her coat and gloves on and rummaged around for her notepad. "I won't keep you long, sir."

"Good, fine."

"No need to be nervous. Just a few simple questions."

"Fire away."

"Where were you yesterday morning between seven and eight?"

"I was making breakfast in here and watching the news."

"Can anyone confirm this?"

"Absolutely not, sorry. I made scrambled eggs and coffee. I'm supposed to be eating porridge to reduce my cholesterol," he said unhappily. "You'd think being a doctor I'd know better."

"We're all allowed a treat now and again, sir."

He looked down at his protruding gut and frowned. "Well, yes… that's sort of why I'm here really. I'm one of those people who can't say no. Very easily addicted to things. I've had a terrible time with prescription drugs. All since the accident."

"The accident?"

He paused. "There was a problem with the anaesthetic during one of my client's procedures. She died."

"I'm sorry to hear that."

"Things went badly for me after that. Especially recently. I had to leave my practice in Harley Street with my partner and take some time out. Things reached a head on Christmas Eve when I was so high I nearly fell off the balcony of my house in Earls Terrace in Kensington. I knew I had to get away."

"Are you originally from London?" she asked.

Wickham looked at her, running his tongue over his lips to wet them before replying. "No, I'm from around here as a matter of fact."

"Where exactly?"

"I'm from Marlborough."

Her eyes widened. "Ah, small world. I moved there recently."

"That's where I went to school," he said dismissively.

"But where did you go to university?"

He paused, took a sip of his coffee and set the cup back down on the side table. "Oxford."

"That must have been a great experience."

He pushed his glasses up the bridge of his nose. "Not particularly. I studied medicine at Magdalen College before moving to London."

She made a note on her pad and then looked up to meet his anxious gaze. "We're taking DNA and blood samples from everyone who was in the vicinity at the time of the murder. Will you give us one?"

"DNA and blood?"

"Yes."

"Is that strictly necessary?"

"It's helping us rule people out, sir."

"Seems rather invasive, but I don't see why not."

"Thank you for your time, sir."

When she stepped out of Wickham's lodge a gust of wind blew more leaves across the isolated path and made her shiver. Looking into the gloom, she saw Jacob's tall, imposing figure making his way over to her from the other lodge and she felt a wave of guilt about Kent and his suggestion that she should spy on him.

"All good?" he asked.

"I think he was high," she said quietly. "Very vague and nervous. What about you, sir?"

"I don't think you would have wanted to meet your hero."

As they stepped into the woods, another light snowfall began to drift to earth through the pine trees surrounding the lodges. Jacob put out his hand, palm facing upwards and caught some of the flakes which quickly melted in the warmth. "You know what?" he said turning to Innes. "I think they might just be right about this blizzard that's supposed to be blowing in."

*

Neil Talbot was cleaning mud off his boots out at his cottage in the woods when he heard something moving around in the undergrowth behind him. A ranger of more years than he could remember, he knew it was a person – too heavy to be a dog and too light to be a deer. With the old potato peeling knife in his hand, now all covered in mud, he turned and stared out into the trees.

"Who's there?"

The sound of the wind singing in the trees was the only reply.

"I know someone's there. Come out! This is private land!"

When the person he had called on stepped out of the trees, the first thing Talbot saw was the matte black barrels of a twelve bore shotgun raised into the aim and pointing squarely at his face.

"Put that bloody thing down!" he yelled. "You could kill someone!"

When the gun went off, Talbot was only dimly aware of the shot tearing into his face and throat, and then he collapsed backwards and smashed the back of his head on the cast iron boot scraper. As he faded away, he caught one more glimpse of his killer, slowly stepping back inside the shadows of the wood.

*

The gunshot split the icy air like an axe slicing through wood. Startled jackdaws took to the air as the shot echoed out across the rolling fields. Jacob and Innes stared at each other in shock, and then the SIO reached for her shoulder and pulled her down into the tangled undergrowth. "Down!"

"What the hell was that?" she said.

"Sounded like a twelve bore." He peered over the fallen trunks and branches. "It was close, too – no more than two hundred yards over there to the west, around Talbot's cottage."

"Bloody hell."

"Normally I'd presume it was just a farmer in a place like this but not after the murder this morning."

Both Wickham and Everett came to their doors.

"Get back inside and stay there!" Jacob yelled, and they both obeyed.

Innes looked up at him. "You think it was aimed at us?"

"No way to know," he said. "Let's find out."

"Are you sure that's a good idea, sir?"

He looked at her, eyebrows pulling down to shadow his eyes. "What do you want us to do, call the police? Come on!"

They got to their feet and cautiously made their way along the path in the direction of the gunshot until they reached the cottage.

"There!" Innes said.

Jacob looked down and saw Neil Talbot's wounded body slumped down between his Land Rover and the front door. He ran over to him and checked his pulse. Lifting his eyes from the horribly mutilated face, he looked up at the young woman. "No, he's gone."

Then he saw it – no more than a shadow running through the woods behind them.

He leapt to his feet. "Over there!"

Innes spun around. "What is it, sir?"

"Could be the killer or a witness. I'm going after them." He ran to the tree line, turning as he vanished into the trees and calling out over his shoulder. "I want back-up here now!"

He watched Innes reach for her phone and then turn to face the woods. The shadow was slipping away to the north now, dressed in black and moving like a demon.

No gun, Jacob thought.

He powered forward, his legs pumping as hard as he could muster as he sprinted along the wooded path. December air clawed at his throat as he gave pursuit to the fleeing man, but he was much faster and had a massive head start.

"Stay where you are!" he yelled. "Police!"

But he was gone and Jacob felt like his heart was going to burst. He slowed and came to a stop, leaning his hands down on his knees as he crouched over to get his breath back. Slowing his racing heart in the middle of the woods, he heard nothing but birds and wind and then another eerie deer bark. Standing back to his full height he turned around on the spot and kicked a rock from the path twenty yards into the trees, cursing loudly.

Another failure.

CHAPTER 23

M organ was sitting at the desk in the MIU when the telephone rang. Already irritated by the lack of progress on the case, the annoying trill of the plastic phone pushed him over the edge. Snatching the receiver from the cradle he whipped it up to his ear and shouted.

"What!?"

"You don't sound like you're having a very good day, Inspector."

"Ah, Mia. Sorry."

"Quite all right. Have you considered a stress ball, or early retirement perhaps?"

"Funny. Unfortunately, I don't think that's going to cut it this time. Something's gone down over in the woods north of Four Sisters. Another shooting, apparently, but we didn't hear anything over here. Anyway, the boss is over there and he doesn't sound very happy."

"Sounds like I've got a busy afternoon ahead of me."

"Looks that way. Anyway, I take it you have something for us?"

"As a matter of fact I do — two major breakthroughs. First, I had a nice visit to a farm this morning and I can tell you that the quad Cooper was driving on the morning of Kieran Messenger's murder is an exact match to the fresh tracks we found next to the body."

"Oh, glory be."

"Second, I've been busy looking at all the CCTV footage of the raid on the pharmacy warehouse up in Swindon."

Morgan felt the clouds in his mind breaking apart and a little light starting to seep in. "Don't stop now, Mia. You know how much I like it when you talk dirty."

"It's good news," she said, ignoring him. "I've used digital reconstruction software to clarify the images and improve the definition as much as I can and I think we have a match for Cooper."

"But they were all wearing masks during the raid."

"But not when they got back in the getaway vehicle. It's not a perfect match but our facial rec software is telling me an eighty per cent likelihood that the man driving the Transit is Dean Cooper, so how do you like those odds, Inspector?"

"I like them very much – and having met the little toerag I'm confident his personality will provide the other twenty per cent."

"Then I would say the case is closed."

"Thanks, Mia. I owe you big time."

"I'll take payment in a pint at the next England-Wales game."

"You're on."

*

Jacob and Innes were standing outside Talbot's cottage watching uniformed constables stretching barrier tape around the crime scene when his phone rang.

"Good afternoon, boss."

"Bill, hello."

"Any news from Talbot's place?"

"Nothing. Someone was up here, Bill. I chased him into the woods."

"The killer?"

"Maybe, he was wearing what looked like a black Chesterfield coat, but he didn't have a gun and we can't find one in the area."

"Good, another job for Sherlock Holmes, then. Anyway, I've got some good news."

"Makes a change."

"Mia called. We've had two major breakthroughs down here and I thought you should know about it straight away."

He glanced at Innes who was staring back at him with expectant eyes.

"What breakthroughs?"

The young detective's eyes darted over to his and she mouthed the words *what's going on?*

Morgan said, "After trawling through the facial recognition system guess whose ugly mug they found?"

"Mr Cooper's?"

"Bang on target, and guess where?"

"Surprise me."

"In the driver's seat of a Transit van on its way out of the Hillmead Industrial Estate in Swindon. He was bright enough to take the number plates off the car but not to hide them well enough to stop an enquiring mind such as Anna Mazurek from finding them."

"Great work, Bill."

"But it gets better. The quad tracks found by Messenger's body only happen to belong to the vehicle Cooper uses for his farm work."

Jacob smiled. "I want everyone in the MIU within the hour for a briefing."

"Will do. Looks like we might be getting somewhere."

*

"Thanks for getting here so quickly," Jacob said. "As you'll all know by now there was a fatal shooting this morning in woods to the north of Four Sisters coppice and Neil Talbot the Forestry Ranger was killed. DC Innes and I were on the scene within minutes but sadly he was already dead by the time we arrived. I saw an unidentified man in the woods behind the cottage and gave chase but was unable to apprehend him."

"We'll find him, guv," Anna said.

"Let's hope so. The CSI team are already over there now investigating the scene and searching the area and will get back to us when they're done." He turned to Anna. "I want you to get on to the National Firearms Licensing Management System and check for anyone around here with a shotgun licence."

"It's a very rural area, guv. There's likely to be a lot of them."

"I know, but you never know what can turn up. As we all know, tracing lead shot to a shotgun is pretty much an impossible task, so the licencing angle is our best bet. In the meantime, I called us all together because we've had a breakthrough concerning Dean Cooper thanks to the work Morgan and Holloway have been doing with Mia and the CSI team."

A murmur of excitement went around the briefing table.

"I'll hand over to Mia."

"Thanks, Jacob. First, it's not all good news. At the moment we can't directly link him or his girlfriend to the murder of Kieran Messenger. The boots we found in the mud around Messenger's body could belong to either a man or a woman. Weathering has distorted the prints so it's impossible to tell one way or the other, so that's a blank and certainly impossible to connect them with a specific individual."

"Great start," Anna said.

"Criminal records?" Holloway asked.

"Here's where it starts to get interesting. Rachel Ryall has previous for dealing cannabis and meth and Dean Cooper has previous for joyriding and arson, only his real name is Richard Dean Cooper."

Jacob looked at her sharply. "Details?"

"Turns out Richard Cooper stole a car and burned it out in a field when he was a teenager, way back in 1992."

"The year of Emma's disappearance."

"And he was inside HMP Erlestoke when she went missing."

"So he's out of the frame for Emma's murder," Jacob said.

"And Talbot's," Morgan said. "He was with me and Matt when that gun went off."

"We *have*, however, identified the quad tracks found near the body as belonging to the one Cooper uses at the farm," Mia said.

"But that could have been anyone with access to the farm," said Anna.

Innes fiddled with her pen. "And none of his previous form points to murder."

"But if you ask me, they are *prime* suspects," Morgan said.

"What about the DNA samples?" Innes asked.

Mia said, "Among the samples we've received in CSI, we've had Cooper's and Ryall's but none from the lodges yet. I'll be processing them as soon as I get back. When will I get the rest?"

Jacob said, "I have a team of PCs collecting DNA and blood samples from everyone in the vicinity as we speak. No one has objected and everyone is cooperating so we should be able to get the rest to you before the close of play today."

"Great, thanks."

"Wait," Anna said, shifting in her seat. "What about Messenger's phone? You said you found an email message on it requesting to meet. Does that link to Cooper?"

Mia Francis shook her head. "Sorry, but we traced the email back to a young woman living in Marlborough. She said she was his girlfriend and they were seeing each other behind his wife's back."

Morgan sighed. "Please don't tell me she has an alibi."

"She has an alibi."

"Which is?"

"Massively hungover at a house with seven of her friends. She'd been at a Hen Party in Swindon the night before."

Anna frowned. "None of this sounds like a major breakthrough, guv," she said. "I'd hate to think you were the type to over-promise and under-deliver."

Jacob managed to crack a smile, but Mia answered. "The major breakthrough can be summed up in just one word – furanyl fentanyl."

Innes looked confused. "Run that by me again."

"It's a version of fentanyl," she continued. "And it was just one part of a massive haul of pharmaceuticals recently stolen from the pharmacy warehouse on the Hillmead Industrial Estate in Swindon."

"I know fentanyl," Morgan said. "Just finished a joint

operation with South Wales Police concerning the stuff. It's very nasty," he said. "A synthetic opioid with extremely high levels of toxicity. GPs prescribe it from time to time as an anaesthetic but it has some pretty chunky side effects ranging from euphoria on the one end and coma and death on the other."

"And it's not just doctors who dish it out," Anna said.

"Quite," Mia said. "Everyone knows how dangerous heroin is, but fentanyl is around fifty times stronger. Even the tiniest quantity of the stuff can be fatal and that's why there are so many users who overdose on it. It can be bought as a powder, cut with heroin or disguised as any one of a hundred tablets."

Anna crossed her arms. "How very reassuring."

"Users can swallow it on blotting paper, snort it like cocaine or they can inject it intravenously as they might with heroin, but whichever way they deliver it to their system they're dicing with death every time. The powdered version is not only cut with heroin, which is quite bad enough, but also with mannitol and paracetamol, among other pharmaceuticals."

Jacob sighed and shook his head. "It comes over from China mostly but it's also stored in warehouses like the one that just got knocked off in Swindon, and on top of that it can be made in home-built labs. After going through smaller distribution centres it winds up in our kids. It's a big problem and it's getting worse every single day and now we have CCTV of Cooper driving a stolen Transit van away from a raid in which an industrial quantity of this chemical was stolen," Jacob said.

"Not to mention fentanyl traces in Messenger's car and Cooper's bloody quad tracks next to his dead body," Morgan said.

"That *is* a major breakthrough," Anna said. "And at this moment I feel I should point out that it's all thanks to me for getting hold of those number plates."

"A round of applause for Anna Mazurek," Morgan said.

Anna slapped her hands and rubbed them together. "So let's go and get the bastard!"

"We'll need a warrant first," said Jacob.

"Dawn raid?" Holloway asked.

"I'd prefer to move faster. You and Innes go around and see if his car's in. If it is we'll move today before dark." He paused. "We're running along two different roads at the same time and it's important not to get confused," he said. "We're still on the Emma Russell case, but after these leads, we have to work even harder to solve the murders of Kieran Messenger and Neil Talbot for the reason we know their killers are alive and quite possibly in the area."

"Or their *killer*," Morgan said.

"Right. Our working hypothesis is that the three murders are linked but if they're not I can't waste resources on a twenty-six-year-old cold case when we have an active killer on our patch. In the meantime, we have intelligence linking Cooper to a serious crime so we go and get him now."

"Good call," Morgan said.

Jacob turned to Holloway. "I asked you to organise another house to house with an extended radius, Matt. Any news on that?"

"Almost finished, sir. It's quite a large area and very sparsely populated but so far nothing has turned up and everyone we've spoken to can account for their movements during the times of the murders."

"All right, keep going – you never know what might turn up out of the blue."

"You can say that again," Morgan said.

"Sorry?"

"And behold," the Welshman said in his gravelly voice. "There arose a great tempest in the sea, insomuch that the ship was covered with the waves, but he was asleep."

"Bill?"

Morgan tapped his knuckles on the MIU's side window. "I present to you Chief Superintendent Marcus Kent, and he looks like he's spent the morning licking piss off a stinging nettle."

*

The presence of Marcus Kent had cleared the MIU like Moses parting the Red Sea, and now Jacob found himself sitting in tense silence as his commanding officer drummed his fingers on the edge of the table and kept his eyes fixed on the plasma screen attached to the wall.

Jacob was sitting opposite him and the two men were both watching aerial footage of Grovely Wood filmed by a BBC news helicopter. The area looked much bigger from the air, but both men were more interested in the bright red news ticker running along the bottom of the images: *THIRD BODY FOUND IN WOODS.*

Kent lifted a compact remote from the desk and muted the reporter's sombre words.

"This is not a good development, Jacob."

"No, sir."

"First Emma Russell's body is found, then Kieran Messenger has his head bashed in and now the bloody Forestry Commission Ranger is shot dead on his own porch."

"Yes, sir."

"As SIO I expected you to be getting out ahead of this by now and making real inroads as far as the Russell murder was concerned. Instead, you've got nothing, and worse than that we now have a second and third murder on our hands and endless talk of ghosts and witches. It's absurd and turning us into a laughingstock."

"We're doing everything we can, sir. We have evidence that a local man was involved in the fentanyl raid in Swindon recently and we're going to pick him up as soon as we can get a warrant from the magistrate."

"That's all well and good, but a drugs bust is not why we're sitting in the middle of these bloody woods, is it now?"

"No sir."

"No sir," he repeated. "It is not. We're here because we're engaged in a triple murder enquiry and all you can come up with is a drugs bust at the other end of the county."

"There might yet be a connection, sir."

"And there might be bloody fairies at the end of my garden," he said angrily. "I'm going to need results, Jacob, and soon, or I'll have to take you off the case."

"But sir!"

"My hands are tied. As I think we both know, rumours are going around about your mental health."

"My mental health?"

"Don't be coy. We both know what's going on here. Word is that you never recovered after the fire and I was wrong to let you back in. We talked about this."

"And who, may I ask, is behind these rumours?"

He paused a beat. "I'm on your side, Jacob. You know that. But I can't support you indefinitely without results. You have to show you're in control, and right now, the way this investigation is currently going I'm not sure you are."

"We're on top of it, sir."

"Don't make me laugh. This whole operation is like a drunk on an icy pavement. All over the sodding place. I've decided we need to give a press conference immediately to try and stem these ridiculous rumours about witches for one thing. We need control. I need you to play it down and whatever you do, *don't* aggravate the killer. He could easily be watching."

"No problem. I'll go down now."

Kent laughed. "If you think I'm letting you out there alone you can think again." He unmuted the TV. A reporter was standing under an umbrella at the end of the road doing a piece to camera, the grim, familiar woodland in the distance over his shoulder.

...there are even rumours that the deaths of all three people were part of some sort of ancient ritual. These woods behind me are said to be the location of the brutal murder of several women in the eighteenth century who were accused of witchcraft following over one hundred deaths by smallpox. Some local people have pointed to similarities between the graves of the women accused of witchcraft and the way the newly discovered bodies were discovered, when asked if there was a danger of more murders, local police said...

Kent sighed heavily and hit the off button. When the screen went black he turned with barely contained anger on his face. "It's not even factually accurate."

"No, sir."

"I mean it, Jacob. I want results or I'm pulling you from the case – got it?"

Jacob nodded but said nothing.

He got it.

"Now, get the press up here."

CHAPTER 24

From her flat in Salisbury, Sophie Anderson watched as Jacob and Kent walked out of the MIU and over to where the press had been corralled behind some barrier tape. It was a much bigger group than she had imagined, with several news cameras and around two dozen reporters huddling under umbrellas in a bid to stay out of the wind and sleet.

With her hands wrapped around her favourite coffee cup, she found herself feeling unusually nervous for him, hoping everything went well. She prayed no one had found out about the pile of police property that was sitting in a cardboard box just beside her television set.

Jacob wore his overcoat and gloves but no hat and he had forgotten his scarf as well. It didn't seem like the cold was bothering him. As he strolled over to the press, Marcus Kent was still flanking him and arranging a thick scarf around his neck. The isolated location meant no members of the public were around, and she thanked heaven for small mercies.

After a flurry of questions, Kent raised his gloved hands and made the 'settle-down' gesture. "I am able at this time to confirm that we have been able to identify the second victim as Kieran Messenger and the third as Neil Talbot. Both men were local and worked together in the Forestry

Commission."

"Did either man know Emma Russell?"

"It's possible," Jacob said. "We're looking into it."

"Looking into it?" the reporter said.

Kent cleared his throat and offered a reptilian smile. "Our CID department is fully utilising all of its resources in a bid to establish if Emma Russell, Kieran Messenger and Neil Talbot were ever mutual acquaintances."

"Has the poacher arrested for her murder in 1992 been found?"

"Jim Latimer was arrested but released without charge at the time as there was no evidence to link him to any crime. We have not been able to locate him."

A murmur of dissatisfaction went around the group.

"On the subject of the more recent murders, Chief Inspector, we've heard there's a consultant on the investigating team – a criminal profiler who specialises in serial killers. Is there any truth to this?"

Marcus Kent looked at Jacob darkly, his brow furrowing as the Chief Inspector answered.

"No."

"Because if that were true would it not suggest either that your department is not capable of solving these murders without outside assistance or that these really are serial killings?"

"It suggests no such thing," Kent snapped. "Now the Chief Inspector will brief you on the details."

Sophie looked on with a strange feeling of responsibility

for Jacob as he started to take their questions. When he spoke about the psychological ideas she had discussed with him, she felt a burst of pride, but then a sense of dread when the next question came.

"Chief Inspector, are you capable of leading an investigation after such a personal tragedy and being out of action for so long?"

Kent stepped in. "We have full confidence in DCI Jacob. Next question."

"Is there anything to the rumours that these murders were part of some sort of religious rite?"

Kent answered before Jacob had a chance to open his mouth. "We have no reason to believe that at all."

*

Jacob braced against the wind whistling through the trees, his only consolation being that he had the toasty MIU to go back into while most of the press had nothing more than their cars. With Kent still at his side, he decided to shake things up. From out of nowhere, he fixed his eyes on the BBC camera and started to speak. "I know you're watching."

Kent turned subtly towards him and tried to catch his attention, but Jacob ignored him.

"I know you're watching me now, and I know you've been watching me since we discovered the remains of Emma Russell. You've been watching all of us, up here as we work and I want you to know something. You're not going to get away with this. You killed a young woman and buried her in these woods and until this week you thought you'd been lucky enough to get away with it."

Kent fought hard to keep the rage from taking over his face.

Jacob hardened his voice. "I'm here today telling you that your luck just ran out. I have solid evidence pointing in your direction. You will be found and you will be brought to justice for what you did."

Kent lowered his voice to the slightest of whispers and leaned into Jacob's ear. "That's enough."

He ignored him again. "I'll say right now that you're not half as clever as you think you are and you will be caught for what you did here this week, and for what you did here all those years ago. I won't sleep until you're stopped for the simple reason I can't. I can't sleep knowing a creature like you is free and walking the earth."

A flurry of wild questions burst from the reporters like frightened birds, but a furious Marcus Kent ended the press conference in a hurry, telling them to move back behind the barrier tape. With a red-flushed face, he steered Jacob back towards the MIU.

"What the hell was that?" he snapped. "I expressly told you to play it down and not aggravate the killer, and what do you do? You march out there in front of the nation's press like Wyatt Bloody Earp and do everything you can to aggravate the bastard!"

"I want him scared."

"And I want you sacked, laddo, so you're bloody lucky the Chief Constable has such a high opinion of you. If it weren't for him you'd be out on your arse quicker than you can say 'where's my pension?' And why the hell haven't I been briefed on this so-called solid evidence?"

"Because there is none."

His cheeks reddened further. "Then what are you playing at, man?"

"As I said, I'm trying to provoke him, get him to make a move, make a mistake."

"You just antagonised a brutal killer, a man who may have been moved to kill again just this week to cover up what he did in 1992. You may very well have put someone else's life at risk."

"We're not talking about an irrational killer sir or an insane serial killer. This is someone cleaning up to protect a very old and very dark secret and we need a way to get to him."

"Last chance, Jacob." Kent pulled on his gloves and told his driver to start the car. "One more error in judgement and I'm handing the case to Morgan. He's a good man and more than capable."

"Look, we're raiding Cooper's place this afternoon. I'm confident something will turn up there."

Kent turned as he stepped out of the MIU. "Last chance."

*

After seeing a fuming Marcus Kent climb into his car and head back up to headquarters, Jacob made a coffee and sat down at the table in the back of the MIU. From the window, he was able to see a short glimpse of a watery sun as it slipped below the canopy of the woods and sunk into a barely-visible cloud-strewn horizon.

This landscape was quiet; most people were safe at home with their families enjoying each other's company and their brand new gifts. But he had a very different afternoon ahead. While the rest of the team were preparing for the raid on Cooper's cottage and with dusk falling early, he had decided to take this moment of peace to once again go through all the paperwork and files that the case had accumulated over the past twenty-six years.

There was unsettlingly little to read.

He lifted the cup to his mouth and swore under his breath as the cheap, scorching coffee nearly burnt his lips. Setting the cup down with a curse, he rubbed his eyes and opened the old manila folder. Inside were the original case notes of Emma Russell's missing person investigation. Her whole life amounted to a small stack of A4 paper less than one centimetre high.

His first reading of it back at the station had been a quick scan to gather the most salient details, but now he pushed back into the chair and made his way through the file in more detail. On the surface of it, everything looked in order: medical student, 23 years old, home from university, goes missing after a night at the pub – but Jacob's eye was sharper than that.

Something wasn't adding up.

He had over twenty years of police experience, and fifteen of them were in detective work. He recalled one of his favourite Sherlock Holmes stories, *Silver Blaze*, and the famous line about the dog that didn't bark. It wasn't the information that was in the file that bothered him, but what was missing from it. After he had pondered it for a few moments he concluded that DI Miranda Dunn had made some serious errors, and the fact there was so little in the file forced him to consider some kind of cover-up as a possibility.

And that meant trouble because her line manager at the time was Marcus Kent.

Back then, when the girl went missing, Dunn was a freshly-minted detective inspector, and Kent, a DCI, was her immediate superior. The two of them had conducted the search for Emma Russell, focussing on Salisbury and Oxford, and then Dunn had filed this report. On the surface every box had been ticked – from the house to house to interviews with old friends from college and university - and yet something didn't add up.

His phone rang.

"It's Mia."

"Hi."

"We're finished up at Talbot's cottage."

"Anything to report?"

"No forensic evidence I'm afraid, and no guns in the woods. There were three shotguns inside a locked cabinet in his cottage but none was the murder weapon. As for the lead shot that killed him, it was a standard non-toxic tungsten-bronze, size five. Due to a very low sectional density, lead shot loses its velocity very fast after leaving the muzzle, so I can say that shot of this size would be bought for hunting game, and most likely clearing rabbits off the land."

"Thanks, Mia. We go from strength to strength."

"But wait till you hear this."

"What?"

"Neil Talbot wasn't his real name."

"No?"

"Nope. We found all the proper deed poll paperwork in his loft. His real name was Jim Latimer."

The words hit Jacob like an ice pick. "Bloody hell."

"He was your original poacher turned gamekeeper."

"And someone didn't want us to talk to him."

*

The man with the pagan tattoo stared at himself in the mirror. He was proud of the ink on his arm, but also disgusted by it and what it had come to represent. Rolling his shirtsleeve down he covered the thing up, and for a moment his dark past went with it. He pulled a cigarette from a crumpled pack on the side of the sink and lit it on the third stroke of the match.

Another death, another kill.

Things had been better.

He considered summoning Artio like a stray dog to meet in the car park of the abandoned ice cream factory where they had met once before.

A phone call would suffice.

"It's me," he said.

"I saw it on the news. Why did you have to kill him?"

He breathed out a cloud of smoke. "I dealt with the problem. It's over."

Almost over.

"You shouldn't have killed him."

"Farewell, Artio. We must never speak again."

He cut the call and closed his eyes and instantly he heard the sound of the screaming in his head. Sometimes, their voices haunted him like phantoms. Once every year, the souls of the dead returned from the underworld and paid a visit to the world of the living. That was what they used to believe. Did he still believe it? He had no idea.

The acrid smell of the struck match still lingered. Oxidised potassium chlorate, sulphur and glass powder. He dragged on the cigarette and felt the chemicals seeping into his bloodstream. Jacob meant business. His latest TV appearance proved that. He was arrogant and unpredictable but he was good, and now he was on a mission.

Things had to change, and fast, but no matter how he looked at the problem the conclusion was always the same – there would have to be more killing before nightfall.

CHAPTER 25

With the dark December dusk once again gathering over the downs, Lucinda Beecham walked back from the lodges after checking the guests were all right and opened the back door of Grovely Manor. Taking her jacket and boots off, she walked into the kitchen and filled the kettle. Choosing her favourite cup, she placed it on the side and began her coffee grinding ceremony.

The murder of Neil Talbot practically on her doorstep had shaken her up and she found herself wishing for something stronger as she filled the kettle.

Then she heard something behind her in the hall leading down to the dining room. The noise startled her and she gasped before trying to calm herself down.

Another sound.

Scared almost witless, she grabbed a knife from the block, but then she discarded it in favour of something more substantial. She walked over to the large handmade wooden gun cabinet her father had made back when she was a child and the property was a working farm. She snatched the keys off the shelf and fumbled to find the right one, certain she had seen something move in the shadows of the fire back in the kitchen.

Unlocked.

She was sure she had locked it, but it had been so long since she'd looked.

She opened the cabinet and pulled out her father's shotgun. It was a twelve gauge, side-by-side double-barrelled Cogswell & Harrison chambered for three-inch cartridges. She hefted it from the cabinet and her mind was flooded with memories of her dad. Growing up on a farm, he had taught her to know the weapon back to front and inside out, and now she rapidly loaded both barrels. Heavy in her hands and reeking of gun oil, she closed it up and made her way back into the kitchen.

Nothing but a kettle on the boil.

She silently disengaged the safety catch and raised the heavy gun into the aim. "Who's there?"

No reply.

"I know someone's here," she said, her voice starting to wobble with fear. "I'm armed and I know how to use it!"

A pocket of sap deep inside one of the logs on the fire exploded. She spun around and aimed both barrels at the fireplace, almost firing.

Jesus, Indie… get a grip.

She looked at the phone and considered calling the police. The man called Jacob who had spoken to her about the murder in the woods had seemed nice. Approachable and fair. No, she decided. If there was no one here she would look like a hysterical fool. This wasn't the first time she'd had burglars at the property, and she'd coped before. Part and parcel of living in a rural location with so few police around.

Another noise, this time from her office where she kept the company safe.

She spun around with the gun, repositioning the weapon's smooth walnut stock against her shoulder and made her way slowly down the hall.

*

Less than half a mile away, Anna Mazurek glanced at her watch and then slipped it off and put it in her pocket. She had been on too many raids to know how easily the glass face could get smashed if there was any trouble. She sighed and tried to make the stab vest vaguely comfortable. She hated wearing them but it was protocol for an occasion like this. Cooper was known to be violent, and the risk of getting stabbed or shot was very real on a raid with someone like him involved.

"I've been looking forward to this," Bill Morgan said, rubbing his hands together. "If we get a result I'm buying the drinks."

"Everyone hear that?" Anna said. "The Inspector here says the drinks are on him."

"If we get a result," he added hastily. "If he slips the net yet again there won't be enough money in the world to drown my own sorrows, never mind all yours as well."

The raiding squad had assembled in the MIU, carefully coordinated by Jacob whose days in the Met and Thames

Valley had supplied more than enough experience. Now they drove around to his property and pulled up just out of sight at the entrance to his drive.

Jacob looked his team in the eye. "All right, listen up! On the surface, Dean Cooper is a hard-working farm labourer. After moving down from Swindon after the joy riding bust he started all over again, and he's generally law-abiding and respected around these parts. But scratch that surface, as we did when we started to look into his life, and you find a much nastier piece of work."

"You can say that again," Anna said.

"We know he can't have killed Neil Talbot, not personally, anyway, and he was in prison for arson when Emma Russell went missing, but there's evidence he was involved in Kieran Messenger's murder – tracks to a quad he had access to were found next to the dead man's body and fentanyl was found in the pickup, plus he has no alibi."

"It's got to be him, sir," Holloway said.

"We'll see what we can get out of him in an interview, but now we also have reason to believe that he's heavily involved in the smuggling and distribution of illegal narcotics across the south of England, especially here in this little corner of it. Thanks to the hard work of Morgan and Holloway and the CSI team we've all seen his ugly mug in the CCTV footage of the raid on the Swindon warehouse, so we know he's in it up to his neck. We can presume that whatever he's up to, it's going to be involving this little cottage of his and tonight's the night we put an end to it."

"What if he gets to his car?" Anna said.

"We've got the end of his drive blocked, so that shouldn't be an issue. All ready?"

"Yes."

"Then let's do it."

*

Lucinda Beecham stepped into the office and saw the French windows were open. Freezing cold air pushed into the house from the icy twilight outside in the yard and two long silk voiles billowed into the room like ghosts drifting in from the December darkness.

Maybe I should have called the police after all.

She moved deeper into the room, noticing that the old Italian oil painting in front of the safe was still in place. She moved over to the wall behind the desk and lifted the painting an inch off the wall. Seeing the safe was untouched she turned around and prepared to walk out into the yard.

That's when she saw him, standing in a long black coat beside her drinks' cabinet.

"What are you doing here?"

"Here." He handed her one of the chunky cut-glass tumblers. "Let me buy you a drink."

"How dare you just break in here!" she said and moved to leave the room.

Still holding both glasses, he moved to block her way to

the door. She felt the hairs rise on the back of her neck and lashed out, swinging the muzzle of the gun through the air. The tip of the barrel caught the tumbler's rim and shattered the top half of it over his gloved hand.

He cursed and hurled both glasses into the carpet where they landed with a muted thud.

"If you touch me, I'll scream." She was breathing heavily now, her heart beating hard in her chest.

The man sucked at the blood on his wrist and then brought it against the woman's face hard and fast, knocking her down to the floor where she dropped the gun. For a few seconds she stayed down in the arctic white plush pile like a deer shot through the neck; collapsing in a snowy field with seconds to live.

As she crawled up to her knees, he studied his wrist wound in detail and saw a tiny shard of glass glinting in the blood. He pulled the splinter from the cut and carefully placed it in his pocket.

As he cursed again, she staggered to her feet, snatched up the weapon. "I'll kill you if you come any closer."

"We both know that's not true."

He took a step closer and she turned, making a break for the open French windows.

The blow came from behind, knocking her forward off her feet and pushing her over the threshold of the French windows. Tumbling out of the door into the yard, she dropped the shotgun once again. This time it clattered to the gravel and fired one of the cartridges. The roar of the weapon cracked the evening like an axe splitting wood as she fell face first and struck the snowy ground. He cursed, picked it up and ran back into the kitchen.

Through the stars in her eyes, she managed to turn around just in time to see his face as he returned and stepped out into the yard. Looming over her, his hands were still hidden in leather gloves and there was a fiendish grin on his face. Was he carrying something new in one of his hands? When she saw what it was, she screamed but her voice was hoarse with terror.

"Leave me alone!"

The man said nothing but raised his arms as he moved towards her.

"What's that in your hand? No… please!"

Her pleas fell on deaf ears, and the next thing she knew she was paralysed with fear. Unable to scream or move or fight him off, she felt the leathery gloved fingers wrap around her wrists. Then he started to drag her by the arms across the gravel drive, moving around the side of the house to where her car was parked. He dumped her numb body down on the ground as he opened the door of the classic Mercedes and then heaved her up over his shoulder before bundling her inside the car.

"I'm so sorry it had to end like this," he said gently.

She strained to speak but no sound came. Her body was frozen and now she was struggling even to breathe. Her head swam and she felt sick. How hard had he hit her on the head? A panic attack loomed as she fought to suck air into her lungs. Why was it so hard to breathe?

"You will asphyxiate before you breathe the smoke," he said. "And certainly before you feel the flames."

Smoke? Flames?

She felt her heart quicken as he moved out of sight. When he reappeared, she saw with horror that he was holding a pressed steel jerrycan. He unscrewed the lid and began to slop the contents over the car's roof and bonnet. Leaning inside the old car, he hurriedly slopped more of the liquid over the top of her and now her sense of smell told her what before she had only dared to fear.

Petrol.

"The tragic end of a burnt-out actress."

How could he do this to me, after all I have done for him?

He pulled a lighter from his coat pocket and dumped the empty jerrycan inside the passenger's footwell. Flicking the spark wheel with his thumb she saw in the periphery of her vision a small flame burst to life.

Her heart thundered like a drum.

She wanted to scream but couldn't move a muscle anywhere in her body, and then he tossed the lit lighter into the car. There was so much petrol everywhere it ignited the fumes before it even reached the leather seat. A savage burst of fire ripped through the cab in a second, barely giving him enough time to slam the door and run away as fast as he could.

She couldn't scream.

She couldn't move.

As she felt the fire dancing all over her body, she could do nothing but stare forward with frozen eyes. The last thing she ever saw was a crescent moon rising over the skeletal canopy of the woods running along the ridge to the south.

CHAPTER 26

Early dusk gathered as the sun slowly sank in the west, streaking the evening sky with deep ambers and glowing ribbons of red. Out here on the downs, the cold of the day was rapidly getting worse, and the scent of damp, rotting leaves drifted on the icy breeze. Where alpine swifts would fly in the summer, now a solitary brambling fluttered over their heads before spinning around and vanishing behind Tithe Cottage. In the distance, the last of the light was swallowed by the dank green rise of Grovely Wood.

The small raiding squad was ready to go, and when Jacob gave the order they crossed the small front yard, led by two officers gripping an enforcer. Informally nicknamed the 'big red key' by the police, the chunky steel battering ram delivered a hefty blow of more than three tonnes of force to any front door.

"Go!" Jacob said.

The enforcer smashed the door open and the team flooded into the house.

"Police officers!"

"Police – stay where you are!"

Radios buzzed as they stormed into the house, one team pounding upstairs two steps at a time while the other worked their way through the ground floor.

"We got him!" Holloway yelled from upstairs.

Jacob moved from the empty kitchen back through the hall just in time to see the young detective marching Dean Cooper down the stairs. He was wearing a black down jacket over a heavy metal t-shirt with a satanic emblem on the front of it and a pair of torn jeans. Behind him, Anna Mazurek was guiding Rachel Ryall in the same direction.

"Where do you want them, sir?"

"Outside."

"We ain't done nothing!"

"Tell someone who cares," Morgan said, and read Rachel Ryall her rights. "Take her away."

As they gathered outside in the gloom, two uniformed constables dragged her kicking and screaming to a police van. Moments later they fired up the engine and pulled away to take her back to the station.

Jacob approached Dean Cooper with his crooked smile. "Now you."

"Piss off!" Cooper struggled in Holloway's arms as he fought to pin his arms behind his back and cuff him. He was pulling up his right arm so hard he thought it might break and grunted in pain as he yelled at him to release it.

"Richard Dean Cooper," Jacob said calmly. "I am arresting you on suspicion of murder and possession with intent to supply. You do not have to say anything, but it may harm your defence if you do not mention when questioned something you later rely on in court. Anything you do say may be given in evidence."

"Murder?! Get stuffed!"

Jacob sighed. "You will now be taken to the nearest police station where you will have your fingerprints taken and you will be placed in custody. You can contact a brief when you get there."

He looked from the struggling, sweating man up to Matt Holloway and the uniformed PC standing beside him. "All right, take him away."

"I can't get the cuffs on him, sir," Holloway said.

"Is that a fire?" Innes said.

Jacob stopped what he was doing and turned to face her. "Where?"

"Over there through the trees."

They all turned to see what she was talking about and then it happened. Cooper's formidable strength overwhelmed the young detective and he spun around, bringing his elbow up into his face. A wet crunching sound filled the air and Holloway grunted with pain before falling back and striking his head on the side of a police car.

With blood pouring out of his nose, the young man slumped down unconscious against the front wheel while Jacob lunged forward to subdue Cooper but it was too late. He'd grabbed hold of Innes and put her in a chokehold and was now walking her back towards the trees. "Stay away from me or I'll break her neck."

Morgan moved forward but Jacob stopped him. "Wait, Bill."

"But we can't let him take her!"

Everything had changed in a second. Not only had Cooper escaped custody and was now holding one of his officers as a hostage, but something very serious was happening over in the retreat. "Anna, call the fire brigade and get yourself over there and see what's happening. We'll handle this."

"Guv."

He watched her jog down the drive and disappear into the woodland dividing the two properties before turning his attention back to the fugitive. "You're not going to hurt her, are you Dean?"

"You leave me alone, and I'll leave you alone! Bloody coppers!"

"Just take it easy and let go of her," Jacob said calmly. "You don't want to add assault and battery and kidnapping to the other charges, do you now?"

"If you stay back, I'll let her go when I'm out of here!"

Now Jacob took a step forward. "That's not acceptable, Dean. I can't let you take her."

Innes stared back at them with horror in her eyes. She had raised her arms and was trying to pull the man's muscly, tattooed arm away from her neck but she was too weak to move it an inch.

Then, through the trees, they all heard a wild explosion.

"Shit!" Morgan said, turning to face the fireball in the woods. "I hope Anna's all right."

Jacob's eyes never left Cooper. "She knows what she's doing, Bill."

Without warning Jacob rushed Cooper, running across the dark garden and piling a hefty right hook into his face.

Cooper grunted and fell backwards but rolled twice in the shadows and got to his feet. He stepped back into the tree line, then in the blink of an eye he darted into the darkness of the woods.

Jacob and Morgan ran forward as a startled Laura Innes staggered away from the trees, gasping and rubbing her neck.

"Are you all right?" Morgan asked.

"I think so, yes."

"Good," Jacob said, grabbing Innes by her shoulders. "I want you to stay here and call an ambulance while you keep an eye on Holloway. Inspector Morgan and I will go after him."

"Yes, sir."

He ran over to the marked police car, swung open the door, opened the glove compartment and pulled out a torch. Checking it was in good working order, he ran over to Morgan and then the two of them sprinted towards the trees and scanned the area for any sign of the runaway. Full-dark now and with no snow in the air, Jacob shone the powerful Maglite into the woods and swept the beam from side to side.

"I know you're in there, Dean!"

His voice echoed through the endless pine trunks but there was no reply.

"We'll never find the bastard in there," Morgan said.

They heard a branch snap off to their left and the two men exchanged a quick glance.

"That way!" Jacob said. "Come on!"

They made their way through a patch of dense undergrowth until reaching one of the many paths that wound deep into the woodland.

"Damn," Jacob said, once again sweeping the torch beam across the tree trunks. "He's gone quiet again."

He turned to see Morgan crouch down on his haunches, carefully examining the lower branches of a pine tree. "He went this way," he said calmly.

"You're sure?"

The Welshman nodded. "Without a doubt. This is a fresh break and there are brand new footprints on the path a few yards ahead."

Jacob nodded appreciatively. "There are some compensations to having a former commando on the team."

The two men took off down the path at a jog, the torch's beam bobbing about ahead of them as they went deeper into the woods. A crescent moon hung above the treetops, offering scant natural light but then they heard the sound of another branch breaking and Cooper swearing in the dark.

"Wait," Jacob said. "That came from further around to our right."

"Little bastard's trying to get back around to the house," Morgan said. "Probably thinks he can overpower

Innes again and get in one of the cars."

Jacob shone the torch down the path and then over his shoulder back up towards the path they had just followed from Tithe Cottage. "Let's keep on his trail," he said. "He could be trying to fool us."

*

Innes saw the flashing blue lights through the trees at the end of the drive and felt a wave of relief as the ambulance turned into the property and drove up to the front of the cottage. Holloway was just starting to regain consciousness when the two paramedics climbed out, and when he was delivered into their care, she decided to execute the warrant and start to search Cooper's home.

The raid had already covered the main house, so now she walked through the kitchen and stepped out into the back garden. Raising her torch to light the path, she made her way down to the bottom of the garden where a substantial wooden workshop was nestling under a line of wild, overgrown Leyland cypresses.

She peered in through the window but realised they had been blocked by black bin bags. She walked around to the double doors and saw they were fixed with a chunky straight shackle padlock. Moving back to the window she covered her eyes and smashed it in with the tailcap of her Maglite. After clearing the remains of the shattered glass and shredded bin bag out of the way she leaned inside.

Sweeping the torch from side to side, she let out a short gasp.

"Bloody hell," she muttered. "I've never seen anything like it."

*

Dean Cooper's blood ran cold when he heard the barking. Was that deer or dogs? With the adrenaline coursing through his system and the blood pounding in his ears it was hard for him to tell. If it was dogs, he had no chance at all. His panicked mind raced.

Were they here to go through his house and locate drugs? Re-tasking dogs to hunt him down would be only too easy. How long before they picked up his scent? The hoarse, hungry barks echoed sharply in the woods and he realised with a wave of relief that they were deer barks after all. He should have known – he hadn't seen any sniffer dogs during the raid.

Trampling and trudging deeper into the trees, he tripped on an exposed tree root. He tumbled down an incline and came to a halt in a patch of hard, frozen mud. "Damn it all to hell," he cursed into the darkness and hauled himself back up to his feet, brushing off the leaves. He let out a sharp breath and closed his eyes. *Keep it together, Deano!*

The cold, harsh scream of a barn owl cut the night in two. It might have made anyone else jump out of their skin but Cooper knew the sound only too well. He'd lived here for long enough to know these birds and animals and their strange ways. He knew the place like the back of his hand, and he knew how to get a load of cops off his trail as well.

If he could get out of the woods and back around to the retreat, there were cars. His would already be impounded and besides, the cottage would be crawling with coppers like cockroaches, but the retreat had several vehicles and she always left the keys in them. It was a long shot but it was all he had.

He could hear the voices of the two older pigs now, working their way closer to him as they fanned out and made their way through the dense woodland.

Now or never, Deano my boy.

He took a deep breath, crawled out of the ditch and walked east towards the retreat. Finding the way through the woods at night was not easy, but tonight a roaring car fire was like a beacon leading him to safety. They had Rach but she would never squeal on him and he couldn't help her if he was in the nick as well.

The fire was terrifying. It looked like the old gull-wing Mercedes she used to swan about in, only now it was a burning wreck of bare paint-stripped steel and blistering, melting plastic. Too bright to look at, his terrified eyes drifted upwards at a thick column of noxious black smoke slowly vanishing in the bright starlit sky. Beyond the blaze, he saw a handful of people he presumed had come from the lodges to witness the horror, and from somewhere behind them, there was another flashing blue light.

Fire.

Ambulance.

Probably more pigs, but he had to push on. After all, when they found the amount of China White in his shed they'd throw away the key.

He raced to the garage, his heart set only on escape and burst in through the side door. As expected, he saw several cars, but instantly settled on the Jaguar F-PACE. A fast and reliable SUV that had the best chance if he had to go off-road. Nothing could stop him now.

Nothing except the copper who had just appeared in the garage in search of a fire hose.

CHAPTER 27

Anna watched in horror as Dean Cooper snatched a chunky wheel nut wrench off the top of the workbench and rushed her. What the hell was he doing in here? He wasn't in here a second ago when she had searched the place for a bucket, so he must have just arrived and was on the run.

And she knew there was nothing as dangerous as a man on the run.

Now he was lunging towards her, swinging the wrench above his head like an axe. Aiming for her head, he swung it down with all his strength. She dodged his lunge and sidestepped him, grabbing a long ring spanner from the workbench and bringing it up into his ribcage.

He grunted in pain and lashed out once again with the wrench, punching one of the steel arms clean through the window behind her. Aware she was alone with a very dangerous criminal, Anna remembered her training and stepped into the fight. As he pulled the wrench free from the smashed window, she thrust her hand forward and grabbed one of his wrists.

Shocked by her bravery, he hesitated before trying to pull his hand out of her grasp, raising his other arm ready to deliver a heavy slap to her face. As she reached down to pull the handcuffs from her belt, the back of his rough hand made contact with her cheek and knocked her down to the polished concrete floor of the garage.

She looked up, dazed by the power of the blow he'd just delivered to her head but still able to see him as he stepped over her and ran to the car. He swung open the driver's door and climbed up into the seat. Firing up the engine he hit reverse and smashed out through the double doors, turning much of them into matchwood and spraying a hail of splinters all over her.

Anna tucked her face down into her arm to protect her eyes and heard the car's wheels spinning on the drive. Smelling burnt rubber smoke, she lifted her head just in time to see the Jaguar reversing down the drive at speed. A handbrake turn spun the large vehicle around one-eighty degrees in a billowing cloud of yet more burnt rubber smoke and it raced away flinging wide arcs of gravel in its wake.

Hitting the road, it bounced on its suspension as the young man slammed the car into third gear. He spun the wheel and pulled the car away on the main road in a wild flash of headlights from oncoming emergency vehicles on their way to the property.

"Bugger it all!" She clambered to her feet and sprinted over to another of the retreat's vehicles, a brand new Volvo estate. Climbing inside, she turned the key in the ignition and took off in pursuit of the Jaguar as fast as she could.

Steering out onto the road, she snatched her phone from her pocket. "Jacob?"

"Yeah?" he said in a breathless voice.

"If you're looking for Cooper he made it to the retreat and has now stolen a car. I'm giving pursuit. I'm driving east and requesting any other traffic units in the area. There's just one on board as far as I know."

"Is he still in sight?"

"Yeah, I'm right behind him, speed eight-zero miles per hour. He's really going for it."

Once again she thought of cornered animals and that was exactly how the driver up ahead would be feeling right now. A few minutes ago he was sitting in his cottage minding his own business and raking in a good source of cash from his dodgy fentanyl enterprise, and now he was on the run from the law after seriously assaulting a police officer.

He had nothing to lose so he was going all out to escape whatever the cost.

He finished tearing past the oncoming emergency vehicles and turned onto a narrow unsealed lane with no streetlights. Plunged into a new darkness, Anna followed the brake lights of the fleeing car as he twisted and turned along the tiny track.

"I think he's headed for the A303."

He vanished around a corner and she speeded up to try and close the gap. Turning the same corner she saw nothing ahead but a silent lane lit up by her headlights.

"Wait, he's gone out of sight."

"Be careful Anna!" Jacob said.

She slowed down and scanned the area for any sign of the other car, and that was when she saw the headlights in her rearview mirror. "I think he's behind me!" she said. "He must have pulled off into one of the fields to surprise me."

She prayed it was just another vehicle, but when it ploughed into the back of her and sent her smashing forward against her seatbelt she knew who it was.

"He's just rammed me!"

Speeding up for a second attack, the Jaguar smashed into her again and knocked her off the lane and careering down into an irrigation ditch. Smashing to a stop, the impact threw her forward, locking her seatbelt and triggering the driver's airbag.

Dazed, and seeing the Jaguar disappearing into the distance, she spoke weakly into the phone on her lap. "I'm off the road."

"Hold on, Anna," Jacob said. "We have other units on the way."

She blew out a long breath and slumped forward into the airbag.

*

Jacob cursed and put his phone in his pocket before posting Innes to watch the workshop and make it a formal crime scene. Then, he and Morgan made their way towards the fire. By now the scene was littered with fire trucks, ambulances and police cars and the night was lit blue and red by the flashing emergency lights.

As they'd walked through the woods he'd had a bad feeling about the blaze and when he saw the fire crew manager's face he knew his instinct was right again.

They'd found someone inside the car.

"What the hell happened here, Mark?" he asked.

Mark Roland took off his helmet to reveal a red, sweat-soaked face. With his team fighting to control the last of the fire, he shook his head and sighed. "Hard to tell until a formal investigation, Jacob."

Morgan sighed. "Come on, man! You've been doing this for thirty years."

"I'm not prepared to go there, Bill. But for what it's worth, I can tell you that the doors were unlocked."

Jacob turned back to Roland. "Surely you can't be thinking it's suicide?"

"It's almost unheard of to top yourself like this," he said, shaking his head. "But I just put the fires out, you find the people who start them and why."

Jacob looked away from the smoking wreck and stared up at the stars. "Ain't that the truth."

"Any idea who it is?" Morgan said.

Before the crew manager replied, Jacob, spoke. "The smart money's on Lucinda Beecham."

He sighed and turned to Morgan. "Come on. Let's go and see what Innes found inside the workshop. I can't stand being around fire."

*

Less than two miles away, Anna's head was still spinning when she saw the blue flashing lights and she realised now for the first time that her wrist was pulsing and throbbing and bright red. She had injured it in the crash. Cursing, she blinked a few times and tried to get her focus back, and the next thing she knew a uniformed traffic constable was opening her door and unbuckling her seat belt. "Are you all right, Sarge?"

"I'm not sure. They rammed me pretty hard."

Steam poured from the burst radiator at the front of the car as the policeman leaned into her vehicle. "Lucky they didn't hit you on your side or we might have needed the fire service to cut you out."

She heard a car skid to a halt behind them and saw two more traffic officers walking over to her.

"Did he get away?" one asked.

"I'm sorry?"

"The scrote you were chasing," he said. "Did he get away?"

"Yes."

"Description?"

"Er…"

"Come on, Sarge! We have a criminal on the run."

"I'm dizzy!" she snapped. "He's IC1, mid-thirties, dark hair. Average height. Wearing a black t-shirt with some kind of band's emblem on it and a baseball cap as well."

"Number plate?"

Anna gave him the number and a description of the car and then gently climbed out of the smashed Volvo.

The traffic officer huffed out a sigh and walked over to his car. Lifting the two-way radio to his mouth he said, "All units, we've got a man on the run in a blue Jaguar F-PACE. Rammed an officer in the pursuit. He's got a fentanyl factory in his back garden so be advised he won't come quietly."

Anna watched him as he slung the radio back inside the car and cursed. "What a day this is turning out to be."

She screamed and kicked a chunk of soil out into one of the fields. The fentanyl find was a solid piece of police work but they still had no leads on the murder and thanks to the blaze at the retreat it looked like the killer might have dialled things up a notch.

She cursed again but then started to feel even dizzier so sat back down in the car. In her mirror, she saw the traffic officer walking back over to her. He crouched down and handed her an ice pack. "Here, hold this against your head."

"Thanks."

Then he turned to his colleague. "And get this woman an ambulance, for Christ's sake."

CHAPTER 28

J acob and Morgan followed Innes into Cooper's backyard workshop and were amazed by the scale of the enterprise they saw before them.

Morgan whistled. "There must be enough fentanyl in here to supply the whole of southern England."

"A good result, Innes," Jacob said. "Well done. It took courage coming out here on your own."

"Thank you, sir."

"I know that face well enough to know you're not happy," Morgan said.

Jacob frowned. "Now we know Cooper wasn't the killer of Lucinda Beecham," he said. "For the very good reason he was being chased around by us at the time of the fire – we saw it light up, after all."

"Could have been a timer."

"He's not bright enough to do that," Jacob said. "But it was meant to look like he was the killer."

Morgan nodded. "His arson record?"

"Exactly – setting a car on fire right next door to a convicted arsonist's house? It's a frame-up, for sure, and whoever did it knew he had the record. That meant he knows Cooper personally, or he's very good at researching through old newspaper archives."

"They're online these days, boss."

"His arson story wasn't," Jacob said. "I checked. It was years before the internet and only featured in two local papers. If the killer wanted to frame him it would have meant sitting in a library going through endless microfiche film."

"There is another explanation."

"I don't want to go there."

Morgan stepped closer and lowered his voice. "It could be someone on the force."

"Yes, but we don't *know* that, not yet. We *do*, however, know Cooper couldn't have killed Lucinda Beecham, and he was with you when Talbot was shot, plus he was inside when Emma went missing. He's looking less like a killer by the hour."

"But if Cooper's not our man, then we need to start looking elsewhere."

"Yes," Jacob said with a sigh. "Yes, we do."

*

Anna waited patiently in the Accident and Emergency Department of Salisbury General Hospital. She knew she hadn't been badly injured and so did the triage nurse, but she had to wait to be seen and signed off by a doctor, nonetheless. As she watched the sea of miserable faces all around her, also waiting mostly in silence under the harsh industrial lighting, she realized she would rather be just about anywhere else on earth than in a hospital, especially at this time of night.

Beside her, Matt Holloway sat with a bloody cloth held to his nose. "I expect they'll be along soon."

"I bloody hope so," she replied, still holding her swollen wrist. He was trying to be as supportive as he could, but it was obvious he hated the place as much as she did. "At least you know it's not broken."

"Yes."

"And that your skull's thick enough to absorb a hefty blow by a thug like Cooper."

"Yes again. I was lucky."

"Sergeant Mazurek?"

She looked up to see a smiling nurse. "Yes, that's me."

"This way, please," he said.

She followed the man along a short corridor and into a small office where a doctor was sitting behind a desk. The nurse explained what had happened and the doctor examined her for a few moments before declaring her fit and well, except for the obvious damage to her wrist which required an x-ray.

She went to another department where there was another short wait and then the x-ray, and then back to the doctor where she was told it was a severe sprain but no fracture. The doctor bandaged it up and put it in a support. After prescribing some heavy-duty painkillers she was discharged from the hospital and made her way back to A&E where Holloway was scrolling through something on his phone.

She kicked his leg with her shoe and he looked up, startled. "Oh, it's you, Sarge. All done?"

"Apparently so. Please get me out of here."

"You don't need to ask me twice, that's for sure. I'll call a cab."

*

An hour after Holloway had dropped her in Swindon and gone off in the cab, Anna's boyfriend had called and demanded to see her. She had relented and they had decided to seek shelter from the snows in a busy pub, surrounded by people drinking real ales and wine and having a good time.

Everyone except Anna Mazurek, who was looking glumly at her wrist brace and nursing her bruised pride. She cursed herself for not being able to apprehend Cooper, and even worse, letting him ram the car. Portman had apparently been easy-going about the whole thing and expressed nothing but concern for her wellbeing, but the car was a write-off and she just knew some of her colleagues were going to make her life hell for it until the end of time.

But judging by the look on his face over at the bar, not half as much hell as Gareth Butterfield was going to give her for the rest of the night. He sullenly padded over to the table with two pints and placed them on the table before sitting down opposite her.

"You could have been killed, Anna."

"It was nothing."

"Nothing? A maniac in a car tried to kill you and you say it was nothing."

She sighed and took the top off her pint. The little snug out the back of the pub was busy, but not as hectic as it got during the summer. She closed her eyes and took a deep breath, wincing as an electric bolt of pain shot through her wrist and up her arm.

"I presume a doctor has seen that?"

She nodded. "Went up to the hospital after the raid."

He sighed again and shook his head at some unvoiced outrage or disappointment while the barman who always smiled at her sauntered around the pub and collected empty glasses off the tables. She lifted the pint of beer to her mouth and took another sip while peering at him over the top of her glass. A little too young for her, maybe? She weighed it up in her mind. The good looks could make up for any other doubts, she was sure.

"Well?"

She flicked her eyes back to Gareth. She knew he'd been talking but her attention had been swept away by the barman who now saw her and gave another smile.

"Wait, what?" she said.

Another sigh and his shoulders slumped down. "You're not even listening. I said it's about time we started talking about taking the next step."

"The next step?"

"Yeah, and I want to talk to you about your job, too."

"Not this again."

"You don't need to work, Anna. I earn more than enough to support the two of us, and it's so dangerous! What about when we have kids?"

The K-word. He'd not mentioned the word kids before and now she was worried. It was true that he earned more than enough. His architecture business was thriving and he'd recently had a massive boost after being featured on a television programme about a young couple building a new home just outside Trowbridge.

"But that's not the point," she said, then her phone rang. "Wait."

She looked at the Caller ID and saw once again a name that made her blood run cold. This time, her ex-husband had left a short message: "I do hope you're not ignoring me."

"What is it, Anna?" Gareth asked.

"Sorry?"

"Who is it?"

"Oh, nothing… I mean no one," she mumbled, slipping the phone back into her pocket.

He sighed. "You were saying something wasn't the point."

"Was I?"

"Uh-huh."

"Oh yes. I work because I love my job and I'm doing something good, contributing to society. It's not just about money."

He snorted. "Just as well."

She let it go, but he hadn't finished yet. "How am I supposed to explain to the kids that their mother's been shot or stabbed or killed in a car crash?"

"We don't have any kids."

"Not yet, no."

She vanished again behind the rim of her beer glass and half-wished she was being chased by Dean Cooper again. The whole evening was getting a little too heavy for Anna Mazurek.

*

An evil life is a kind of death.

The man in the car blew out a deep breath and tried to steady his nerves. He opened the glove compartment and pushed the glass bottle and syringe deep inside, before pulling off his leather gloves and throwing them in on top. Closing it with a chunky click, he put his hands on the steering wheel and tried to think about something else, but the image of the dying woman rose in his mind like a spectre.

Ovid knew it well enough, and now he did too.

He picked up his phone and made the call.

"It's done."

"I know. I watched the car burn. It's over now."

"We will not speak again. I expect the others to stand

by their oath."

He cut the line abruptly and the electronic trill of the end-call tone filled the silent car like a warning siren. *It's over now.* The words echoed in his mind like a mantra, delivered over and over again until he thought he might go insane.

He turned on the ignition and the engine roared in the cold. Checking his mirror, he gently pulled away from the side of the lane and followed the signs back to the main road, making sure to drive in the opposite direction from the chaos back at the retreat.

Nor tardier fruits of cruder kind are lost, but tam'd with fire, or mellow'd by the frost.

Tamed with fire indeed, but something told him it was all far from being over.

CHAPTER 29

Saturday, 29ᵗʰ December

After midnight, and Jacob was standing alone in the courtyard staring at what was left of the burnt-out Mercedes. Hands thrust in his pockets and plumes of breath condensed in the air as he breathed, he shivered with the cold of the night but his mind was fixed firmly on the heat of what happened here earlier today.

How a woman had been trapped in a car and consumed by fire.

He shuddered and pulled up his collar.

His fiancée had died in a fire just over a year ago and he still found it difficult to think about, never mind being confronted by yet more evidence of its hideous destruction.

He turned his mind to work.

In the hours after the blaze, there had been progress. Amongst the charred remains, a watch found by the fire crew had potentially identified the victim as being Lucinda Beecham. Formal identification would be made by DNA analysis in the morning, but his instinct told him it was her, and with luck, Mia's CSI team who were now combing through the property would be able to collect more evidence in their case against the unknown killer.

295

With Anna and Holloway packed off to the hospital to have their injuries assessed, Morgan and Innes had interviewed the three guests in their lodges, and none had an alibi. Each one claimed to be alone at the time when the blaze started, and then all three came out and walked through the woods to see what had happened. Finding the burning car, they had spoken and Bryony Moran had called the emergency services. Phone records would at least confirm the call.

Morgan wandered over, hands in his pockets and his square face framed by a thick woollen scarf stuffed down into the top of his coat.

"Boss."

"Bill."

"I sent Innes home."

Jacob nodded.

"And I just got a message from Hampshire Police."

"Sending their Christmas greetings?"

"Better than that. Their traffic boys found a blue Jaguar F-PACE upside down in a ditch on a B road heading into Southampton. Inside was one Dean Cooper, knocked out and sleeping like a baby. Naughty boy had been going a bit too fast in his zeal to get away and start a new life somewhere else and skidded on black ice."

"Oh dear," Jacob said.

Morgan shook his head. "What a shame."

"How sad," they said together.

"Where is he now?" Jacob asked.

"Southampton General Hospital. They're driving him up in the morning providing the quacks say he's good to go."

"Something to look forward to."

"That's just what I thought," Morgan said. "What about his missus?"

"Not said a word since we took her in, apparently. We'll split them up tomorrow morning and see what we can get out of them."

"You sent Anna and Matt to the hospital, I presume?"

He nodded. "I told them to go home afterwards."

"You big softy."

"She could have been killed."

"We're talking about Anna Mazurek," Morgan said.

"What are you saying?" Jacob asked. "That she's invincible?"

"I'm saying that no way did she go home after the hospital. She'd have gone straight to the pub."

Jacob smirked, but it was a hollow gesture. "It's after midnight, Bill. Go home."

He watched the Welshman pad over to an unmarked Insignia and climb inside. Headlights on and then after a tight circle on the gravel drive, he was gone on his way back to his semi in Swindon. Walking over to his car, he briefed the uniformed constables that he was leaving and that no one was to enter the property as it was a major crime scene.

Climbing into the car, he received a text. Checking the phone, he saw it was Sophie. She wanted to speak with him.

She said it was urgent so he gave her a call.

"Hi, Sophie. It's after midnight – what is it you want to talk   about?"

"It's the tapes from the archives that you got me from the original enquiry back in 1992."

"What about them?"

"I've gone through all of them, both the formal interviews and the televised appeal."

"And?"

"It's not good. We need to talk."

"What's happened?"

"I'm now sure someone in the police was involved with the disappearance of Emma Russell."

The words hit him like an ice pick in the chest. "Say that again, slowly."

"I've been analysing them and I think you might have a real problem here."

He already knew, but he had to ask. "Who?"

"The same person whose statements were dodgy. Detective Inspector Miranda Dunn."

His mind spun with fears, real and imagined. "I'm calling Bill Morgan. If what you say is true we're going to need to be on the same page from the very beginning."

She paused a moment too long.

"What?" he asked.

"How much do you trust him?"

"I trust him with my life."

"I hope so, Jacob, because this thing could go sideways

like a car on black ice in no time at all."

"I do. You and Bill both live at different ends of the county and the roads are all clear, so we'll meet at my place as soon as possible. If you get there before me there's a spare key under the plant pot to the right of the front door."

*

Driving through the night, Jacob used his hands-free kit and called his old friend. "Where are you, Bill?"

"Still on the road, approaching Tidworth. Why?"

"You need to take the next left and get over to my place."

"I know you're lonely, Jacob, but don't you think this is going a bit far, man?"

Jacob rolled his eyes and smiled. It was good to know Morgan never changed. "Just be there Bill. I've just had Sophie on the phone and there's something you need to know before work in the morning."

"But it's the middle of the night."

"It's about your favourite ex-copper."

Morgan's tone changed. "Is it now?"

"Yes."

"Like old times you mean, working through the night?"

Jacob smiled. "Like old times."

"I'll be there within the hour."

*

When Jacob pulled into the Old Watermill he saw Sophie's Audi parked up near the front door and the kitchen light was switched on. She had found the spare key and let herself in as he'd suggested and when he opened the door she was asleep at the kitchen table with a stack of CDs and VHS cassettes in a box in front of her and a cold cup of coffee at her elbow.

When he clicked the door shut she flicked her head up, startled. "Oh, it's you."

"It *is* my house," he said, throwing his keys on the side.

"Sorry, I fell asleep. I was at my parents' place when I called you so I got here in no time."

He nodded his head at the box on the table. "I see you brought the goodies."

She gave a nervous smile. "Yes, most are CDs but some are still on video, so *please* tell me you have a VHS player."

Jacob paused. "Now you're asking."

*

He climbed down the loft ladder twenty minutes later with an old, dusty VHS player under his arm and a victory smile on his face. "Success!"

"That's brilliant!"

"I thought they'd copied all of these old tapes from the archives onto CDs a long time ago, to be honest," he said, pushing the ladder back up through the hatch and shutting it up.

"Maybe these were deliberately left?"

He shook his head. "Occam's Razor says they were just forgotten or overlooked. If anyone wanted them not to be seen it would be easier to take them home one night and throw them on the fire."

They walked back downstairs and into the front room where Jacob lit a fire and Sophie connected the VHS player to the television set.

A knock on the door.

"That'll be Bill."

He returned a moment later with the former commando at his side.

"Well, isn't this cosy?" the Welshman said.

"We're ready to start," Sophie said with a smile.

Morgan clapped his hands together. "Great! Anything to eat?"

Sophie looked at him with confusion on her face. "It's two a.m."

"And?"

Jacob slapped him on the back. "Pizzas in the freezer."

"Good stuff," said Morgan, padding back down the hall. "I knew you'd have something here."

*

With hot pizza slices on every plate, Jacob, Sophie and

Morgan settled down to watch the video cassettes he had liberated from the archives. Most were straightforward interviews of various witnesses and Jim Latimer, the local poacher who had reinvented himself as Neil Talbot and retrained as a forest ranger after his experience as the prime suspect. But the most damning was the TV appeal for witnesses organised by the police a week after Emma Russell's disappearance.

"Watch carefully," Sophie said.

They were looking at a trestle table with a blue cloth draped over it showing the emblem of Wiltshire Police. Behind the table were Emma Russell's parents and Detective Inspector Miranda Dunn, the SIO of the original case.

"I'd forgotten how she used to look," Morgan said. "She looked hard even then."

Jacob watched Miranda Dunn closely as she sat beside Emma Russell's parents and talked to the cameras. Then, Sophie paused the old videotape footage, rewound it a few seconds and turned to face Jacob. "Hear that?"

"What?"

"She starts to speak and then stops very suddenly and goes off in another direction. This is what we call a false start. It's what people do when they're lying and they suddenly realise they've said the wrong thing. The first thing they utter – even if it's just a couple of words – often has critical information that they're trying to cover up."

Jacob took another bite of the pizza. "What did she say

in the false start?"

"*Those…the person or persons responsible for this*," she said. "That's the false start, right there. It tells me that she's attempting to modify what she says by restarting her sentence because the first thing she said was the truth, but the second thing was a managed response, the creation of a new impression that she wants to give."

"This is starting to give me a headache," Morgan said with a smile.

"When she diverts the sentence, *those* becomes *the person or persons responsible*. In other words, she starts talking about a group of people – *those* – and then quickly tries to hide that fact by making it look more ambiguous. She's trying to make it look like she doesn't know how many people were responsible for Emma's disappearance but the false start tells us she knows it's more than one person."

"And you're sure this is what it means?" Jacob asked. "That she really knows more than one person was responsible for Emma's disappearance?"

Sophie nodded. "And there's more. Here she's talking about two witnesses who said they saw her later that evening after she left the pub in Salisbury."

"That's odd," Morgan said. "I don't remember them from the archived files."

"Me neither," Jacob said. "She must have removed them."

Sophie frowned. "Well, when she points at the map of the area where they said they saw her, which was on the

A36 to Southampton, it comes a second after she describes it as the new search area. She's lying. If she was telling the truth the action and the words would be simultaneous. I would suggest that the fact the gesture comes a second later than the description means what she's saying just isn't true."

"That those witnesses never existed?" Morgan asked.

She nodded. "Or that they did and she falsified their testimony to justify misdirecting the search."

"To get everyone away from Four Sisters," said Jacob.

Morgan sucked his teeth. "But the witnesses would know she was lying about what they had said."

"No," Jacob said. "The real witnesses would have no way to know if other people hadn't come forward with new statements about seeing her on the A36."

"So you're saying that she's lying?" Morgan said to Sophie.

Sophie nodded. "This time, I think so, yes."

Jacob whistled. "I hope you know what you're talking about."

"I do," she said with confidence. "And there's more. Look at her eyebrows here, notice the way they're perfectly symmetrical when she's expressing sadness about Emma's disappearance?"

"Yes, I can see that."

"It's genuine sadness. If she were simply trying to look sad out of respect, one would be higher than the other, just by two or three millimetres, but there's perfect symmetry."

"Maybe she was genuinely sad," Jacob said. "A young woman had just gone missing, after all."

"She was definitely genuinely sad – I'm asking you if you think she's the kind of person who would be genuinely saddened by the disappearance of a woman she never knew."

"No chance," Morgan said. "Not only was she hard as stone to start with, but she was a copper and we can't do our job if we let our emotions get in the way."

"I'm not convinced," Jacob said. "Have you got more?"

"Sure." Sophie ran the tape forward a few seconds. "Watch this section here. Notice that when she says she's doing everything she can to find Emma, she moves her shoulder ever so slightly."

He squinted at the television set and leaned forward in his chair. "It's hardly at all."

"Those few millimetres are a big deal. What she's actually doing there is called gestural leakage."

"I'm tempted to make a joke at this point," Morgan said. "But I'll refrain."

Sophie rolled her eyes. "Thanks."

He laughed and finished his slice of pizza. "As you were."

She smiled and gave a polite laugh, but it was late and they were all exhausted. "This gestural leakage is a negative contradiction of the positive statement she's making at the same time. It's a very strong indication that she's deceiving the press and the public. It is my opinion she certainly was *not* doing everything she could to find Emma."

Jacob lowered his head and rubbed his temples. "I'm not liking where this is going. Just pray to God it doesn't go any higher than Dunn."

Morgan looked over at him with a cynical expression. "If we're reduced to praying… wasn't your father a vicar?"

"No," he said with a smile. "Dad was an engineer. Your thinking of my grandfather John Jacob. He was the churchman."

"I knew someone was," the Welshman said. "You think he could help us now?"

Jacob shrugged and laughed. "I don't know anything anymore – this is like a nightmare that never ends."

"In that case, I'm sorry to say the nightmare hasn't ended yet."

She ran the tape forward again, watching the timestamp until the right moment and then hitting play. "This is another classic sign of deception. When one of the reporters asks her if she believes Emma is still alive, she answers that yes she is and that she has every reason to believe she will be found alive and well."

"Problem?"

"Problem is that when she says *yes she's alive*, she shakes her head very slightly. It's very slight, almost imperceptible but it's there, and it's contradicting the affirmative statement that Emma's still alive. Her body language is telling us not only that she thinks the opposite of that but that she *knows* she's not alive."

"But at this stage of the investigation, no one knew whether she was alive or dead."

Sophie crossed her arms over her chest and nudged her chin at the TV. "*She* did."

CHAPTER 30

Jacob immediately understood the import of what she was saying. Miranda Dunn had been a respected member of the CID and had retired shortly after the Russell disappearance. She was decorated with the Queen's Police Medal for saving the life of a pregnant woman during a bank raid in Trowbridge. To suggest she had been anything less than above-board during a major investigation would rock a lot of boats.

"I think we need some sleep," he said, turning to Sophie. "There's a spare bedroom upstairs."

"No," she said. "I want to keep going."

"Bill?"

"Bugger that," he said. "I want my beauty sleep. I'll see you two kids in the morning."

He padded off down the corridor leading to the western staircase while Jacob and Sophie went back to work, carefully scanning every inch of videotape and CD footage of the original investigation until the entire archive had been studied. The conclusion was that Miranda Dunn was guilty at the very least of knowing much more about the disappearance than she had put in her reports, and Jacob knew she would have to be interviewed.

He stretched back on his leather wingback and yawned. Got up and put another log in the burner and swung the cast iron door shut. Yawned again as he crashed back into the chair. He looked at Sophie as she leafed through some of the investigation's paperwork and was impressed by her commitment and focus.

It made him think of Jess sitting on the window bench seat of their Oxford home, reading her Kindle in the evening sunshine. She sat there for hours sometimes, not even noticing that the sun had gone down, a glass of wine untouched at her side. He knew he'd lived that life with her, but now it seemed like nothing more than a dream.

When Sophie spoke, it startled him back to reality with a jolt.

"I'm sorry?"

She smiled. "I knew you weren't listening."

"I was just… I'm tired."

"If you want to sleep I don't mind going on alone."

"No, really…" and, an hour before dawn he was sleeping.

*

Bill Morgan heard the phone ringing but decided to ignore it. He turned his attention back to the pan of frying bacon and eggs in front of him. Working all night had already given him quite an appetite and he'd gone the extra mile and helped himself to some of Jacob's expensive Wiltshire pork sausages, tucked away at the back of the fridge.

He won't mind, he thought with a mischievous smile, *he's a good lad.*

All that remained was the eating, and then back to work.

He set about transferring the food from the various pans to three plates and then poured three mugs of steaming builder's tea. Turning the gas off and pushing the empty frying pan to the back of the stove, he set the full plates on the table, walked across the kitchen and down the hall to the front room where Jacob and Sophie were still asleep.

The boss was in the armchair by the fire and she was stretched out on the leather sofa with a throw over her. When he'd left the room last night to go up to the spare room there had been no throw, so he guessed either she had woken in the night and tracked one down or the boss had put it over her. Maybe he was coming back to life again, after all this time.

"Wakey, wakey," he said, his heavy Welsh accent filling the room. "Eggs and bakey."

Two sleepy heads turned and looked in his direction.

"What is that amazing smell?" Sophie said.

"A proper cooked Welsh breakfast."

Jacob squinted, his hair messed up after a night in the chair. "Aren't they traditionally called English breakfasts?"

"Not when I make them, now get up the table before it gets cold."

They followed him through to the kitchen when the phone rang again.

"Did I hear that a minute ago?" Jacob asked.

"I let it ring off," Morgan said. "You looked so peaceful when you were asleep," he said with a twinkle in his eye. "Beautiful even."

Jacob gave him his best withering look. "It might have been important. Hang on – are they my sausages?"

"I doubt it," Morgan replied, moving things swiftly along. "If it was important it would have been my phone ringing."

He rolled his eyes and snatched up the phone. Checking caller ID he sighed. "Kent."

"I didn't know he did a wake-up service," Morgan said. "Such a nice man."

Jacob ignored the comment and spoke into the phone. "Good morning, sir."

"Is it? I heard all about the car fire last night."

"Yes, that was very nasty. Lucinda Beecham was killed in it."

Kent sighed, and Jacob imagined him reaching for the headache tablets in his top drawer. "I do hope you're not going to tell me it's connected with the woods murders?"

"Sorry, sir, but I think it's connected with the woods murders."

"A fourth dead body all tied up in the same case?"

"I believe so, yes sir. Any word on Cooper?"

Kent spoke wearily. "He's back at the station. Minor head injuries and a bit of whiplash. He's awaiting your company in Interview Room 2. You'll be pleased to know that CSI found fibres from one of Kieran Messenger's jackets in his pickup."

Jacob was disappointed. "Is that it?"

"It's better than nothing. Go and rattle his cage and see what you can get out of him. You know the drill. I thought I'd set it up first thing so they're already waiting for you. No sense delaying things."

Jacob looked longingly at the plate of eggs, bacon, sausage, grilled tomatoes, fried mushrooms and hot buttered toast Morgan had just set down on the heavy oak table.

"How thoughtful, sir."

"You know me, Jacob. It's the thought that counts."

When Kent disconnected the call, Jacob relayed the news of Cooper's arrival at the station to the others. Tossing a house key to Sophie, he told her to lock up when she'd finished breakfast.

"What about me?" Morgan asked, staring hungrily at the food on the table.

"You're coming with me."

Morgan threw down his knife and fork and pushed back from the table. "Bloody hell. Looks like I'll have to make do with just the one rasher." He snatched it off his plate as he stood up and pulled his coat off the back of the chair. "Bloody Marcus Kent."

*

Innes was unusually nervous as she drove into work. Like

everyone else on the team she had already been briefed that Cooper was in custody and that the interview would take place this morning. Craning her neck to see herself in the rear-view mirror she could still see the red marks on her throat from where he had gripped her last night.

She thought about Jacob and how he had saved her life with no consideration of his own safety at all in the face of a very real threat. Kent had described a man almost on the edge, a rule-breaker with no regard for protocol, but she had seen another side of him last night.

The idea of getting onside with the Chief Super and having a fast-track to DS appealed a great deal, but her conscience nagged away at her. It was stopping her from knocking on Kent's door and helping to bring the axe down on Jacob's career. He had been kind to her on a personal level and helpful on a professional level. He had made her laugh and tried to make her transition into the team as easy as possible.

More than that, she now knew all about what had happened to him and his fiancée last year in the fire. She wasn't sure how she would react to a tragedy like that but she had nothing but admiration for the way he had pulled himself together and got back to work in one piece. When you got right down to it, expediting her career essentially meant ending his, and she wasn't sure if that were something she could live with or not.

As she pulled into the station, her mind was still buzzing with uncertainty and indecision.

*

In the interview room back at HQ, Jacob set up the tape recorder while Anna Mazurek arranged the chairs around a little table. It was an uninviting, windowless space with grey walls and the only feature besides the table was an old-fashioned iron radiator covered in chipped paint.

Cooper and his solicitor took their seats on the far side of the table while Anna slipped off her jacket, hung it over the back of one of the chairs and sat opposite them. Jacob also removed his jacket and loosened his tie and top button but chose to lean up against the door and cross his arms over his chest.

The solicitor was a woman named Natalie Abbott who had travelled down from Swindon just for the occasion. She was a slender woman in her late thirties with a blonde bob and a neat navy blue suit. On her pale wrist was a tasteful Cartier watch which glinted in the greasy yellow glow of the overhead strip light.

All of this was in stark contrast to the dishevelled slob she was representing, who was now slouched in his bucket seat in a pair of torn jeans and the same down jacket and occult t-shirt he was arrested in.

Jacob now wandered over to his chair and sat down. Due to a problem with the furnace in the basement, the room was like an oven, and he ordered a young PC to wedge open the door. Dean Cooper looked less than impressed with the ad hoc cooling arrangements and muttered a few words of complaint into his brief's ear before turning two flinty eyes on his hosts. "Ready when you are, Chief Inspector."

Jacob returned the smarmy look and leaned back in his chair to study the man opposite him. His clothes were still covered in mud, as was his sneering, fuming face.

"Good morning, Dean," Anna said. "Know anywhere I can buy some fentanyl? It's just that I'm in quite a lot of pain because some idiot drove me off the road last night." She raised her wrist brace up into his face.

"We're not disputing the drugs charges," Abbott said. "Although my client denies his girlfriend knew anything about the workshop."

Jacob raised a sceptical eyebrow. "What about the other charges? There's assaulting two police officers, car theft, dangerous driving and Kieran Messenger's murder."

"I didn't murder Kieran!" Cooper said. "He was my mate! We used to hang around sometimes."

Abbott moved to silence him. "My client denies only the murder charge, Chief Inspector, and I do hope you have something substantive against him in relation to that charge," she said haughtily. "Christmas is a very bad time to be disturbing and harassing people with false charges in this way."

"I had perfectly reasonable grounds for the search and the arrest," Jacob said. "I have a match for tracks of the quad he was driving a few yards from the dead man's body, and hot off the press I also have a fragment of the dead man's coat found inside your client's pickup truck."

Abbott sighed and leaned back in her chair. "All circumstantial evidence. My client hasn't denied knowing Mr Messenger, and neither has he denied that the dead man has travelled in his vehicle as part of his business ventures in the area."

"You mean supplying drugs?"

Abbott leaned forward and glowered at Jacob with eyes of flint. "Now, you tell me how this means he murdered the dead man because I'm having trouble seeing it."

A smug smirk spread over Cooper's face. "Yes, Chief Inspector. I would be very interested to hear how I'm supposed to have killed Kieran Messenger. Surely you're not suggesting I killed one of my best mates?"

Jacob gave a wry smile. "If you'd be so kind to tell me where you were specifically between seven and eight on the morning in question we'll be happy to remove you from our list of suspects for the murder charge."

"I already told you, I was at work."

"Not good enough," Jacob said. "We have spoken with your employer and he said you went out on the quad during that time. You could have easily killed Kieran Messenger while you were up in that area fixing fences and gone back to the farm in plenty of time."

Cooper and his lawyer had a quiet consultation, and then he said, "I was up there, all right? I saw his pickup driving up to the woods and the bastard owed me five hundred quid for some pills I got him so I went up there to have a word with him. He'd been avoiding me so I thought I'd have it out with him, but when I got up there he was nowhere to be seen."

"I advise you to stop there," Abbott said.

"No, keep going," said Anna.

"I went to his truck to see if he was there and I opened it up and had a look around for any drugs or money but there was nothing there, or so I thought. On the way back I found him in the snow and mud. His head was smashed in. I didn't know what to do so I decided to leg it. That was after eight and I swear to god I never laid a finger on him."

"Call me crazy for not taking your word for it," Jacob said. "But you still haven't said where you were between seven and eight?"

Cooper looked down at the ground. "I was round at Freeth's place doing his missus."

Jacob and Anna exchanged a glance. "Mrs Freeth, the farmer's wife?"

"That's the one, and she'll back me up. She hates the old sod."

Anna raised an eyebrow. "She's nearly twice your age."

"No law against that," Abbott said. "Now my client has told you where he was when the murder took place, and he has also said very clearly that he can prove it. I would suggest you drop the murder charge before I start thinking about police misconduct and harassment." She looked from Jacob to Anna and then back to Jacob again with

317

goading eyes. "Well?"

Jacob gave a businesslike smile and kept his voice calm and level. "I'll drop the murder charge when his alibi checks out." He walked over to the door, stopped and turned, fixing eyes of steel onto Cooper. "But the other charges aren't going anywhere, and neither are you."

CHAPTER 31

Jacob scanned the faces of his team as they gathered in the MIU briefing room deep in the woods. Three days of searching through woodland, poring over witness statements and doing house to house interviews had taken their toll and they looked exhausted and frustrated with the lack of progress. Many had pinned their hopes on Cooper being responsible for the murder but when his alibi with the farmer's wife checked out, it was as if Operation Grovely had been put back to the beginning.

"So, we're back to where we started," Holloway said.

"Not at all," Jacob said. "We've had a result, just not the one we were hoping for. Dean Cooper is a nasty piece of work. He was involved with one of the biggest smuggling gangs in the south of England. Thanks to what we've pulled out of his flea pit near the woods, we know he was the main distributor of not only fentanyl for half the county but CSI also found spice and meth. Unfortunately, there was no sign of the other drugs, but he's still looking at a nice long stretch behind bars, and so is Rachel Ryall for supplying, so well done everyone."

"He is a proper scumbag, all right," Morgan said. "But not our killer."

"No," Jacob said. "But he was responsible for the raid on the warehouse in Swindon. With that kind of form and finding his quad tracks near Messenger's body, it wasn't unreasonable to suggest he might have killed him. Unfortunately, he had plenty of cast-iron alibis up his sleeve. He was in prison when Emma Russell was murdered, he was with us when Talbot was shot, he was in his cottage under surveillance at the time of Lucinda Beecham's murder, and he was otherwise engaged with Mandy Freeth when someone was smashing in Kieran Messenger's head."

A titter of laughter rippled around the room.

"All right everyone, settle down."

"Like the boss just said, we got the bastard on the drugs charges though," Morgan said. "And that's something."

Anna waved her braced wrist in the air. "And the assault and dangerous driving charges, too."

"Yes, it looks like we've got him nailed down on all of those. The evidence on the drugs production and distribution is watertight and it looks like we're going to be able to put a very strong case to the Crown Prosecution Service. Well done everyone."

A half-hearted cheer went up, but the mood quickly dampened again when Jacob brought them back to business.

"But that brings us back to the murders and the fact that with Cooper out of the frame we just lost our prime suspect."

Anna flicked her pen onto the desk and lifted a foam coffee cup to her lips. "What are those lyrics – if it wasn't for bad luck, I wouldn't have no luck at all…"

Morgan was impressed. "Albert King," he said. "Born Under a Bad Sign. A very cool song, if I might say so."

"I'm sure it is," Jacob said, "but as my grandfather used to say, you make your own luck."

"Maybe Mandy Freeth is lying to cover for him?" Holloway said. "Wouldn't be the first time."

"Plus he seems to spend a lot of time hanging around the woods," said Innes.

"Possible, but it's getting desperate," Jacob said. "Anna, how did the shotgun licence search go?"

"As expected, too many to count but our friendly local farmer Mr Freeth is the closest to the murder scene."

"The Freeths come up again," Holloway said.

Jacob considered it. "Any number of people on his farm could have used the weapon, so collecting alibis is going to be a big job. I'll get a warrant and I want you to go down and take his guns but make sure to get any cartridges on the property. Give it all to Mia and see if she can work her magic."

"Okay, guv."

"All right, now we need to move our focus to others. Anna, what about the three men Emma did her Oxford Uni ghost-hunting with?"

Anna shook her head. "All have solid alibis. Razey was in Paris, Mitchell was with his family in Belfast and Hendry was with his wife who was giving birth in the John Radcliffe hospital."

Morgan grinned. "Which as alibis go…"

"Another dead end," Jacob said. "So let's go back to work again."

With that, he turned to the whiteboard where beside Emma's and Kieran's faces, fresh photos of Neil Talbot and Lucinda Beecham were now staring back at him. "Neil Talbot," he said. "The strong but silent type who worked as a ranger for the Forestry Commission. It was Mr Talbot who helped excavate the remains at the start of the enquiry, but now we know he'd reinvented himself."

"The original poacher-turned-gamekeeper," Morgan said.

"Mia already made that joke, sorry."

Morgan shrugged. "You have to try though."

"His real name was Jim Latimer, and before he retrained he was a bit of a vagrant drifting around the area, and yes, he was a poacher. He was interviewed under caution and arrested during the original investigation but always swore he was innocent. Yesterday, someone shot him at point-blank range with a twelve bore double-barrelled shotgun and killed him on his doorstep out at his cottage in a coppice near the lodges, not too far from where we're sitting now."

"Someone wanted to keep him quiet, sir," Holloway said. "It's obvious."

"Maybe, but we have to keep an open mind. As you know, Innes and I were at the scene just minutes after the gunshot and I gave chase to a man in a Chesterfield coat

322

but he evaded me. I've put his description out but it's vague."

"And nothing back yet, either guv," Anna said. "I checked in this morning, but I did find out that Adam Dawes, the other forester, was at home with his family when the shot was fired."

Jacob sighed. "There's no doubt Talbot was murdered and at this point, we have to presume his death is strongly linked to the others. Unfortunately, he was a loner and kept himself to himself. No real friends and rarely spoke even to his foresters unless he had to. I don't think we're going to be able to dig up too much dirt in his direction."

"Which is too bad," Morgan said.

"Moving on…" He turned to Lucinda and keeping his personal sense of failure to save her life to himself, he wrote her name in capital letters beneath the picture.

"Lucinda Beecham, known as Indie to her friends and family," he began. "forty-five years old and a former TV and film actress. By all accounts, she was very highly respected both professionally in the entertainment world and for the work, she did running the retreat."

He felt another wave of failure rise in his stomach. "She died late yesterday afternoon at dusk in what at the moment looks like the most horrific of circumstances, burning to death in her car. Unfortunately, the fire service was unable to stop the blaze before the body was very badly damaged. This greatly restricts what the pathology department can provide us in terms of evidence or leads but we do know that the doors were unlocked so I'm looking for some ideas."

"Suicide?" Innes asked.

Jacob shook his head. "Mark Roland, the crew manager who attended the scene last night told me it's practically unheard of for someone to kill themselves by sitting in a car and then setting the thing on fire. Much easier and less painful to run a tube around from the exhaust and do it that way."

"That's right," Anna said. "Self-immolation usually represents around one per cent of suicides. It's not unheard of, but it's very rare."

Holloway frowned. "Maybe someone locked her in it and after she was dead they used a remote to unlock the doors to make it look like suicide though?"

"Good thinking but no," Jacob said. "First it would be too risky to plan on the locks still working after the fire had got going and second the car was from 1959 and all the locks were manual so she couldn't have been trapped inside it against her will."

He threw the pen on the desk. "My thinking is that this was an attempt to frame Dean Cooper. We all know he did time for arson, specifically burning out a stolen car when he was younger. Whoever did this wanted us to think he killed her."

"I agree," Morgan said. "We should rule out suicide, and as she wasn't locked in against her will by the killer, it must mean one of two things. One, she was unconscious at the time of the fire, or two, someone killed her in another location before dragging her out to the car and torching it."

"But why bother doing that?" Jacob asked. "What was the point of going to all that effort?"

"Some sort of ritual?" Anna asked.

Jacob shook his head. "I'm no expert on ancient rituals but I'm sure they didn't involve gullwing Mercedes Benzes." He looked at the solemn faces of his team, struggling with images of Lucinda Beecham burning to death in the car. "But what if the car wasn't important?" he asked. "What if the fire was the important thing?"

"Go on, guv," Anna said.

"Say you want to kill someone but destroy some evidence relating to the crime. We all know fire is a reliable way to do that, but if you try and torch a house you can't be certain the fire will take hold and do its job before the fire service turns up and puts it out."

"I think I know what you're getting at," Morgan said.

"Right – torch a car and it's going up in seconds. Everything you're trying to hide or destroy, including the body, is almost certainly going to be gone long before anyone can put it out. It's a smaller object to burn and the petrol tank is full of the world's best accelerant."

"So the killer was trying to hide something?" Innes asked.

"I think so," Jacob said. "He put her in that car and torched it because he wanted to hide something – something he couldn't take with him. Whether or not she was dead at the time of the blaze might not be strictly relevant."

"So what was he trying to hide?" asked Holloway.

"That's what I want you all to think about while we're getting on with the investigation," Jacob said.

"Suspects?" Morgan asked.

"The only other people we know who were on the site at the time the fire was started were the three guests in the luxury lodges – Bryony Moran, Simon Wickham and Richard Everett. The problem we have is that each one of them claims to have been in their own lodges at the time the fire was set."

"All in it together?" Anna said.

Morgan shifted in his seat. "Yes, a conspiracy."

Jacob didn't like the word but had already considered it. "It's possible, but that's going to take us into a totally different place. What sort of motive would be required for three people to act in concert in this way and murder someone in such horrific circumstances?"

"It's very rare for murders to be committed by more than one person in a conspiracy," Morgan said.

Jacob nodded. "We'll look into it, but my hunch is that as far as the murder of Neil Talbot is concerned we're looking for Mr Chesterfield, and as far as Lucinda Beecham is concerned we're looking for a single killer, acting alone, and right now the guests in those lodges are looking like the most likely."

"You think one of the guests and Mr Chesterfield is one

and the same, sir?" Innes asked.

"Only Richard Everett fits the man I saw running," Jacob said. "He's starting to look like a real problem, but I want all three of them re-interviewed on site. Any funny business, threaten to take them up to the station and grill them there. That usually does the trick."

"Got it," Morgan said.

"But we may have another direction to go in."

"What's that?" Innes asked.

Jacob now paused and took a breath. It was time to tell them about Sophie and what she had discovered when reviewing the police archives, but he was unsure how they would take it.

"Now, the reason I wanted to meet here in the MIU rather than in the station is a very sensitive one."

The mood changed again.

"I'm sure you all remember Dr Sophie Anderson, the forensic psychologist and criminal profiler who approached me at the beginning of the case with an offer to help."

Morgan and Anna exchanged a knowing glance.

"That's the woman who used to work for the FBI, isn't it?" Holloway asked.

"And the Met, although well after my time there," Jacob said. "You will also know that Chief Superintendent Kent refused my request for her to help us on the case."

"That doesn't sound like him, sir," Holloway said, raising a laugh in everyone except Innes who now gestured with her hand to get Jacob's attention.

"What has this got to do with the enquiry, sir?" she asked.

"Against the Chief Super's orders, I decided to bring Dr Anderson into the team after the murder of Kieran Messenger." He let the news sink in. "I can see some of you are shocked, but due to the possible occult nature of the murders, not to mention the possibility of a serial killer at work, I thought a specialist in criminal profiling could only help us. I thought Chief Superintendent Kent's decision was wrong and I take sole responsibility for Dr Anderson being involved in the investigation. None of you will take any responsibility for this."

"Bloody hell, sir," Holloway said. "He'll go wild."

"Nevertheless," Jacob said. "I feel it was the right thing to do, especially after a meeting between Dr Anderson, myself and Inspector Morgan last night."

Holloway turned in his chair. "You knew about this too, sir?"

The Welshman nodded once. "Guilty as charged."

"And I did, too," Anna said, turning from Holloway to Morgan. "On the upside, looks like I might get DI after all – when you get sacked, I mean."

"Ouch," said Morgan.

"No one's getting sacked," Jacob said. "As it turns out, Dr Anderson was able to provide some very useful leads in the investigation."

"Which is very good timing considering we just lost

Cooper," Morgan said.

"Are these leads pointing to the guests in the lodges, sir?" Holloway asked.

Jacob sighed, aware of the gravity of what he was about to say. "No, they're not. A few days ago, Sophie Anderson requested to see the archived case files relating to the disappearance of Emma Russell back in 1992."

"Please tell me you didn't hand them over to her, guv," Anna said.

"I handed them over to her."

"Make that DCI," she said, looking at Jacob. "When you get sacked, too."

Jacob rolled his eyes. "Thanks for your support, Sergeant Mazurek."

"You're welcome."

"What did she find in the files, sir?" Holloway asked.

Jacob paused again. "What I'm about to tell you doesn't leave this team, is that clear?"

A series of solemn nods in reply, but no one spoke.

"Good," he said shortly. "After reviewing all the case files, including interviews and the TV appeal, Dr Anderson concludes that the SIO on the case at the time, DI Miranda Dunn was somehow involved with the murder."

A shocked silence was finally broken by Anna. "Bloody hell."

"I'm sure Sergeant Mazurek speaks for us all when she says that," Jacob said, trying to break the tense atmosphere. "Now you all see why I wanted to meet here in the MIU and why it's so important this stays in the team until we have figured out exactly what Dunn's involvement was. If she was involved, it's possible other officers were involved too. At the time, her line manager was Marcus Kent, who was a DCI at the time. Like Dunn, he also left after the case but took a promotion and transfer to Cumbria Police."

Innes had paled. "This is starting to make me nervous."

"Don't let it," Jacob said. "We're doing the right thing here. We follow the evidence no matter where it leads. If it turns out anyone at the station was involved in the Russell disappearance then they will be treated the same as any other suspect."

Morgan played with an unlit cigar. "So what now?"

Jacob turned to face his old friend. "You worked with Miranda Dunn a long time ago, so I want you to get hold of anything you can find with her name on it, not just the Russell files. Be subtle and don't let anyone know what you're doing, especially Kent and Portman. When you have it, bring it to me. It's looking increasingly obvious the original case wasn't handled properly and I want to know why."

"Righto – just leave it with me."

"Anna, I want you to take Holloway and Innes and re-interview the guests in the lodges. Lean on them a bit and see if you can get anything out of them. It's just instinct but something's not right in that neck of the woods if you'll excuse the pun. One of them is involved in this somehow, I just know it."

"Guv," she said. "What about you?"

"I have a personal appointment."

CHAPTER 32

Jacob had always hated doctors, and maybe he hated waiting rooms even more. Sitting outside the police psychologist's office in Bradford-on-Avon was no exception and he tried to pass the time by flicking through a pile of old magazines on the table beside him.

It didn't work; there was just too much on his mind. A few days ago he had sat on his own not three miles from here in the Old Watermill, staring out at the snow in his garden while others celebrated Christmas morning with their loved ones. For him, the day meant less than nothing. Jessica had died on Christmas Eve in a terrific blaze at their Oxford home and he had been unable to find her in the blaze and carry her to safety.

His life as he knew it had ended that night and he knew he had not properly recovered. Seeing the car fire at the retreat brought that home to him in a big way. He still had dreams where she visited him, always smiling and laughing. He reached out to her but then he always woke up, just before he could touch her. He had nightmares too. Terrible, tortured nightmares where he was lost in the house fire and unable to find her as she screamed in the smoke. He woke up from those, too, covered in sweat. The most recent one had been just two nights ago.

He wouldn't tell Dr Amelia Lovelace about that one.

Then there was the murder investigation. A cold case going back over a quarter of a century had exploded into what was starting to look like a quadruple murder enquiry with an active killer on the loose and not a solid lead in sight. Aside from the fentanyl bust and a vague suspicion about the guests in the retreat all he had to go on was the word of a criminal psychologist who was adamant a retired cop was lying during the original TV appeal.

It felt like the world was crashing down on him, and now his superior officer and line manager had decided he was still unfit for work and ordered him to seek medical help again.

"Jacob?"

Someone was calling his name. He turned to see the smiling, homely face of Amelia Lovelace standing in the door to her office.

"Sorry," he said, rising to greet her. "Just got so much on my mind I tuned out a bit."

"When sorrows come, they come not single spies but in battalions," she said, quoting Hamlet to perfection. "Please, come in."

He emerged into a sunlit room and was surprised to find himself relaxing. He had expected to tense up but instead, the opposite happened and he felt his neck and shoulders loosen.

He settled in his chair and studied her office. It was a large space with a thick plush pile carpet and original watercolours of various local scenes on the walls. A large window on the south wall gave a view over the River Avon and light from the sunny morning flooded into the warm space and increased his comfort.

"Nice to see you again, Tom," she said.

"I wish I could say the same."

She gave a polite laugh but quickly grew serious. "Mr Kent was very keen we should talk again. Didn't you find our previous sessions helpful?"

He stared ahead and watched a colourful narrowboat moving along the river. "I'm just not the sort of person who likes to talk about these things. Don't take it personally."

"Would you have talked about something like this with Jess?"

A daring opening gambit, he thought.

"That's different."

"That's the problem, Tom. The one person in the world you could share the most intimate things with is gone."

Gone.

"Burned to death," he said sharply. "She didn't just disappear one day."

Amelia gave a short sigh and regrouped. Tom Jacob was one of the more complex cases she had worked on, and certainly, he had suffered more tragedy than most of her patients. In her opinion, he had an extraordinary mind capable at once of making sense of large quantities of disparate information but at the same time being able to connect with every sort of person under the sun. She

334

wished he would lower his guard and start connecting with her but getting inside his mind was proving harder than anything she had ever done before. Maybe Kent had been right to refer him back.

"I know you've heard this a million times before, but you need to drop your guard if you want me to help you."

"Who says I want you to help me?"

Another sigh, and then a laugh. "All right, it's *me* that wants to help you, but seeing the way you're reacting to me today I'm starting to think Marcus is right and perhaps you need to talk with me more. What you went through was traumatic, and my professional opinion, if it means anything at all to you, is that it's possible you have not processed it properly yet. What do you think?"

His response was blunt and unexpected. "I think you're right."

She paused. "Tell me, are you still single?"

He shot her a glance. "What's that got to do with anything?"

"In terms of how you're moving on from Jess's death, it's got everything to do with it."

"It was only a year ago," he muttered, thinking back to last night with Sophie. "As a matter of fact, someone has walked into my life, but I know almost nothing about her."

She gave a gentle nod. Finally, something to write down and work with. "This is good, Tom, but be careful. Does she know about your past?"

"Yes, she does. I think she understands. As a matter of

fact, she's a psychologist like you. We're working together."

"On the Witch-Hunt Murders?"

He winced. "Please, it's Operation Grovely."

"Fine, but how do you feel about this person?"

He shrugged. "I fail to see…"

Her sigh cut him off. "You have to work with me, Tom."

"You know, you're the only person who calls me that."

"Am I?"

A brief nod. "Everyone just calls me Jacob, even Sophie."

Her eyes widened. "That's her name, Sophie?"

"I let that one slip out, didn't I?"

"As in Dr Sophie Anderson?"

He frowned. "Yes."

"I know her, or at least *of* her. She's a very talented psychologist. Wasn't she connected to the Keeley case?"

The ticking sound of the walnut veneer tambour clock on her windowsill grew louder.

"Yes, she was. She asked if she could be a part of the investigation but my boss said no."

"Chief Superintendent Kent refused your request?"

He nodded.

"How did that affect you?"

"I asked her to work on the case."

She sighed. "The word maverick has become a cliché, but it really does fit the bill where you're concerned."

"Thanks."

"It wasn't a compliment. You attract trouble like a magnet attracts metal."

"I know."

"I stress again that the only reason you're in here talking to me again is on the insistence of Marcus Kent, but if I report that you need more sessions, then you're going to have to come back and talk to me."

"Kent is a fool."

"He has concerns regarding your attitude in the workplace."

"I'm pleased to have made such a good impression."

"You have to play by the rules, Tom."

"*He's* not playing by the rules."

"Your boss?"

He paused. "No, the killer."

She closed her pad and frowned. "What do you want to do next?" she asked.

"I've got a briefing at the mortuary."

"I didn't mean that."

He smiled. "I know."

That seemed to be the right place to end the session.

*

Sophie pulled up in the small Forestry Commission car park and turned off the engine. She unbuckled her belt and emerged into a cold, bright and cloudless day. The weather report this morning had said the mighty blizzard they'd been warning about for so long was still building off the coast and would hit any moment now, but there was no sign of it today. Maybe, she thought with a shudder, this was the calm before the storm.

She arranged her scarf and woolly hat and, thrusting her hands in her pockets she made her way over to the Roman Road that cuts through the middle of Grovely Wood. Growing up not too far from here, she'd heard about this place over the years but it wasn't until this case that she had done any serious research into it, and what she found wasn't easy reading.

At least five people had been murdered in these woods in the last three hundred years – seven including Emma Russell and Kieran Messenger. The first four were the Danish sisters who had been bludgeoned to death by locals on suspicion of being witches following a smallpox outbreak.

She shuddered thinking about that bloody day and looked over her shoulder. Somewhere here were four old beech trees marking the graves, and in the back of one of the trunks was a hollow where people visiting the dead witches would leave offerings.

The fifth was either a poacher or a woodsman who was hanged here for stealing. She looked around again at the trees looming above her; some of them were hundreds of years old, so for all she knew he was strung up from one of the very trees she was looking at now.

She heard a noise behind her and spun around.

Desperately scanning the murky woodlands on either side of the road, she saw nothing and returned to her walk. The eerie feeling of being watched was another of the things she had researched when reading about this place. Grovely was notorious for it.

And then there were all the reports of seeing things in the shadows. The murdered poacher leaning against a trunk somewhere off the beaten track, watching you as you made your way through his woods.

She shivered against the cold as she reached the site of Emma Russell's shallow grave. Blue and white barricade tape was still blocking the area, designating it as a formal crime scene. Police – Do Not Cross. The ragged ends of the tape fluttered in the icy wind as she peered down inside the stump hole and tried to imagine what had happened here so long ago.

Then she saw him, a man in her peripheral vision.

She turned sharply, half expecting to see the hanged poacher but instead she saw a man in a bobble hat making his way towards her. In his hands, he held a heavy-looking metal detector and he smiled cheerily as he drew closer to her.

"Hello."

She felt uneasy. This was the sort of place where no one heard your screams, and she cursed her curiosity for coming here. All she wanted to do was try and get a better understanding of the case, see if anything might jog her mind, and now she was alone with a stranger.

She took a step away from him. "Hi."

"Sorry if I startled you," he said, lifting the detector in the air so she could see it more clearly. "But I'm a bit of a nerd. I'm hoping to get a big find one day like you read about in the papers."

"Ah, I see."

He looked at the hole behind the tape. "I found her, you know."

"I'm sorry?"

He nudged his chin at the stump hole beyond the barricade tape and took a step closer to her. She wondered how much a metal detector weighed, and whether it could be used as a weapon. Hadn't Jacob told her that Messenger's head had been caved in with a metal bar?

"I found the poor thing's remains."

"Yes, I read about it." She glanced through the trees at the Police MIU and wondered if anyone was inside it. "It must have been very traumatic."

"Shocked me, I can tell you. To think of all the times I've been detecting up here and I go and find that on Boxing Day of all days."

Sophie listened with a rising sense of anxiety. It was stupid, she knew, but the woods had put her on edge. She had read the reports and knew who Philip Croft was, and she also knew that he was fully alibied and of no interest to the police. Then again, was it possible they had made a mistake? A lie somewhere, hiding in the pages, deceit blowing through the trees on the winter wind?

"I'd better be going," she said, taking another step away from the man with the metal detector in his hand.

"Oh, cheerio," he said, pushing his glasses up the bridge of his nose.

An irruption of waxwings almost startled her out of her skin as she made her way back to the path, determined to look unruffled. "Good luck!" she called back over her shoulder.

"Thanks."

When she turned, she saw he wasn't using the metal detector, but holding it in both hands like a club and staring at her as she walked away. Never had she wanted to get into her car as much as she did right now.

CHAPTER 33

With a crisp clear sky above them and a balmy twelve degrees Celsius, Jacob had relented to Innes's demands that they should drive with the top down on his vintage Alvis. It wasn't the first time he had driven the convertible with the roof down in the winter, but he guessed from the look on the young woman's face beside him that she had never experienced it before.

He picked her up from HQ on his way down from Bradford-on-Avon, and now freezing air whipped around the windscreen and scratched at her face like birch branches. It was icy cold but nothing could wipe the smile off her face as they powered south away from the downs and headed back to the hospital in Salisbury.

Drawing closer to their destination, she turned to him and raised her voice. "Sir, what would happen if the Chief Super found out about Dr Anderson being involved in the case?"

He shrugged. "I don't know him that well yet, but from what I've gathered so far I'm guessing his head would fly off his shoulders like a champagne cork."

Innes laughed. "I'd like to see that."

"I'm not sure you would, but seriously you don't have to worry about it. It was my decision and mine alone, and

I've deliberately made sure no one else has worked directly with her apart from me and Bill Morgan. You're safe from any accusations."

"I wasn't trying to protect myself."

"Well, you should be. You're young with your whole career ahead of you. Don't look at me for inspiration, whatever you do. I'm a disaster."

"You have one of the best arrest records in the force, sir. You're respected not only in Wiltshire but in the Met and Thames Valley."

"Maybe, but I rub people up the wrong way. Forging a successful career is as much about politics and diplomacy as it is about policing." Looking up into the clear sky, he breathed a sigh of relief. "Could be warming up after all."

"Reports still say the blizzard is on the way," she said.

"Maybe, maybe not."

He steered into the hospital car park and slowed up to a stop. Climbing out of the car, he pulled the roof back up with a glance at the clear blue sky. "But you never can tell."

*

"You don't need me to tell you that this person died from death by burning."

Ethan Spargo gently pulled back the plastic shroud sheet and grimaced. Jacob had previously been looking at the latest novelty bow tie, covered in tiny snowmen, but now his eyes were drawn to the horrific, charred corpse on the gurney.

"Good God."

Innes covered her mouth and turned away.

"Quite," Spargo said. "It's one of the worst injuries I've ever seen."

Jacob said nothing in reply.

Spargo turned to Innes. "Are you all right? If you want to leave…"

"No," she said, composing herself and turning back to the gurney. "I want a career in CID. I need to prove I can handle anything."

Spargo nodded. "If you're sure. What about you, Jacob? You're turning green."

"I'm fine, Ethan. Thanks for your concern." He got out his notepad. "I'm presuming there's not much you can get from a body in this state?"

"You presume correctly. It's in a terrible condition, but having said that, I can tell you that she was struck from behind by a heavy blunt instrument that fractured the skull. I suspect it would have rendered her unconscious before the fire."

"Thank heaven for small mercies," Innes said.

"But she was alive – there's evidence of smoke inhalation in what's left of the lungs."

"My God," Jacob muttered. "ID?"

"Yes. I've already run a DNA test and using a sample taken from a hairbrush in Grovely Manor by one of your constables I have been able to formally identify the body as belonging to Lucinda Beecham."

Jacob gave a simple nod. "My instinct told me that."

"You and your instinct," Spargo said, rolling his eyes. "I suppose I'd better get used to that."

Jacob managed half a smile. "You'd better, yes. Tell me, is there any way this person was drugged before being burned?"

"Perfectly possible," he said flatly. "There is any number of ways to render someone unconscious before killing them, ranging from a simple knock on the head all the way through to quite sophisticated drugs."

"Where could you get these drugs?"

"Your local pharmacy," he said without hesitation. "Some of the more heavy-duty anaesthetics are off-limits to Joe Public, of course, but many things purchased in a high street pharmacy would do the job just as well."

"And they wouldn't wake in the fire?" Innes asked.

He weighed the question. "Depends on the quantity of the drug, unfortunately, there is no way for me to tell if this person was drugged or not. The damage caused to the body by the fire was just too great. I'm sorry. As I say, it's more than likely the head injury incapacitated her before the fire."

Jacob considered his response. "All right, thanks, Ethan. Could you put together a list of drugs capable of knocking someone out or sedating them to the point they wouldn't be able to help themselves even if they were in a fire?"

"You'll have it before the day is out."

"What about the ranger?"

"Much simpler," he said, moving over to a second gurney. "Direct hit to the chest, throat and face with a twelve bore shotgun. He would have been unconscious within seconds due to blood pressure loss and dead a few minutes later. Gruesome, but on reflection probably a better way to go than the car fire."

As Spargo pulled the cover over Talbot's face, Jacob sighed and turned to the young woman at his side. "Let's get out of here."

*

As soon as he entered his office in HQ, Jacob saw the report. Someone had left it right in the centre of his desk with a yellow Post-It note stuck on the front. He slipped off his jacket, sat down and flicked the radio on. Vaughan Williams's pastoral symphony filled the air as he pulled the note off the folder. It was from Mia Francis, explaining that it was the CSI report on Dean Cooper's property. She'd even drawn a smiley with a cigarette hanging out of its mouth to accompany the sign-off.

Jacob crumpled the note and tossed it in the bin. He sipped his coffee and started to look through the folder. It was substantial and the report was just as he'd known it would be – meticulous detail and highly professional. Both the house and gardens, including the workshop, had been subjected to a comprehensive fingertip search by her team but there were few surprises. Alongside the fentanyl, meth and spice, there were also traces of cocaine found in one of the bedrooms, but he still had questions so he picked up his phone.

"Mia – thanks for the report."

"Good afternoon, Chief Inspector. It's a real page-turner, isn't it?"

"If you say so. You didn't find any of the other stolen drugs on the property?" he asked.

"If you're talking about the methadone, morphine and anaesthetics, then no."

"But they were stolen in the raid, so they have to be somewhere."

"He could have sold them."

Jacob sighed. "Maybe, but either way, what this report is telling me is that you found nothing at all connecting him with any of the murders?"

"Correct. We found all sorts of samples in there but they all belonged to Cooper or his girlfriend or members of their families. I thought you'd pretty much ruled him out, anyway?"

"I had, but there's always mindless hope."

"Sorry, but aside from what we already know, there was no forensic evidence to place him at any of the crime scenes, and neither is there any forensic evidence that either of the victims was ever in his house. We can only place Messenger in his pickup."

"Which is of no use as they knew each other. What about in that workshop though?"

"I already wrote this all down in the... did you *read* the report? It's all in there."

"I like asking questions, Mia. It's how I do things. It's how I learn."

"But all the answers to your questions are in the report."

Jacob smiled. He could see he was going to have some fun with her over the years. "Yes, but I said I like *asking* questions, and I like *listening* to answers. It's different."

"I'm so glad I spent three hours putting my report together for you."

"My question?"

She sighed. "No, nothing to place him or anyone other than Cooper and Ryall in the workshop."

Morgan poked his head around the door and waved a manila folder. "As requested, boss. Gimme five."

Jacob acknowledged him with a silent nod. "Thanks, Mia. Gotta go."

*

When Morgan reappeared in his office he was equipped with a greasy paper bag containing two substantial beef and vegetable pasties and a cheese and onion bake from a local bakery. Jacob picked up one of the pasties with a white paper towel and glanced at the bake. "Isn't that overdoing it?"

"Not for a growing boy like me, boss."

Jacob took a bite and opened the latest Dunn file. "Anything good?"

"Some accusations about her conduct were buried pretty deep – bribery and corruption and so on but nothing ever stuck. Beyond that, if there was anything funny going on there's barely any trace of it in these files."

"Barely?"

"For a start, they could have done more in the early part of the investigation. I was a uniformed PC at the time and not working on this case. I thought it was odd that more of us weren't drafted in at the time, but at that age, you don't question the decisions of your elders and betters. Seems to me like Dunn just sort of let the case fade away."

"Between what you just said and Sophie's work I'm harbouring some very bad feelings about Miranda Dunn. If there *is* anything dodgy about her I'm praying it doesn't go all the way to Kent. I know he's a bastard but that would just rock the whole force."

"And ruin public relations," Morgan said. "It's bad enough as it is these days, that would just about do us in, but unfortunately, there's more."

"Do tell – this pasty is excellent by the way."

"I think so. Not as good as my mam's though. Anyway, after Sophie found that tape with Dunn talking about the two witnesses, I decided to chase it up. As I said, they weren't in the original files, so I had a think and decided to call up an old friend of mine who was a sergeant back during the original case."

"Was he any help?"

Morgan nodded. "He most certainly was, boss. He was able to give me the names of the two men who had come forward."

"So they were real?"

"Yes, and both local – a farmhand and an old boy who used to walk in the woods with his dog. Thing is, they both committed suicide not long after the case was closed."

"Both of them?"

"The farmhand cut his wrists open and the old boy hanged himself in his shed."

Jacob stopped chewing and set his pasty down on the desk. "I don't like to use the word, Bill, but I'm starting to think we could be facing some sort of conspiracy."

Morgan looked at his boss for a second, stopped eating and put his pasty down next to Jacob's.

"I thought you didn't like that word?"

"I don't, but something tells me we need to go and see retired DI Dunn, don't you?"

Morgan winced and looked at his watch. "I've got to see my solicitor about the divorce. Leanne's raising hell over my pension. Could you take Anna instead?"

Jacob gave him a look of pity as he picked up the phone and dialled through to her number. "Sounds like I got the better deal this evening if that's where you've got to go."

*

Professor Hugo Winter closed his office door in the Stonehenge Visitor Centre and picked up the phone with the usual fear and trepidation that was connected with the number he was about to dial.

"What is it, Fagus?"

Hugo swallowed. "I'd rather you didn't call me by that name."

"I insist on your calling me by mine."

"Magalos, you mean?"

"What do you want, Hugo?" the voice said, totally ignoring him.

"You know what I want," he said, opening his drawer and pulling out a half bottle of whisky. Taking a small slug from the bottle he slowed his breathing. "You murdered her."

"It was necessary to frame the drug dealer."

"And how well that worked out," Hugo said. "I've just seen the news and they say they're continuing their enquiry. You killed her for nothing. This is spinning out of control."

"Just stay calm, and you'll be all right."

He sighed and rubbed his tired, red eyes. "No. This has gone on long enough. I'm going to speak to Jacob. I'm going tell him just what the hell has been going on for all this time and bugger the consequences."

"I'm not sure that's a very good idea," said the rich, gravelly voice of Magalos. "I don't like it one little bit."

"I don't give a damn about that. It's time to do the right

thing."

"Don't do anything silly until we've had a chance to speak. Where are you?"

The man took another inch out of the bottle as he listened to the reply. "At work, but we can't meet here. I'll call you when I get home."

"I'll be waiting, Fagus, and don't do anything silly in the meantime."

CHAPTER 34

The village of Castle Combe was one of the prettiest in the county. Just outside Chippenham, the idyllic chocolate-box charm of the twelfth-century settlement had brought it worldwide fame in the movies, often being used for location shoots. Tonight as Jacob and Anna drove into the heart of the village, the entire scene was framed by a wild spray of stars littered haphazardly across the early winter twilight sky.

"It's crawling with tourists in the summer," Anna said.

"You've been here before then?" Jacob signalled to pull off the main road and followed the satnav back out of the village along what looked like a farm track.

"Oh yeah," she said. "The racetrack is just outside the village on the old wartime airbase. There are some major motorcycle race meets here."

"Ah, of course. I forgot you were a bit of a petrolhead. Is it a Kawasaki you own?"

"No, a Ducati."

He slowed as they moved deeper into the village. Anna, who was watching a couple walk along a frosty pavement, turned to him. "So what do we know about this woman?"

"Not much, but the more I'm learning about her the less I like her. As you know, Morgan says she was never very popular, but he didn't work with her for long because she retired not long after he started."

"I guess it was long enough to give him an idea of what she was like."

"Seems that way. He says she was one of those managers who somehow always finds a junior colleague to take the blame for their own screw-ups, but I think it went a lot further with her. He found some accusations of corruption and bribery in the files."

"Yikes."

"Needless to say, she retired with full honours and an even fuller pension."

"Naturally."

"And now we have increasing evidence she wasn't on the level, at least during the Russell case back in ninety-two. Sophie is sure she was lying when she gave the TV appeal and it looks like she was taking stuff out of the files, specifically witness statements."

"That's not good." Anna's phone rang in the cosy amber glow of the Alvis. "It's a text from Mia."

"What does it say?"

She frowned. "You're not going to like it."

"Then it'll fit right in with everything else."

"None of the guns at Freeth's farm have been recently fired and none of the shotgun cartridges on the farm was a match for the type that killed Talbot."

He turned to her with a cynical expression on his face. "Thank her for her time."

"Will do."

He pulled into the road and slowed down to a crawl. "Listen, this is how I want to play it. We get in and have a chat – nothing that's going to spill the beans and upset her. You go upstairs and have a look around and see what you can find. Many former coppers keep personal records of their cases. See if there's anything on the Russell disappearance."

"I'm absolutely sure that's illegal without a warrant."

"Problem is, Anna, we don't know how high this goes. It might end with her, or it might go up to Kent or even higher to Portman, although I find that hard to believe. But if that's the case and we go and request a search warrant for Dunn's place, then we're not likely to find anything, are we now?"

"She'll have the law on her side if it comes to trial."

"I'm not worried about the law," he said flatly. "I'm worried about getting justice for Emma Russell and the other victims of whatever the hell went on in that wood." He killed the engine and turned to her, fixing his blue eyes on hers, unblinking. "Are you with me?"

She nodded. "Can't let you get all the glory, besides – I want to know what she's been up to."

"If she has any evidence in there."

"Of course."

They walked up the path and rang the doorbell. When the former Detective Inspector opened the door she was holding a menthol cigarette in one hand and a vodka in the other and looked half asleep. "Now, I know when I see a copper, and right now I'm looking at two. Am I right?"

He flashed his ID. "DCI Jacob, and this is DS Mazurek. Got a minute?"

*

Miranda Dunn sat back in her armchair and sucked on the cigarette. A blue glass ashtray was balanced on one of the arms and now she flicked some ash into it without taking her eyes off Jacob. "So, how can I help you?" she asked coolly.

Jacob studied her with care. She wore makeup but her eyes gave her age away – soft purple bags underneath a criss-cross grid of crow's feet. Thin, gaunt almost. Cigarettes suppressing appetite, he thought. Lots of rings on thin fingers and sharp, jerky body movements vaguely redolent of a garden bird hunting for worms.

"We're here in relation to the Russell case," he said.

"I thought you might be," she said. "It's all over the news."

"It is. I was wondering if you could help me with the enquiry?"

She dragged on the cigarette, exhaling and filling the room with more of the minty smoke. "Good God, you're going back a bit. Tell me, how is PC Bill Morgan?"

She's changing the subject.

"He's good. He's a DI now."

"A DI?" she said, cocking a quizzical eyebrow. "I

always knew he'd go far. Wish I'd had him on my team during the Russell case."

A smoky silence in the cramped room. "Thanks for seeing us today, Miranda."

Had she bristled when he used her name? Tough, he thought. He sure as hell wasn't going to call her madam. Even Mrs Dunn seemed too respectful.

"I always like to help the police," she said with a slurred laugh. The vodka sloshed around in the tumbler before settling back down over the chunks of chipped ice. She saw him looking at the glass and waved it in the air. The light from her Tiffany lamp caught the cut-glass and sparkled in her hand. "Are you sure you won't have a drink, Chief Inspector?"

"Yes," he said flatly. "Very sure, but thanks. Now, let's talk about the Russell case."

"I barely remember it."

As Anna took out her notebook and crossed her legs, Miranda caught her eye.

"Sergeant Mazurek. Is that a Russian name?"

"Polish," she said, surprised she had asked.

"Ah, my first husband was Russian."

"If you must know, my grandfather came over in the Second World War to fly Spitfires in 303 Squadron."

"How fascinating," she slurred.

"And where's your second husband?" Anna asked.

"Keith, my third husband, is out at his Golf Club. Some bloody Christmas thing."

"And what does he do?"

"He's a GP."

Jacob cleared his throat. "But the Russell case was one of your most important cases."

"It was one of my biggest failures."

Jacob nodded. "You never found her."

"No, but the last time she was seen was leaving a pub in Salisbury. We focussed the investigation on there and Oxford. We had no reason to search those woods."

"Are you sure about that?"

Dunn's eyes crawled over the carpet for a few moments as she thought of a response. Jacob hadn't seen the former top dog before, but he instantly recognised the shifty, searching look in her eyes that Morgan had described.

"What do you mean by that?"

Another drag.

"In the TV appeal, you spoke about two witnesses who saw Emma later in the evening on the A36 heading to Southampton."

"Did I?"

"Yes, but for some reason, their statements aren't in the files. Any idea why?"

"It was a long time ago. Can you remember every last detail from your old cases?"

Anna stood up and looked at Dunn with a question on her face. "Where's your..?"

"Top of the stairs and turn left."

*

When Anna closed the door behind her, Jacob got up from his chair and started to peer inside the large Welsh dresser beside a fake plastic Christmas tree.

"Sit down, for god's sake. You're making me nervous."

He spoke without turning. "Have you any reason to be nervous?"

A long drag. "Of course not."

He continued to study the dresser. Pictures of old friends, ornaments, cherished cards, all neatly wrapped in bright red and silver tinsel. Christmas cheer, wrapped in cigarette smoke and tension.

He turned. "Do you remember interviewing those two witnesses?"

"No."

"Both men killed themselves shortly afterwards, did you know that?"

"No, I don't even remember interviewing them, like I just told you. It might not even have been me."

"I think it was you," he said. 'In fact, I'm sure of it."

"Ah yes, that's right – I remember. They said they'd seen her in a car going south, I remember now."

She sucked the cigarette back to the filter and stubbed it out in the ashtray. Reaching for the packet, she pulled out another and slid it up onto her lip. "Yes, that's right, but it was all so long ago."

Anna Mazurek saw the bathroom at the top of the stairs, but that wasn't her destination. Reaching the top step, she turned one-eighty degrees and walked along the carpeted corridor running parallel to the steps. On her way, she craned her head into each room until she found what was obviously the study.

It was a plush space, but modest in size as was normal for such an old house. A sloped ceiling with exposed beams overhead, and a hardwood desk beneath the lead-lined window. A filing cabinet stood beside a glass-fronted bookshelf. She tried it, but it was locked so she went through the desk drawers instead but found nothing except old bills and personal documents.

Back to the filing cabinet, she pulled two paperclips out of a novelty desk-tidy shaped like a wheelie bin and went to work on the cabinet's tiny lock. She inserted one of the clips into the lock and pushed it up and around to the left and then slid the second clip into the lock plug. Then she started to rake the top across the pins until they were pushed down and lined up with the shear line. When the final pin was aligned she swung the first pin around in a clockwise arc as if it were a key and the lock clicked open.

"That never happened, Ania," she whispered to herself, using the name her grandfather had always called her.

Peering inside the filing cabinet she discovered yet more household paperwork, but then had an idea when she remembered a raid she'd done on a fraud case in Swindon. Pulling the bottom drawer all of the way out and taking it off its runners, she found what she was looking for – a pile of folders underneath the bottom drawer, resting on the carpet.

She pulled them out and opened them, and quickly realised she had struck pure gold.

"Oh my *God*." She stared down at the documents in her trembling hands with horror, instantly realizing the implications of what she had discovered. Without wasting a second, she pulled her iPhone from her pocket and snapped a picture of several images and papers before sliding it back onto the carpet and putting the drawer back on its runners and shutting it again.

There was no way to lock the cabinet back up again with the paperclips, so it was a matter of praying that Dunn wouldn't remember whether she had locked it or not. Judging from the amount of vodka she drank she thought she might just have luck on her side and slowly walked down the corridor to the bathroom. She flushed the toilet and took a few seconds to compose herself before walking down the stairs and going back into the front room to join a tense conversation.

Dunn was lighting a second cigarette and sipping the vodka. "Not sure what you're driving at, Chief Inspector."

"Don't you?" Jacob said darkly. "I don't think those two witnesses saw Emma on the A36 at all, do you?"

"What are you talking about?"

"I think those two witnesses placed her in Grovely Wood and that you took their statements and falsified them to keep the search away from where you knew the body was. Then you removed any trace of them from the file and somehow arranged for them to be killed to silence their testimony forever."

She stood up, her face reddening as Anna walked back into the room.

"Nice wallpaper in the bathroom," Anna said.

Dunn was shaking with anger. "Get out of my house!"

"Ah."

*

Outside in the car, Jacob turned to his sergeant. "She denied everything and tried to hide behind how long ago it was, but she's hiding something. I can't prove it yet, but I just know it. Did you find anything upstairs?"

She handed him her phone with the picture she had just taken on the screen. "You could say that."

Jacob stared at the images with disbelieving eyes. He was looking at pictures of Miranda Dunn out in the woods with various other people, their faces obscured by shadows, all of them dancing around a fire. "No sign of Emma though."

"Keep going."

More fires, more people in the woods. "My God, this looks like some sort of ritual."

"And it gets worse."

Swiping through the phone, he saw another image – a copy of Sir Walter Scott's *Letters on Demonology and Witchcraft*.

"Swipe again and read the inscription in the front of the book."

He did as she said and was horrified by what he saw next.

Your very own copy to keep you in trouble, love Emma xxx

"My God, she knew her."

"And that's a big problem," Anna said. "If she knew the victim she shouldn't have been on the case, let alone SIO. Conflict of interest."

"I think it's a much bigger problem than that, but we can't move until we have all the facts."

*

Miranda Dunn watched Jacob and Anna get back into the car and leave the cul-de-sac. When they were safely out of sight, she slipped her mobile phone off the side and scrolled through the contacts until finding the number she was looking for.

"I told you never to call me again," the voice said.

"We've got trouble, Magalos," she said quietly. "Big trouble… he knows."

CHAPTER 35

Sunday, 30ᵗʰ December

"**G**ood morning, boss."

Jacob squinted at his clock and wondered how Morgan could be so cheery at eight on a Sunday morning. "Bill."

"Not up yet? You'll miss church."

"I take it there's a reason for this gross intrusion?"

"That there is. Guess what we found first thing this morning creeping around Grovely Manor?"

"Surprise me."

"A man in a Chesterfield coat. I think you should get down here sharpish."

*

Jacob arrived at the HQ building less than thirty minutes later, bursting through the reception doors and marching down to the interview rooms like a man possessed. Seeing Bill Morgan standing outside Interview Room 4, he approached him with a blend of excitement and anger rising inside him.

"So who is it?"

"That's the sad part, boss. It's one Magnus Rhodes, a private investigator, and unfortunately a former Detective Inspector I used to work with."

"Ah."

"Exactly, sir. We found him after Ted Farnham the estate's gardener caught him sniffing around the manor first thing this morning, and even better than that he had a nice little folder in his car, all stuffed full of goodies from his employer."

"Don't tell me."

"Ian Russell. He hired him after the remains were identified, and you won't believe why."

"Time for a chat, I think," he said, slamming open the door and storming inside.

During Jacob's absence from the force, Magnus Rhodes had become a detective legend, gaining a reputation for being an unparalleled genius when it came to solving serious crimes and rapidly clocking up the best arrest rate in the county. It had all gone wrong during a high profile kidnapping case and he had left the force under a cloud. A tall, strong man with square features and a no-nonsense air, Jacob knew to take him seriously.

"Mr Rhodes."

"DCI Jacob, I presume?" Rhodes said, unruffled.

Jacob spun a chair around and sat down opposite him, with his arms draped over the back. "What the hell has been going on, Magnus?"

Rhodes raised his palms. "It's all above board and

legal."

"Except for the trespass and failing to report a murder."

"Yes, except for that."

"What were you doing out at Talbot's property?"

"Just watching him as per Ian Russell's orders."

"Why?"

"Because he was convinced Talbot was guilty of his daughter's murder and he wanted justice."

Morgan nodded his head and Jacob knew the Welshman understood what Ian Russell must have gone through over these last years.

"Did you kill Neil Talbot?"

He shook his head, his face a stony, inscrutable wall. "No."

"Did you see who killed Neil Talbot?"

"No. I watched him for a few moments and then I heard someone slamming a door. It sounded like it had come from the lodges, so I turned and walked away through the trees. That's when I saw you and a female officer leaving the lodge area. Then I heard the shot. I was a good detective, Mr Jacob, and I knew what it looked like, so I made a break for it. Then you gave chase, and the rest is history."

"And yet you were caught sneaking around at Grovely Manor."

He shrugged. "Talbot's shooting simply convinced Mr Russell that others were involved in Emma's death, so he asked me to delve deeper. It's how I put bread on the table these days."

"And that's the extent of your involvement in all this? If there's more I want to know and I want to know now."

"There's no more. It's perfectly simple like I said. Ian Russell hired me to locate the killer before you could."

Jacob sighed. "Because he had no faith in the police after the failure to find his daughter the first time around?"

Rhodes leant back in his chair and sighed. He looked tired not just of the day, but of his life. "Partly, Jacob, but mainly because he wanted to kill him."

Jacob looked up at Morgan and the Welshman raised an eyebrow. "I did say you should get down here sharpish."

*

Back at his desk, Jacob's fury was interrupted by his phone ringing.

"Hi, Mia."

"Jacob."

"Please say you have something for me."

"I have something for you."

He rolled his eyes. "Please elaborate."

"With pleasure."

Jacob waited as the other end of the line went dead. "Mia?"

"Sorry, just sipping my coffee. It concerns the murder at the retreat, which we've been going over with a fine toothcomb while you sit around eating pasties."

"Is that what you think I do all day?"

"I've been to your office and seen your bin, and Bill's too. I know he's the ringleader."

"I hope you're putting your forensic skills to more use than just stalking my wastepaper bin."

"I am. Turns out your fourth victim wasn't as innocent as you might have liked."

"Lucinda Beecham?"

"At least you can count."

"But can you get on with it?"

"We have a piece of rather damning evidence implicating her in the murder of Kieran Messenger, I'm pleased to say. Our fingertip search of her property – and you might remember it is a *very* large property – revealed one Angry Jester 24" breaker bar with a substantial quantity of Mr Messenger's hair, blood and bone fragments on it. It also had Lucinda Beecham's fingerprints on it."

"A breaker bar?"

"It's a non-ratcheting bar used when more torque is required than a socket wrench can deliver."

"I know what it is," he said. "I'm merely expressing surprise."

"That a mere woman would have one around the house?"

"Hardly. Where was it?"

"In a disused well on the western edge of the property, and there's more."

"Go on."

"Lucinda Beecham had a side-by-side double-barrelled Cogswell & Harrison shotgun in a cabinet in her kitchen. Twelve-bore and chambered for three-inch cartridges. It's a good match for the weapon that killed Talbot, but more than that, the cartridges we found in the cabinet were a perfect match."

He narrowed his eyes. "Lucinda Beecham killed Neil Talbot?"

"That's your department."

"You know what this means?"

"With luck, I can finally go home and enjoy what's left of my Christmas."

"What it *means*," he said with emphasis, "is that this confirms our multiple killer hypothesis so it looks like we have another killer on our hands."

"Sounds like progress."

"Yes. We now know that Lucinda Beecham killed Kieran Messenger, and possibly Neil Talbot, but we have no idea why. We also have no idea who killed her."

*

That afternoon, Jacob stirred his coffee and looked out through the Old Watermill's kitchen window. It was a view he had seen so many times he could describe it in infinite detail with his eyes firmly shut – the chestnuts to the north, the gentle camber of the lawn, the crumbling bricks of the walled garden. Everyone who came to the house was

369

always in awe of it, but to him, it was just a rambling old building where he'd grown up. Nothing more.

Lifting the cup to his lips he took a sip and tried to clear his mind. He'd had several emails over the last few days from old colleagues in Thames Valley and the Met asking how his new life was panning out, but he hadn't answered one. It wasn't that he didn't care, but that there had been no time. His first week back in the county had dawned with the discovery of Emma Russell's body up in the woods, and since then things had only got faster and more out of control.

"Everything all right?"

Startled, he turned in the chair to see Sophie standing in the doorway. She was holding a cup of steaming coffee in her hand and looked about ready to drop. She'd driven over after he'd called her to tell her that she had been right about Dunn and broken the news about Rhodes to her.

"Nearly," he said.

No one spoke, and for a few moments, the only sound was that of the antique carriage clock on the mantelpiece as it ticked away the day. Jacob waved the Rhodes folder in the air before dropping it back on the side table. "Decided to use the time catching up on the case."

"You need to get some rest."

"I can't," he said. "Not while I know he's still out there somewhere," Jacob said. "Right now."

"I feel the same way about Keeley."

"Except Keeley is locked up."

"You're right," she said. "I know, but I still worry."

"I'm sorry."

"Look, I should go."

"You don't have to."

"I think I do. You need to be alone."

He watched her pull out of his drive and then he walked around the back of the mill. He felt the cold air rush over him as he walked away from the house. Ducking his head under the box hedge archway, he walked along an overgrown path before finding himself in his mother's beloved sunken garden.

What had once been a perfectly manicured landscape of angelface, lavender and Japanese catmint was now a tangled, wild mess of neglect. Nature had reclaimed it with a vengeance and now it was hers once again. Not even the paths were properly visible.

He blew out a deep frustrated breath and folded his hands behind his head as he paced up and down beside the empty, cracked koi pond. The garden had grown over any trace of his mother's hard work in the same merciless way the trees had enveloped Emma Russell as she lay crushed under the ancient woods.

"Where are you, you bastard?" he called out to no one.

But there was no reply.

*

The distant October night all those years ago rose in

Magalos's mind like a spectre. His eyes clamped tightly shut, he could smell the damp air and the earthy scent of the dead leaves mulching on the forest floor. The sharp, trilling call of a nightjar emanated from the darkness somewhere in the dormant boughs above his head.

Their heads.

There were six of them there on that fateful night. Young and with their lives stretching out ahead of them, full of promise and adventure.

And then it happened, and everything changed in a heartbeat.

He opened his eyes and lifted a cigarette to his lips. He flicked the spark wheel and a tiny flame appeared above the hood. He fired up the shreds of tobacco at the cigarette's tip and sucked on the filter until the hot, blue smoke filled his mouth. Exhaling it into the room, he stretched his neck to relieve some of the terrible tension that had been building there since Boxing Day and tried to settle his mind down to business. He was sure he had made no mistakes, and he was sure none of the Grove would speak of that night, but one thing was certain.

That bastard Jacob wasn't giving up and he'd have to be dealt with, but first, there was more pressing business. Firing up the ignition of his car, he pulled off onto the road and headed to Stonehenge.

CHAPTER 36

With the second wave of the blizzard gathering strength off the coast, Jacob had piled up another couple of logs on the fire and made himself a cup of fresh coffee. Just after five and the end of another long day. He sipped the coffee and pushed back into the leather chair and thought back over the original day from hell.

Most of his time had been spent on Rhodes who had turned out to be a major wild goose chase. He'd never met him before today, but there was plenty of talk in the station – the sad story of a good copper broken by tragedy and leaving by the back door. As a former DI, he'd known the risks of overstepping the line in his new chosen profession and now he was facing several charges. But that was *his* problem.

Jacob had enough of his own. Now, as the light failed, the blue sky they had enjoyed over the last day or so would soon be swallowed up by another bank of heavy, grey clouds pushing their way over the land, laden with snow and dimming the sun.

He looked at the file they had found in Rhodes's car and started to leaf through the paperwork Ian Russell had given him but kept from the police. He'd told Rhodes he'd found it during the recent renovation of their home. A bag tucked away in a wall cavity for over a quarter of a century. Lost, covered in dust and full of memories. He continued to look through the box file – a diary, mementoes, old, yellowed photographs.

Ian Russell had been reluctant to share too much information with the PI, but from what he could gather from the diary, their daughter had hidden some of her belongings in the wall cavity to keep them away from the prying eyes of her parents. A casual glance through some of the entries revealed lots of talk about how she felt suffocated and how she couldn't wait to leave home.

Jacob looked down at some of the photos of Emma Russell. Young, fresh and her life before her. She stared out of the pictures at him, her bright intelligent eyes almost imploring him to catch her killer. In one, her blonde hair was tied up in a neat bun and secured with chopsticks. She was wearing a formal dress and holding a glass of wine up to the camera.

Turning it over he read the inscription on the back. Written in smudged black ink, it said *Graduation Day*. He knew the rest of the story from her official file – this was taken at the end of the clinical stage of her medical degree at Oxford.

He turned it back over and shook his head. She would have been no more than twenty-three in the picture and with no idea of the horror life had in store for her so soon.

And then he saw it.

The tattoo.

The simple, fine lines of the circle with the two lines in the centre. "Wait, what's this?"

He set down his coffee cup and leaned in closer to the picture. Not close enough. He moved over to the side table and opened the drawer, rummaging around for a few seconds for his magnifying glass. No luck, so he pulled his mobile phone from his pocket and snapped a picture of the tattoo, then used the zoom facility to magnify it.

"My God," he muttered. "I've seen this tattoo before. She must have known him."

His mind shifted back to the day he interviewed Richard Everett in his lodge and the celebrity's photographs on the chimney of his central fireplace. The famous actors and smiling TV stars, and the shot of Everett on the tropical beach, stripped to the waist and the tattoo on his arm.

With his phone still gripped in his hand, he felt an ice-cold chill run up his spine and around his neck as he dialled his old friend.

"DI Morgan."

"Bill, it's Jacob. I know why they burnt Lucinda Beecham in the fire."

"What are you talking about, man?"

"To destroy a tattoo, Bill!"

"What?"

"It's Everett. We need to bring him right now. Get everyone on the team to the MIU!"

*

Hugo Winter finished tidying his desk and picked up his car keys. Well after five now, the Stonehenge Visitor Centre was closed to the public and as silent as the grave. Both the security guards who were on the night shift had clocked in and were out in their Land Rover checking the site.

Then from outside his office, he heard what sounded like the main entrance doors sliding open.

He raised his voice. "I'm sorry but we're closing up for the day."

"Not to me." The words rolled off his tongue like warm honey.

Hugo fought back the urge to take a step back. "What the hell are you doing here?"

"I've come to discuss our little problem."

"This is my place of work, and lower your voice for God's sake. What if one of the security guards has come back?"

"Oh, don't worry about them, Hugo. They only just started on their rounds."

"What's that in your hands?"

The man lunged at him, pushing a needle into his neck and Hugo felt himself falling to the floor.

"What was that?" he said, his voice already reduced to a whisper. "What have you done to me?"

"The problem I have, Hugo," the man began, "is that I simply cannot allow you to destroy my life over what

376

happened all those years ago."

"You're insane..."

"No, in point of fact I am totally sane. An insane man would not be able to do what I am doing now, carefully removing the weakest link from the equation."

Hugo felt his heart slow down, not in the usual way that comfort or relaxation brought but in a hideous, dying way. He knew he had seconds to live, and so did the other man. They saw it in each other's eyes at the same second. In one, a deep, dreadful fear of what was about to happen. In the other, the blank, measured stare of a killer.

He slowed his breathing. The man in front of him stared. He felt his fear rise.

He turned to flee the office, but the man rushed him and grabbed hold of the back of his tweed suit jacket. Spun him around and knocked him down. Then he was on the floor but this time Magalos was on top of him and his hands were around his neck, pushing down into the soft flesh of his throat.

He fought back hard, but then he felt himself losing control. It was as if someone had cast a spell over him, and suddenly Magalos was too powerful for him now that the poison was in his system. He was choking him with one hand while he used the other to bat Hugo's arms away from his face, and then he pinned both his hands down above his head and waited for the drug to finish its devilry.

When he heard his last sigh he released his arms and staggered to his feet.

The past should stay in the past, he considered.
And now it would.

CHAPTER 37

"All right, this is it."

Jacob looked at the faces of his team members and felt a wave of pride. Approaching seven o'clock on a freezing, snowy night in December and yet they had mobilised in less than two hours and were all ready for the raid on Everett's lodge.

"I can't believe the bastard's still staying there, after what happened," Holloway said.

"The lodges are well away from the main house so he's nowhere near the crime scene," Jacob said. "And from what I gather Lucinda Beecham permitted him to use it as his home until he found somewhere else. He has nowhere else to go. He's not breaking any laws on that one, Matt, sorry."

"And he's definitely in now?" Holloway asked.

Jacob nodded. "He was out earlier today because he was clocked driving past Stonehenge on the A303 an hour or so ago by a traffic camera, but now he's safely tucked up in his lodge and he doesn't know what's about to hit him."

"Have we got the place sealed off?" Innes asked.

Jacob nodded. "There's only one way out of the retreat by car and that's this main driveway," he pointed to the map on the wall in the MIU and traced his finger along the winding private road. "It's half a mile long but if he gets hold of a car and tries to make a break for it, he's out of luck. We're blocking the entrance up at the main road with two unmarked cars, and the men posted there are authorised firearms officers in case he tries to ram his way through."

"Is that necessary, sir?" Innes asked.

"He's the prime suspect in a major murder enquiry and something tells me he's not going to go quietly. He won't be fired on unless he puts the officers' lives or the safety of the general public at risk, but I think it's a sensible precaution until we have him safely in custody. Are we all ready?"

A round of nods was his answer.

"All right then everyone," Jacob said firmly. "Let's go get our man."

*

When Everett slowly pulled back the curtains of the luxury lodge's hallway, his worst fears were confirmed. His mouth dried and his heart rate quickened as he wondered if his past had finally caught up with him. Squinting in the darkness, he studied the shape of the figures trudging up his path. It was impossible to be sure but it didn't look like Jacob. Maybe the Welsh inspector and one of the younger detective constables.

Time's running out, Rich.

"The mistake you made was to come back here," he

muttered.

He had to act fast. Walking into the kitchen, he pulled open one of the drawers and scanned the cutlery tray for a suitable knife. Finding nothing worthwhile, his eyes crawled out of the drawer and along the countertop until stopping on the beechwood Wusthof Classic knife block beside the sink. Say what you want about old Indie Beecham, but she knew how to organise the décor.

Sliding a six-inch *kiritsuke* knife from the block, he tested its substantial weight in his hand. The blade glinted in the calming blue neon glow of the LED underlighting and without realizing it, a grim smile had appeared on his face. It felt good, and he considered bringing the meat fork with him too, but there was such a thing as overkill, he considered.

No, he'd stick with the knife – but could he use it?

Only if he had to, he decided, but he knew he could. After all, he'd done it before, he recalled with dark, cold satisfaction.

A stark, hard rap at the door jolted him from his thoughts.

"Mr Richard Everett?"

Had one of *them* squealed on him?

"We know you're in, sir. Please come to the door."

He was right about the inspector. The Welsh accent gave him away. He cursed under his breath, remembering what Dean Cooper had told him when he'd delivered some drugs a couple of days ago. He'd told him he'd seen a Royal

Marines tattoo on Morgan's arm. A commando dagger inked into his flesh for eternity as a not-so-subtle warning to others to keep away, a reminder that if there was a disagreement, they were going to come off worse.

"Come to the door please, sir."

"Yeah, right," Everett muttered, recognising Jacob's voice now as well. With his profile, disappearing would be hard but not impossible, especially if he could get out of the country to somewhere where he was unknown. It was either that or going inside for the rest of his life. He walked to the back door, stopping for a moment to admire his reflection in the hallway mirror. "With a face like that, you'd never last a day, Ritchie."

"Go around the back, Holloway."

"Sir."

Too late.

Everett dumped the knife in a bag, slipped out of the back door and into the snow, already knowing his destination. Tucking behind a pine trunk to keep out of Holloway's sight, he watched the young DC cautiously approach the open back door. "Mr Everett?"

But he was gone, fleeing along the short forest path to the shed where the retreat kept its maintenance equipment – ladders, bolt-cutters, axes, shovels and forks. His dark eyes lingered on a twelve-inch steel billhook blade hanging off the back of the door. There would be no messing with that, commando or not, and he decided to bring it with him, throwing it into his bag alongside the knife.

Scanning the shed beyond the tool storage area, he quickly found why he was really here – the quads – and ran over to them. As he moved through the dusty shed, he heard Holloway call out to Morgan back over at the lodge. "Over here, sir! The back door's open!"

Four quads were three too many as far as Richard Everett was concerned, and now he unscrewed the fuel caps and made a quick check of their petrol tank levels. Choosing the one with the fullest tank, he rolled it away from the shed and out into the snow.

He straddled the seat and flipped the handlebar switch to 'run' before kick-starting the engine. A stench of two-stroke oil floated up to him as he pulled in the clutch and kicked the left foot pedal down once, to shift into first gear. The noise of the engine seemed incredibly loud in the darkness of the night, but he had no other choice.

No one could ever know what he'd done.

Gently releasing the clutch he squeezed the throttle with his right hand and felt the biting point. A bit more throttle and the machine started pulling away from the shed.

*

Morgan and Holloway were about to enter the house when they heard the two-stroke quad engine firing up a few hundred feet from the lodge.

"Sounds like the bastard's nicked a quad," Morgan said.

"Anna, call in a chopper," Jacob said as they ran down to the shed. "If he's gone rogue on one of those bloody things he could be anywhere. We're going to need some backup and some thermal imaging cameras."

"On it, guv."

He saw Morgan climbing onboard one of the other quads. "What are you doing?"

"I'm going after the little sod."

"You can drive one of these things?"

"Of course, I can," he said. "I grew up on a farm."

"Easy to learn?"

"Left foot controls the gears, kick down for first and then up for the rest. The right-hand controls the throttle and the left-hand controls the brake. You think you can remember that?"

"Just watch me."

CHAPTER 38

E verett's eyes strained in the darkness as he searched for a way through the woods. The track was clear enough to see but easy to follow him on, especially if any of them could ride quads. He passed a trembling hand over his face to calm himself. It smelt of engine oil he'd picked up from the machine's cold alloy handlebar and made him feel momentarily nauseous.

He was on the retreat's southern perimeter where it started to incline up towards the main part of Grovely Wood behind him and offered a good view of the surrounding countryside. Over the top of the retreat's main building, the lights of Hanging Langford were dimly visible in the snow, but beyond them, he saw nothing but whiteout.

The blizzard was finally coming in.

His mind raced with thoughts of escape and terrifying visions of his capture, but he could never let that happen.

Was that a way out of the woodland without using the main track? It looked like it, but it wasn't going to be easy. One mistake and he'd get thrown from the seat. As he weighed up the risks, the quad's 450 cc engine idled in the chilly gloom, echoing off the trunks of the surrounding pine trees. It wasn't the most powerful of machines because farmers preferred reliable, easily serviced models to the racier ones found on the quad-biking centres, but no matter. It was a damn sight faster than being on foot like Jacob and the rest of his team and by the time they got up here, he'd be long gone.

He twisted the throttle and the quad's engine roared in response.

Time to go, Ritchie, he said and steered down towards a farm.

*

Jacob climbed on board the Yamaha ATV, kickstarted the engine just as Morgan had shown him. He pulled the clutch in and flicked up the shift lever with his shoe, engaging first gear. The quad jerked forward as he steered away from the shed and out to the snowy path leading into the woods. Rapidly changing up through the gears with the shift lever, he was soon racing deep into the woodland just behind the Welshman, both in close pursuit of the fleeing Richard Everett who was by now half a mile further along the track.

Blinking in the swirling snow and struggling to keep his eyes on the path, he powered the quad forward with only Morgan's rear lights to act as a beacon in the night. Somewhere further ahead was the man they had been chasing for days and he was finally in their reach. He knew whatever he did now, he couldn't let him get away again.

*

Anna Mazurek got off the phone to find a concerned-looking Laura Innes standing beside her. "That was the NPAS," she said. "They've already re-tasked a chopper from Salisbury. It'll be here in minutes."

The National Police Air Service provided air support to all forty-three police forces in the country, and now all they could do was hope it could get here in time to help Jacob and Morgan track down Everett before he got too far away.

*

The Airbus H135 utility helicopter raced over the downs less than a hundred feet below the cloud ceiling, effortlessly scanning the expansive landscape for any sign of the fugitive. Powered by two Pratt & Whitney turboshaft engines, it rapidly reached the coordinates above the woodland and began closing in on Everett. Using the thermal-imaging camera, the crew easily located him as he raced along a path deep in the woods.

The pilot radioed the rest of the team on the ground. "We have him at the western edge of the retreat's woodland."

"Received, thank you."

"He's on a track running through the middle of the woods. It's a right, right, right. He's now left the central road and gone onto a track heading west."

"Received."

"Be advised he's heading towards the open fields to the west of the woods."

The pilot maintained his course while a tactical flight officer operated the thermal imaging camera, keeping it fixed squarely on the fleeing man down on the quad. "As they say in the movies," he said in a slow Wiltshire drawl. "He can run but he can't hide."

*

Jacob heard the pilot's transmission on his radio and scanned the woods for a way to turn right. "This way, boss!" Morgan called out.

Spying a narrow footpath, he steered off the track and headed west, instantly skidding down a steep slope and hitting the brakes. Shifting down a gear for some extra torque to climb the other side of the ditch, he found himself near the western edge of the woods and saw Everett as he made a desperate last attempt to escape the pursuing police.

"I see him!" he called out.

*

Everett heard the helicopter's rotors and started to panic. Driving down the ridge he slipped on some ice and the quad spun out of control. He swerved violently to the right before one of the front tyres hit a rut in the mud and flipped the machine up on its front axis, hurling him into the air like a straw doll. He crashed down into the frozen mud and realised he'd sprained his ankle.

Grunting with pain, he crawled away from the wrecked quad and started to stagger across the open field. It felt like his heart was about to burst open in his chest. Somewhere over his shoulder, he heard once again the sound of the police helicopter's rotors as it flew over the ridge behind him and closed in on its prey. He turned and saw the aircraft's lights flashing in the snow clouds and realised he had no chance of escape unless he could evade the thermal-imaging technology.

Then he saw his chance. Up ahead was a barbed-wire fence which divided the field from another further to the north, and inside it, he spied a cattle shed belonging to one of the farms. Many of the farmers around here often out-wintered their beef cattle but due to the much lower temperatures this year he guessed they had decided to house them inside.

Fine with him. This was exactly the opportunity he was looking for.

Reaching the barbed-wire fence, he dropped to the ground and crawled over the frozen mud, scarred and rutted by the endless trample of the herd earlier in the year. The roar of the helicopter was louder now, and when he glanced over his shoulder he saw it was almost on top of him, its mighty downdraft blasting the hawthorn hedges in the corner of the field and clearing the air around him of the swirling snow. Beyond it, still up on the ridge but breaking the tree line now and getting closer by the second, he saw two men on quads and guessed it was Jacob and the commando.

He had to hurry.

Away from the fence, he scrambled across the rest of the field before reaching a wide area of tarmac just in front of the cowshed. He searched for an entrance and found one on the western end of the large building. When he got inside he was greeted by the faces of countless cows who all turned to see who the intruder was.

He limped through the shed, panicking about his next move. The body heat from all the cows would help disguise him for a short time, but he had to think fast. Reaching the far end, he peered through the door at the farmhouse and saw a series of vehicles parked up in a line. If he could break into the farmhouse and get the keys, maybe get a hostage...

It's now or never, he told himself and made one last break for it.

*

Jacob swerved to a halt beside Morgan a few yards south of the cowshed. "I see him, boss! He's over there on his hands and knees."

Jumping off the quads and running over to the shed, they found Richard Everett crawling through the mud with his sprained ankle, desperately trying to reach a gate leading to the farmhouse.

Making their way through the snowstorm they closed in on the forlorn, broken figure who now turned and looked over his shoulder. Visibly deflating, he crashed back down in the muddy snow with a howl of despair, pounding his fists on the frozen earth.

"I never meant to kill her!" he shouted. "I'm not a killer!"

"It's over," Jacob shouted through the swirling snow. "There's nowhere else to run to."

"It was an accident!" he yelled back, his voice hoarse and weak.

"Richard Everett, I am arresting you on suspicion of murder. You do not have to say anything, but it may harm your defence if you do not mention when questioned something you later rely on in court. Anything you do say may be given in evidence."

Everett pounded the ground again, each strike a little weaker than the last until finally, he crumpled down into a heap like a pile of rags, sobbing and mumbling to himself.

Morgan grabbed his hands and cuffed them behind his back before pulling him up to his feet. "You always were a terrible performer."

CHAPTER 39

New Year's Eve, 31ˢᵗ December

Richard Everett cut a pathetic figure as he sat behind the desk in the MIU's incident room, one bandaged ankle resting on a chair under an ice pack to ease the swelling. Stripped of his previous glory as one of the nation's darling celebrities, he was a shadow of his former self, a study of sunken cheeks, nervous leg bouncing and a wild, aimless stare into the middle distance.

With the rest of the team waiting in the adjoining room, Jacob started proceedings with a heavy sigh, operating the PACE compliant recording device and falling into his chair. "It's quarter past midnight and DCI Jacob and DI Morgan are present with Mr Richard Everett. A solicitor has been called but cannot attend until the morning due to weather conditions. That meeting will take place, weather permitting, in the headquarters building in Devizes."

Everett sneered. "I want it on the record that I was badly injured during the course of my arrest."

"You were fleeing the police in the course of their duties," Jacob said. "You skidded on some ice in a field and crashed the quad you had stolen to escape on."

"Nevertheless, I'll be ordering my brief to file a…"

Without waiting for the end of the sentence, Jacob cut

him off. "When we took you into custody you were formally charged and processed in the correct way, including taking your fingerprints."

"I'll be going through the entire process with a fine toothcomb," he said. "Including why I'm being interviewed in a lorry in the middle of some woodland instead of a proper police station. This alone causes me concerns."

"We're here because the road to Devizes is blocked with snow," Jacob said calmly.

"I'll be taking all of this forward in a formal complaint."

Jacob ignored him. "Let's talk about your tattoo."

"What?"

"The one you have on your upper right arm."

Now Morgan leaned back in his chair and crossed his arms behind his head. "I didn't think a bigtime celeb such as yourself would come over all shy. Go on – show us your tattoo."

"I'm under no obligation to remove my clothes and show you anything."

Jacob slid the photo across the desk. "Don't worry – we've already seen it."

Everett stared at the photo with widening eyes. "This is from my lodge!"

"And was obtained just now during the raid under the authority of a properly issued warrant."

Everett grew smaller in his chair, then a loud knocking on the door made him jump.

Jacob turned. "Come!"

The door opened to reveal Anna Mazurek. Jacob recognised the look on her face at once.

"What is it, Sergeant?"

"A word, sir. It's important."

Jacob said nothing but pushed away from the desk and walked over to the door. Here, he turned and fixed his eyes on Everett. "Time's running out, Richard. You may as well come clean."

He closed the door gently behind him and turned to Anna. "What have you got?"

She handed him a print-out. "It's the Europol report you ordered. You won't believe your eyes."

Jacob's eyes danced over the lines of text and then widened like saucers. "Is this on the level?"

Leaving Everett in the company of a uniformed PC, Morgan joined them. "What's all the fuss about, then?"

Anna explained. "Double-checked and confirmed by Mia Francis. The fingerprints we took from Richard Everett when we nicked him are a perfect match for a set taken by the Italian police on a sexual assault and murder case dating back to 1997. This Europol report confirms it."

"Hells Bells, he's killed in Italy, too," Morgan said. "I said there was something dodgy about the bastard the minute I laid eyes on him, didn't I?"

Anna rolled her eyes. "Listen to the Wise Sage."

The Welshman showed his hands in a gesture of despair. "If only people did, Anna… if only people did."

Jacob turned to go back into the incident room when he saw Holloway walking quickly towards them with a piece of paper in his hand. He had paled but looked excited.

"What's the matter?" Jacob asked, glancing at Anna.

"Another body's been found, sir," he said.

"Where?"

"At the Stonehenge Visitor Centre, sir. Victim's name is Professor Hugo Winter. He's some sort of archaeologist who's been working at the site temporarily."

"Who called it in?"

"One of the security guards. Says he saw him alive at around five or six but reckons he's been dead since not long after then. He says he was a medic in the army so knows what he's talking about."

Jacob looked at his watch. "It's just after midnight now, so that's around six hours ago."

"Exactly when Everett was driving back on the A303," Anna said.

Morgan frowned. "Which just happens to go right past Stonehenge."

"And another thing, sir."

"What?"

"It might be nothing but the guard who phoned said his colleague has gone missing on one of his rounds and that he's seen a pickup truck parked up on one of the lanes to the north of the site."

"At this time of night?" Anna asked.

Morgan sighed. "It's not Magnus Bloody Rhodes, is it? He was released on bail."

Jacob looked at his watch, gave a sharp sigh and ran a hand through his hair. "Damn it, it's after midnight and Mia lives in Bath. Is the A36 still blocked at Warminster?"

Anna nodded. "No way is she getting through tonight unless we task another helicopter."

"Yeah, right," he said with a snort. "What's the road to Salisbury like?"

"No reports of anything."

His mind buzzed with solutions. "Get Ethan on the phone, quickly. He lives just outside of the city and could be up here in twenty minutes. I want everything I can to throw at this bastard. Tell him to get up here now, if the roads are clear. I want him briefed on the situation and then to get his arse up there as fast as he can. You and Holloway go with him. I want something forensic I can use to get a confession."

"Guv."

"And get Kent on the line. He needs to be updated and I see no reason why we can't wake him from his beauty sleep."

"I already tried, boss," Morgan said. "No answer. Just keeps on ringing."

"That's odd," Jacob said. "And wait for a second – where's Innes?"

"On her way home to Marlborough," Anna said. "I sent her home a little while ago after the raid."

"Depending on how far along she is, she might be the closest to Stonehenge. Give her a call and if the conditions are clear send her to the murder scene as fast as possible."

"Okay, guv."

Jacob and Morgan exchanged a knowing glance and returned to the incident room. "Now, Mr Everett, have you ever been to Italy?"

Everett sighed. "What's that got to do with the case at hand?"

"It has everything to do with it," Morgan said. "Because when you went to Italy you were a very naughty boy, weren't you, Richard?"

Everett slumped in his seat. "You know."

Jacob said, "Your prints returned nothing from the UK database, but then I had them sent to Europol. Turns out they were found at the scene of a murder in Rome way back in 1997. A brutal stabbing."

Everett sucked in a deep breath and said, "I need to stop this interview and wait until I can have a private consultation with my brief. This is a new accusation and we need to…"

"We know you did it, Richard," Morgan said firmly. "Your prints were all over the woman's apartment, only they never found you because you fled the country."

"All right," Everett said quietly. "I was there that night, in Aventino but it was an accident, I swear!"

"I smell bullshit," Morgan said. "And I'm not just talking about your new aftershave."

"Is that sort of talk strictly necessary?" Everett said.

"Not strictly, no," Jacob said. "But I don't think Inspector Morgan likes you very much."

"Very perceptive," Morgan said. "That's why he's a DCI, you see."

Jacob leaned back in his chair. "So at this time, Mr Everett, you're the prime suspect in five brutal murders. Maria Innocenti in Rome in 1997, Emma Russell in 1992, and this week Neil Talbot, Lucinda Beecham and now Hugo Winter up at Stonehenge. I'd say you're looking at a whole life order."

"Hugo's dead?"

"Do you know him?"

"Well…"

"Don't play games," Jacob said.

"I went to speak with him earlier but decided better of it…"

Morgan gave a cynical laugh. "They'll throw away the key, man."

"I never killed any of those people, only Maria and that was an accident."

"Why did Lucinda Beecham kill Kieran Messenger and Neil Talbot?" Morgan asked out of nowhere. "Are you in it together?"

"I want a break, please."

"And why did you kill Lucinda?"

He had now turned ashen. "I really need a break."

"Fine," Jacob said. "You can have twenty minutes to

get your head straight and then I want some answers."

*

After failing to get in touch with Kent a second time, Jacob stood with Morgan outside and watched Anna and Holloway climb into Ethan Spargo's luxurious S Class Mercedes. After a brief discussion, the Home Office Pathologist had refused point-blank to travel in any of the available police cars as none of them had heated seats.

Now, with a roll of his eyes, Jacob watched through the snow as they pulled away from the MIU and started on their journey to Stonehenge.

"I just hope they can get there before the snow gets too bad," Morgan said, finishing his cigar. "Now let's go and crack that murdering bastard."

CHAPTER 40

DC Laura Innes strained to see through the windscreen as the snow fell harder and faster. She flicked her headlights onto the main beam and increased the power of the wipers to medium. She had the radio on for the weather report but now switched it off in case HQ called again on the two-way. They had already requested she divert to Stonehenge to attend another murder, and she was almost there.

She dropped into fourth gear and slowed for the next bend. Checked her mobile but still nothing else concerning the murder or Everett from anyone at the MIU.

Her mind was racing with too many thoughts. To be the first on the scene was exciting but scary and she felt her nervousness rising in her stomach. Yes, she was trained for all police work, but coming face to face with another victim of one of the county's most notorious murderers was another matter altogether. One thing was for sure, life in CID was shaping up to be more than she thought possible.

And then there was Jacob. She knew in her heart that Marcus Kent was a bastard but he had offered a fast-track to detective sergeant if she provided the evidence required for him to bring down the DCI. The only problem was even though he was a maverick and pushed his luck more than was safe for him, Jacob was a good man. He had offered her a massive break by accepting her into the team and had already taught her so much.

Could she go to Kent and give him what he was looking for? Jacob had, after all, hired Sophie Anderson as a consultant against Kent's express orders. He'd stolen police property and taken it off-site and he'd ordered Sergeant Mazurek to conduct an illegal search of DI Dunn's private property. It would be enough to give Kent what he needed. The name *Judas* rose in her mind as she shifted up into fifth and accelerated along the final straight. Up ahead was Stonehenge.

And a man in the road.

In the swirling snow, he appeared like a wraith.

She had razor-sharp reactions and instantly checked the mirror. No one behind her. Hitting the foot brakes at this speed on snow would be too dangerous. She shifted down into third and then second. The Vauxhall's 1.3-litre engine growled in response and she felt the car slow rapidly as the engine braking kicked in.

Much slower now, she tapped the foot brake and slowed again. The wraith had turned into a tall man in a long black overcoat. He was wearing a black beanie pulled down over the tops of his ears and only an inch above his eyebrows. He waved his hands in the air as he walked into the middle of the road and flagged her down.

She brought the car to a halt less than twenty metres from him and instantly picked up the two-way radio. "Dispatch this is DS Innes, be advised I've been flagged down by a man on The Packway."

"Received…" and then static.

She was all alone.

*

Jacob walked into the cramped incident room, dismissed the uniformed police constable and restarted the recorder. Glancing at his watch he said, "Interview resumes ten past one a.m."

He took a seat beside Morgan and crossed his arms over his chest. "Now then, Mr Everett. You were about to tell us why you murdered Emma Russell before moving to Italy and then went on a killing spree this week."

"I never killed Emma Russell or went on a killing spree."

"More bullshit," Morgan said.

"It's not bullshit," he insisted.

A long silence followed, each man only slowly realising just how much the wind had got up outside the MIU. It beat hard against the side of the large truck, rocking it back and forth on its suspension and howling like ghosts through the antenna array on its roof.

"Well?" Jacob said. "This doesn't end until you tell us what we want to hear."

Everett finally broke, visibly crumpling down into his seat. "We called ourselves The Lucus," he said at last.

"Say again?" Morgan asked.

"*Lucus*, Inspector. It's Latin for a sacred grove, and that made sense because we're in a Grove."

"In a Grove?"

"It's an ancient druidic term. When druids gather in larger groups they're called Orders, but we were much smaller and smaller groups are called Groves."

"And was Emma Russell in this *Grove*?"

He nodded. "Yes, she was."

"And how many others are in it?"

"*Were*. We broke apart after Emma's death and never spoke again."

"I asked how many."

"Just a small group of us," he said, darkly. "We gathered most weeks after we'd all returned from our various universities. Just stupid stuff, mostly. A vague interest in black magic, Wicca, druidism. All just silly nonsense with no real understanding of any of those things. We just conflated all of it together and had some fun with a few drinks, but then one night it all went wrong."

"Don't stop now, Mr Everett."

A weary, nervous sigh whistled through the prisoner's lips. "Emma had heard about the women who were murdered in Grovely Wood in the eighteenth century. A tragic story, but some of us in the Grove took it more seriously than others. The decision was taken to go up there one night and see if we could summon them."

Morgan shook his head. "What a load of bollocks."

Jacob raised a hand. "Let him finish, Bill."

Morgan pushed back into the plastic bucket seat and crossed his arms over his chest. "Sorry, boss."

"What happened when you summoned them?" Jacob asked him.

Everett snorted. "Nothing, at first, but then the decision was taken to take some drugs and see if that helped."

"Brilliant," Morgan said. "What a university education buys you…"

Jacob shifted uneasily in his seat as the wind howled outside. "You keep saying *the decision was taken*, Mr Everett," Jacob said. "Who was taking all these decisions?"

Everett's eyes flicked to the floor and his leg began bouncing even more violently. "The Chosen Chief."

"A name, please, Mr Everett."

He started rocking back and forward on his chair and shaking his head. "No, I'll never give the name up. It would be a death sentence."

"You're already facing a life sentence," Morgan said. "After a few years in stir, you might wish for the other, especially when the other lags find out you're in for sex crimes and murder, believe me."

"Maybe death would be better if it were to be a painless and quick death, but that's not what would be waiting for me if I betrayed the Chosen Chief."

"Is this *Chosen Chief* the killer?"

"Yes."

"And are you afraid to give up his name?"

"You don't understand, Chief Inspector. Each member of the Grove took a sacred oath never to reveal what happened on that dreadful night, and never to implicate any of the others. We were all destined for greater things and we knew we had to take the secret to our graves. It's very much a case of united we stand or divided we fall."

"And you're prepared to go to jail for this, are you?"

"I never murdered any of these people."

"That's to be proved one way or the other," Jacob said. "But one thing we are sure of is that you committed the murder in Rome in 1997. That's not going to look great on the evening news, is it? National TV celebrity subjected an innocent woman to a brutal sexual assault and then stabbed her and knocked her down a flight of stairs, breaking her neck."

Another long pause. "If I help you, will I get some sort of immunity?"

"This isn't America," Morgan said. "And you've already confessed to a murder."

Jacob said, "But if you were to help us significantly in our enquiry and give us the identity of the killer I'm sure something can be arranged." Without hesitating, he added, "I've asked you before and this time I want an answer. How many, exactly, in this Grove?"

"There were six of us. As I said, we met after university through a shared interest in paganism and the occult. The Chosen Chief gave us the names of ancient Celtic gods and goddesses as a form of initiation, and after that, you had the right to wear the tattoo. Emma was Meduna, the goddess of mead. She liked a drink, you see. Indie was Artio, the Celtic goddess of wildlife and bears because she'd grown up in the woods."

"Who else?"

"Miranda was Divona, the goddess of the sacred spring."

"Miranda Dunn?"

He nodded. "One of yours, I believe."

"She'll be arrested in the morning for an accessory to murder during and after the fact," Jacob said without emotion. "Which *god* was Hugo Winter?"

"Fagus, the god of beech trees, only he hadn't been initiated by then so he never had the tattoo."

"And now with the news of his death from Stonehenge, I'm guessing there are only three still alive."

"That's correct."

Morgan shook his head. "What was your little nickname?"

"I was Dullovius, the forest god. The Chosen Chief found it amusing – the forest reference was obvious but *dull...* he said this described me perfectly."

"And the Chosen Chief?" Jacob said. "What name did he give himself?"

"Magalos, the hunter god."

"Don't you think that was a bit childish?" Morgan asked.

"It's not childish at all," he said. "They were powerful

Celtic deities."

Jacob crossed his arms. "I thought the Celts came much later, well after the Iron Age druids."

"Very little is known about the Iron Age druids, so we settled on using the names of Celtic gods and goddesses. It worked for us."

"Still say it's childish."

"It was far from childish. In fact, right now your people are in danger, Chief Inspector."

Jacob narrowed his eyes. "What are you talking about?"

"The people you just sent up to Stonehenge, they're in great danger. All of them."

"How?"

"He's up there, at Stonehenge, watching them."

"Who?"

Everett gave a grim smile. "Magalos, of course. He's everywhere."

Jacob stood up and grabbed his phone. "Watch him, Bill. I need to call Anna in a hurry."

CHAPTER 41

Anna Mazurek reached for her phone and saw from the caller ID that it was Jacob. She turned to Holloway in the back seat. "It's the boss."

"Hopefully, Everett has confessed," the young detective said. "That'll make everything much easier."

Spargo sighed. "It might make your life easier but it doesn't make mine any easier. I'm still expected to produce the same quality of work whether he confesses or not."

Anna took the call. "It's me, guv."

"Anna, it's Jacob. Where are you?"

"Still on our way."

"How far out are you?"

"We'll be there in less than ten minutes."

"And where's Innes?"

"Last I heard she was ahead of us but I can't get through to her."

"Neither can I." He blew out a breath of anxious frustration. "You need to find her and tell her that she's in danger. You're all in danger. Everett has confessed to the Italian murder but swears he's innocent of the woods' murders. He's just told me that he knows the ID of the killer and that, likely, he'll still be up there somewhere. It's the same bloke the guard saw lurking in the truck."

"Do we have an ID on him?"

"Not yet. I get the impression Everett is scared of him. I don't want to go there but it could be Rhodes."

"Jesus… all right – thanks, guv."

Anna Mazurek cut the call and slipped her mobile back into her pocket. She turned to Spargo and Holloway, a look of grim reality on her face. "He says Everett confessed to the killing of the woman in Italy in ninety-seven but is adamant that he is not guilty of any of the other murders."

"And Jacob believes him?"

"He says the real killer is going to be up at Stonehenge, waiting for us and that Innes is up there somewhere on her own."

"Bloody hell," Holloway said. "I wish we were armed."

"There's three of us and one of him," Spargo said.

Anna gave him a brief sideways glance struggling to picture him in an altercation with a killer. "How much longer till we get there?"

"Still around ten minutes."

Her phone rang again. "It's dispatch."

"We're all go tonight," Holloway said.

"Tell me about it," said Spargo. "I was in bed an hour ago."

Anna rolled her eyes. "Go ahead, dispatch."

"We just had DC Innes call in. She says she's just been flagged down by a man on The Packway."

"The Packway?" Anna said. "That's to the north of Stonehenge and well off the main road. What the hell is she doing out there?"

"There's been an RTC on the A303 and the road is closed. She took the side roads to get to the murder scene."

Anna absent-mindedly scratched her forehead. "All right, thanks."

She cut the call. "I think we need to get over to The Packway fast, Ethan."

"You can say that again," Holloway said. "She could be in real danger."

Spargo brought the car to a slow stop at the side of the road. "But that's well to the north of the Stonehenge site."

"I know. We've been called to attend a dead body and that's a priority, but on the other hand, Laura is out on her own and after what Everett said about the killer being up there, I think she's in real danger."

The corner of Spargo's mouth turned up in a gesture of indecision. "Left or right, Anna... it's your call."

*

Out on The Packway, the wind howled through the small gap Innes had left at the top of her window.

"I need your help," the man in the beanie said.

Laura noticed blood on his cheek. The faintest touch, three thin red lines that looked like scratch marks. "What's happened?"

"My pickup." His breath plumed in the swirling snowy air as he pointed down the road. "I came off the road on the next bend and almost went into a ditch. Got scratched

410

by hawthorns on the way out. I just need someone to give me a push start and I think I can get on my way."

"Have you called for assistance?"

"Mobile's not working," he said, looking up at the leaden sky. "I guess because of this."

"I'm having the same problem," she said. "I just called dispatch and I'm not getting through."

He looked at her oddly. "Dispatch?"

"I'm a police officer," she said confidently, showing him her ID. "DC Innes."

"Ah, even more useful! The car's just around the next corner."

Laura Innes looked up at the man's cold, desperate face and for a moment was unsure what to do. In normal circumstances, she would simply help push-start the car and get about her business. But these were far from normal circumstances. First, the blizzard was almost unprecedented in its fury, and second, she knew there was a killer in the vicinity. On the other hand, she knew she couldn't leave the man stranded out here. She had identified herself and he would surely make a complaint.

"All right," she said, thinking on her feet. "You walk ahead and I'll follow in the car. When we get to your vehicle we'll take it from there and I'll try HQ one more time."

"Thanks," he said. "It's just around the next bend."

She pushed up her window and watched the man in the black coat trudge away in the snow. She felt no guilt about not offering him a ride. If the broken-down pickup was as close as he had claimed he only had a short walk to the next bend.

But after that, she had no idea what she was going to do.

Into first gear, she crawled along behind the man in the snow and tried the radio again, but there was nothing but static.

*

The wind rose to another eerie howl outside the MIU as Everett shifted in his seat, his hands still handcuffed together in his lap. "What do you know about the Age of Pericles, Chief Inspector?"

"Enlighten me."

"It was an unprecedented time of learning in ancient Greece. The Golden Age of Athens which gave us so many wonders… including Hippocrates."

Morgan shifted angrily in his seat. "What are you talking about?"

"I swear to fulfil, to the best of my ability and judgement, this covenant…"

"Stop wasting our time, man." Morgan turned to Jacob. "He's out of his mind."

Jacob kept his eyes locked on Everett.

"Do you like lasagne, Chief Inspector?"

Morgan snorted. "If this is some sort of pathetic attempt to go for an insanity plea…"

"It's not," Jacob said flatly.

Everett smiled. *"I will remember that there is art to medicine as well as science, and that warmth, sympathy, and understanding may outweigh the surgeon's knife or the chemist's drug."*

Morgan snorted. "Then pardon my French but what the buggering hell is he going on about?"

"I will prevent disease whenever I can, for prevention is preferable to cure."

As Everett stared serenely at the two policemen, Jacob's eyes widened with horror. "My *God…*"

"Boss?"

"He is quoting from the Lasagna Oath."

"I don't understand."

"Louis Lasagna was an American doctor and a professor of medicine. He revised the Hippocratic Oath into a modern version, the one that doctors use today. I know because Jess was a doctor."

"You've lost me, boss. Maybe we should lock him up for a bit and see if that clears his head."

Jacob's blue eyes were fixed on Everett's macabre smirk. "Don't stop him now. He's telling us who the killer is."

"Who?" Morgan asked.

Jacob's voice was as cold as steel, calm and measured. "Ethan Spargo."

Morgan stared at Jacob with saucer eyes. "What?"

A fiendish grin spread across Everett's face. "Full points, Chief Inspector, only his divine name was Magalos, the hunter god. I trust my assistance will be reflected in the sentence should I be found guilty. By crossing the Chosen Chief, I have put my life in jeopardy tonight."

"Don't count on it," Jacob said, getting up to leave.

Hearing the confirmation, Morgan's face was once again stricken with a mix of disbelief and abject terror. "Bloody hell… he's out in the storm with Anna and Matt, boss! They're all alone out there with him."

"Not for long they're not," Jacob said. "With me, now."

He and Morgan left the constable in the interview room as they walked out of the room and along the narrow corridor at the side of the MIU truck. A stark, unwelcoming place lit by harsh strip lights and made even more unpleasant by the wind driving snow against the side door.

"Get the armed response team from the raid back here now and I don't want any excuses about the weather. We know their last position on the road to the west of Stonehenge, and we know the body is in the visitor centre. We also know there's no way Spargo is going to kill Anna and Matt unless they find out he's the killer."

"What about you, boss?"

"I'll go on ahead," he said, pushing open the door. A flurry of snow blew into the MIU and settled on the cheap Persian blue carpet tiles. "I just hope we're not too late."

CHAPTER 42

With Holloway desperately trying to get a signal on his phone in the back seat, Anna Mazurek strained to see the road through the blizzard. Even the main beams were now acting against them, illuminating the snowfall directly in front of the car and simply bouncing the light back into the cab.

"I see the Visitor Centre!" she said.

"Can you?" Holloway asked. "I can't see a bloody thing."

Anna pointed into the snow. "It's there to the left, but only just. Someone's waving a torch!"

Spargo saw it now. "Okay, got it."

Ahead of them, a man in a black beanie was waving his arms in the air and shining a torch into a corner of the car park."

"Must be the English Heritage security guard who called it in," Anna said. "I think he wants us to park over there."

Spargo raised an eyebrow. "I can see why they made you a sergeant."

Anna sighed. "Just park."

Spargo followed the man's instructions as he directed them along the now invisible road leading up to the centre. Using his torch like a man guiding an aircraft onto the parking apron with marshalling wands, he was able to get them safely to the car park.

Pulling the car up outside the visitor centre, Spargo killed the engine. Switching the lights off, his face was momentarily illuminated by a soft blue glow from the dashboard lights. "We made it."

"And the job hasn't even started yet," Anna said. "We still have a corpse waiting for us."

He stifled a laugh. "Oh, happy life…"

The moment was ended by the sharp rapping of the security guard's hand on the driver's window.

Spargo opened his door. "Good evening."

"Can't believe you got here," the guard said, his face pinched red by the cold.

Anna opened her door and stepped out into the snow. "We very nearly didn't. Now, where's the body?"

"It's at the back of the centre," he said.

"Inside or outside?"

"Inside, in the office section. Just go through the front door and go past the ticket desk and then turn left."

"Can't you show us?"

"I need to clear the road for the ambulance. It's getting worse by the second."

"Aren't there supposed to be two of you on duty?" Anna asked.

"There are, but Dave went out on his rounds to check out the pickup we saw hanging about. It's only a short trip but then this nightmare blew in. I'm guessing he's got stuck somewhere."

"Helpful."

"Anyway, as I said, I'm going up to clear the road again so the ambulance can get in."

"Good idea," Anna said. "You've got more than one snow shovel I presume?"

"Of course."

She turned in her seat and gave Matt Holloway her best smile. "Glad you brought your coat now?"

"Thanks a lot, Sarge."

*

Jacob changed down into second gear and swerved around a bend in the lane. Stonehenge was only around fifteen minutes' drive from the MIU but the blizzard had blown in early and was now racing across the downs with a vengeance. Driven by a fierce December wind, sleet and snow whipped across the landscape so fast it was almost moving horizontally. He shifted the windscreen wipers to full power but they were barely able to cope, only just clearing the glass before the next flurry of snow piled down onto it.

"Siri, call Anna Mazurek."

Gripping the smooth, wooden steering wheel he shifted down and roared around another corner, the headlights sweeping along the snow-packed hedgerows.

"Come on!"

No signal.

"Damn it to hell! Siri, call Matthew Holloway."

He raced along the deserted road, drawing closer to the ancient monument as the modern electronic dial tone filled the interior of the vintage car.

No signal.

He stamped on the throttle and the three-litre engine growled like a hungry beast. Jacob felt his heart pounding in his chest and knew there was nothing he could do but drive and hope the roads stayed clear. Weaving the car around endless twisting lanes as he raced towards the ancient monument, he saw the fuel gauge on the Alvis was almost on zero. He cursed again and smacked his hand down on the wheel. He'd left the MIU in such a rush he hadn't checked how much petrol was in the car. With the needle dipping below empty, he could do nothing but pray it would be enough to get him all the way to Stonehenge.

"Come on!" he muttered. "Don't let me down now."

The storm gathered strength as the fuel gauge dropped lower, then, another half mile up the road he finally saw the sign for the visitor centre. Turning left onto the slip road he was almost there when the car started to sputter and eventually stalled completely. His prayers had been ignored and the car had run out of petrol at the last hurdle. He cursed again, and steered it over to the side of the road, bringing it to a stop just on the snowy verge. Climbing out of the car, he saw a glimpse of the ancient sarsens around a mile to the northeast.

He ran to the boot and pulled out a hefty tyre iron. The snow swirled in his face and nipped at his ears. He felt the cold snapping at him, and with only his feet to carry him, he made his way towards the approach road.

*

Anna watched Holloway pad away with the security guard, a snow shovel over his shoulder as he made his way towards the approach road. "All right, I suppose we'd better go and see what's waiting for us."

Spargo looked at her. "I'll get my medical bag."

They walked into the empty visitor centre and followed the security guard's instructions around to the office section. Smooth stone floors and wide silent corridors stretched before them as they drew closer to their destination. Turning a final corner, they saw another corridor with five doors.

"This way," Spargo said, pushing open one of the doors. "It's just through here."

Anna followed him and saw the dead man, hanging from his belt. Even after all this time, it was a shock, but she quickly pulled herself together. "All right, let's get on with it. The boss wants everything we can get to help nail Everett."

"You'll have to help me get him down," Spargo said, placing his medical bag down on the desk.

She was walking over to the hanging corpse when she

felt her blood run cold.

It's just through here.

Ice ran up her spine as she turned to face the pathologist. "Wait, how did you know which one his office was?"

Spargo turned to her. "I'm sorry?"

"You walked straight to this office, but there were five doors. The security guard never told us which one."

She didn't need to say anything else – the devilish smirk on his face was the only reply she needed to see.

"That was a silly mistake to make," he said, darkly.

Anna took a step back but he stepped in front of her and slammed the door.

She looked down in his medical bag and saw a syringe and black leather gloves. "Oh my God, it was you all the time."

*

When Jacob ran further up the approach road he saw Laura Innes's Corsa parked up on the side of the verge. She was walking with a man in a thick black coat and beanie hat. The road was blocked with snow, but further ahead two more men were working hard to shovel it out of the way.

"Innes!"

She turned, and so did the man.

"Sir!"

"What's going on?" he asked, looking at the man.

"This is Dave," she said. "He's one of the on-site security guards. He was on his rounds to check out the pickup truck they'd seen. It turns out it was broken down – the owner had left a note on the windscreen."

"And then my pickup only went and broke down too," Dave said with an eye-roll.

"So I gave him a lift back," Innes said.

As she spoke, the two men with snow shovels drew closer and Jacob recognised one of them as Holloway.

"Sir!" Holloway said.

"Where's Anna?" Jacob shouted.

"Sorry?"

The wind swirled.

"Anna and Spargo, where are they?"

"Up in the visitor centre, sir," Holloway said. "She's securing the crime scene while the doc does his medical magic."

Jacob raised his voice to a shout to cut through the roaring snowstorm. "We have to get up there! Spargo's the killer!"

*

"I expect you think I'm some sort of monster, but I'm not." Spargo loomed over her with the medical bag in his hand. "I only killed Emma because I was out of my mind on drugs. We all were. It was a crazy night a long time ago but I can remember it like it was yesterday. It haunts me. It

421

turned me into an insomniac."

"You get away from me."

"The six of us in the Grove were all up there together. It was a wild night. I'd taken too large a dose of LSD and gone off into the woods in search of the witches – or at least, their ghosts. Then I saw one of them. She rose from the grave and ran towards me with her dead, withered hands stretched in front of her. I chased her through the woods and then I picked up a rock and smashed her in the head, and when she fell to the ground I stabbed her and stabbed her... I was delirious."

He stopped and glanced around the office as the wind howled in the eaves.

"But when I came down from the trip I saw it was no witch I had killed, but Emma. You can't imagine how I felt. A strange cocktail of guilt, horror and power. It changed me forever, Sergeant."

Anna's mind spun like a Catherine wheel as she took in everything he was saying. She remembered her training and knew she had to stall for time. "And you all buried her up in the woods with the hope no one would ever find her?"

"We all had very promising careers ahead of us. Poor Hugo here had just been accepted into Cambridge to study archaeology. Miranda was already in police college and Richard's TV career was finally starting to get off the ground. Even poor old Indie had so much to lose. Her parents would never have left her the estate had she been convicted as an accessory after the fact. You know how it goes. As for me, I was about to finish at Oxford and start a very promising career as a police pathologist. Can you imagine the fallout had we gone to the police and confessed to what had happened that night?"

"So you just left her there to rot? You let her family live with all that doubt for so many years?"

"Collateral damage, just like you."

She shook her head in disgust. "What about Kieran Messenger?"

"Haven't you worked it out yet, Sergeant? Indie killed him when he tried to blackmail her. He told her that he knew what had happened, that he knew she was involved."

"How?"

"He was always in the woods as a teenager, trapping birds and small animals. A real weirdo by most people's standards. He told her that he'd seen our rituals around the fire and always wondered why we'd stopped meeting there so abruptly. Even when he heard about Emma's disappearance on the news all those years ago he didn't put it all together, or at least he had no evidence. If you ask me he lusted after her. He let it go, but when those fools with the metal detectors found her he finally put two and two together."

"Not so stupid then."

"I would disagree. He asked her for a quarter of a million pounds. Said she was rich enough to be able to afford it and if she didn't pay up he'd go to the police and point them – *you* – in our direction. She snapped and killed him with a breaker bar instead. Unfortunately, the bloody ranger saw the whole thing and it was left to me to sort out the mess. As the Chosen Chief of the Grove, I decided to kill Talbot and frame Indie for it, using Cooper as the patsy."

"But you didn't know we were raiding him, and in the process giving him an alibi?"

He shook his head. "No, sadly I was left out of the loop on that one. A tragedy, considering the planning I'd put into it. Just as I had carefully planned Talbot's murder to make Indie look like *his* killer. I stole her shotgun and shells when she was up at the lodges and used that as the murder weapon. Then I put it back when I broke in to kill her. She only used the thing to kill rabbits at the end of the season in February so I knew she wouldn't miss it for a few hours. She killed Talbot and then Cooper killed her. It was choreographed to perfection."

"Including planting a beech tree on Emma's grave to hide it?"

He looked at her oddly. "No, that was pure serendipity." As he spoke he reached into his medical bag and started to put on some black leather gloves. "Now, it's time to make your peace with God."

She staggered back to the door but he lunged forward, black-gloved hands reaching out towards her.

*

424

Jacob led the others up the approach road, running through slush and dirt as they drew closer to the visitor centre. The wind had gained strength and was driving an ever thicker blizzard into their faces as they made their way through the night.

"How much further?" he called out.

"Not far," Dave shouted back, burying his face down into a thick black scarf. "In these conditions, I'd say another five minutes. If you look over there you can just see the outline of the main centre."

Jacob followed his pointing arm, but another wave of snow had already obscured the building.

"We have to hurry," he shouted through the snow. "He's got nothing to lose now."

CHAPTER 43

Anna Mazurek struggled with the much stronger man as he forced her backwards away from the door. Grabbing her arm, he twisted it behind her back until she screamed in pain. "I'll break it if you don't stop resisting."

"You can't get away with this," she said, desperately stalling for time. "Jacob and the rest of the team are on their way. They know who you are and what you've done." It was a lie, but it was all she could do. As far as she knew, Jacob was in the MIU and all the roads were blocked by the snow.

"Hush now, Sergeant Mazurek," he whispered in her ear. He was standing behind her now. With both her arms pinned behind her back with one of his hands and the other arm clamped around her throat he pushed her towards Hugo's desk. He brought his arm around from her neck and unzipped the medical bag a little more to make a wider opening.

"Just another sad police suicide," he whispered breathily.

She turned her head and watched as he fumbled with the small bottle full of clear liquid she had seen in the bag. On the label was the word *succinyl chloride*. She didn't know precisely what it was but she knew enough to understand what was coming.

"Something to stop you struggling."

Then it struck her like a hammer. Staring at the drug, she said, "My God, you killed those two witnesses as well! They never killed themselves! You paralysed them and made it look like suicide."

"You always were very observant. Both those men reported seeing Emma walking to the woods to meet with us that night. Unfortunately, they told Miranda Dunn, who in turn told me. She then falsified their evidence to move the search away from Grovely Wood. When the world had moved on to the next tragedy she destroyed their statements and I paid them both a visit and silenced them. You surely would have made a wonderful DCI."

"Please! You don't have to do this," she said.

"I wish that were so, Anna," he replied, pulling a syringe from the bag. "But we both know I have no choice." She felt his breath on her ear as he spoke, his words calm and measured.

He brought the bottle around to her back and she felt him push against her as he filled the syringe with the liquid. Then, without another word, she felt the sharp, metallic sting of the needle piercing her neck. She gasped as she felt the cold liquid pumping into her artery, and then he released her and stepped away.

"Off you go to the Summerland."

She thought he'd made a mistake and not given her enough, but then she turned to confront him and felt her body responding to the powerful drug. As she reached out her arms towards him, she realised she could barely focus her eyes on him and that she could no longer move her hands. The potent sedative was coursing through her entire system now, gradually shutting down her ability to control her own body. She wanted to scream, but no sound came out of her mouth, and then she was unable even to move her mouth.

And then her legs gave way and she slumped to the floor like an empty suit.

He walked over to her and her brain told her to run as fast as she could, but nothing responded. Not a single muscle moved.

"Don't worry, the dose isn't strong enough to shut your lungs down… yet."

Frozen by the sedative, she was unable to respond. Her only choice was to sit in silence and stare unblinking at him as he spoke.

"It's a very powerful drug, and a full adult dose would shut down your respiratory function and kill you instantly, but I gave you an even smaller dose than I gave poor Lucinda, and she was able to breathe right up to the moment I ignited her car." He sighed and pursed his lips for a moment. "You too will be alive when you commit suicide by slashing your wrists at the monument. How romantic."

He got up from his chair, gently replaced the bottle and syringe in his bag, pulled a scalpel out and walked over to her. "It's time now, Anna."

He hoisted her over his shoulders in a fireman's lift and walked to the door.

She wanted to scream, to lash out and punch him and kick him, but her arms and legs responded like they were tied down with lead weights, with only the slightest responsive movement. Then he pushed open the fire exit door and stepped out into the blizzard.

*

When they finally reached the visitor centre, Jacob led the way inside and they rapidly followed Frank and Dave, the two guards, to Hugo Winter's office.

"They're not here," he said.

"Where the hell could they be?" Holloway asked.

"The fire door's been opened," said Dave. "Maybe he went outside?"

Holloway frowned. "Could be a false trail."

"Maybe, we'll need to split up," Jacob said. "Innes, you and Frank check the entire visitor centre and Matt, I want you to check the car park with Dave in case he's trying to make a break for it."

"What about you, sir?"

"Emma's murder was in an important location to him – it had symbolic value. Now, he knows it's the endgame and he wants to go out in style. It's just a hunch, but I'm going to check the monument."

*

As useless as a puppet with its strings cut, Anna watched in horror as Ethan Spargo reached the top of the slope and approached the ancient monument. The blizzard was blowing hard now and everywhere she looked snow was scarring the night.

With dry, unblinking eyes, she stared down at the ground from her position over the man's broad shoulders. As he walked, he hummed a classical tune she vaguely recognised, coming to her intermittently through the gusts of icy wind. Now they moved through a gate and were moving up the main path leading to the monument, and she was just able to make out the enormous sarsens as he carried her over the final few yards.

Hanging limply, she stared at her arm. She tried to move her hand with every ounce of strength she could muster. There was a little more movement this time but straining with everything she had only shifted her fingers a fraction of an inch. The rest of her hand was still numb and lifeless, just like the rest of her. If the drug were wearing off, she wondered if it would be in time to save her life.

He stepped inside the monument's outer horseshoe and walked to the centre where the altar stone had once been. "If it's any consolation," he said calmly, "you'll be the last."

With bulging, bloodshot eyes, she stared up at the sky. He had released her and yet she still could not move a muscle. Spargo looked at her terrified face and then down to the slender blade in his hand. His lips moved rapidly as he mumbled some sort of mantra.

Cortisol pumped through her system as the sheer terror of what was about to happen to her intensified. She strained against the effects of the drug but it was no use, her entire body was paralysed. She felt like stone as she gasped for air, her lungs slowly shutting down because of the drug. She felt her eyes stinging with fear, dry, burning and red and fixed in position. Her world was limited to the tops of the giant dolerite bluestones above her head and the face of her tormentor as he lifted the surgical blade into the air and prepared to kill her.

She wanted to scream but she knew there was no one else here. No one else knew where she was. Would Matt and the security guard return from clearing the roads quickly enough to investigate what had happened? Even if they did, how long would it take to find her? In this weather, it would take them an age to get out here and now she realised with a stomach-turning horror she had only seconds left to live.

As the terror grew inside her, Spargo was still mumbling his mantra. The ancient words fell from his lips like blood from a fresh cut as he readied himself for one final sacrifice. Her mind raced with panic as she considered her last moments. No chance to say goodbye to her loved ones, no way to tell anyone that Ethan Spargo was the demented killer they had been hunting all week.

New thoughts of dread filled her mind. Would she be conscious when he plunged the knife in and cut her wrists? Would the anaesthetic numb the sensation of the blade? She saw him now, moving around in her peripheral vision, stalking in a circle like a lone wolf measuring his prey. If only she could talk to him. Use her training to talk him back from the edge, but her lips didn't move. Her tongue was numb and useless.

No way to delay the inevitable.

"Unfortunately, you discovered the truth about me," he said. "Most unfortunate because now I will have to silence you."

Her thoughts ran wild. *Please, you don't have to do this…*

He leaned down, a depraved snow-covered face. "I always liked you, Sergeant Mazurek – or can I call you Anna in this last moment?"

If I had my strength, you son of a bitch!

The snow whipped across them harder now, driven by the harsh wind scratching across the wild, surrounding downs. Spargo pulled up his collar and readjusted his scarf. Gripped the blade in his hand.

"Goodnight, Anna Mazurek."

Then she thought she saw lights bobbing about on the horizon.

Please, let it be someone! she thought.

Anyone at all.

*

Jacob reached the top of the slope and took in the awesome sight of the ancient stones, standing like giant sentinels in the blizzard. In the middle of the inner horseshoe, he saw Ethan Spargo, standing over Anna with a scalpel raised above his head.

He felt his heart pounding in his chest like a drum as he staggered through the snowfall and weaved his way between the enormous sarsens.

"Get away from her!"

Spargo's head jerked up and scanned the inner horseshoe for the man who had called out. Seeing Jacob's imposing figure padding towards him with a tyre iron in his hand, he staggered to his feet and lunged towards him with the blade.

Spargo was a big, strong man, and when he fought he meant business.

Jacob shot his hand forward and grabbed the other man's wrist, twisting it around anticlockwise until the joint of Spargo's thumb had fully rotated, breaking the joint entirely and shattering all of the bones in his wrist.

Spargo grunted in pain, thrusting his good hand into Jacob's face in a bid to break his jaw. The aim was good but it lacked the power to dislocate the jawbone and slid past his head, giving Jacob time to step closer into his opponent's personal space and land a hefty uppercut into the centre of his face, smashing his nose. Before he could react, Jacob spun around and planted the tyre iron in his stomach, badly winding him.

Spargo fell to the ground, blood from his broken nose spilling out onto the freshly fallen snow as he doubled up and tried to re-inflate his lungs. He lunged forward again, slashing the air in front of Jacob's face with the scalpel.

Dimly aware of Anna's lifeless body on the frozen ground, Jacob now saw headlights from a distant vehicle cutting the night, the main beams lighting up the swirling snowflakes as the two men fought in the centre of the monument's ancient horseshoe.

"There's nowhere to run, Ethan!" he called out in the storm. "Those lights are Morgan and the armed response team. Throw the weapon down!"

Suddenly aware of the flashing blue neon of the emergency vehicles' LED lights, Spargo twisted his head towards the visitor centre and saw a group of police cars and an ambulance. Then, the bright haloes of the marksmen's arc lights appeared on the perimeter of the monument.

"It's over," Jacob yelled through the snowy wind. "Give me the knife, Ethan. We have marksmen all around you."

Spargo's eyes widened with terror, glancing from Anna's numbed body back up to the police cars and then Jacob. Without warning, he raised the scalpel and charged toward Jacob with a blood-curdling scream.

Cut short by the surgical crack of three rifle shots, Spargo's attack was over, and his dead body fell to the floor, the sound of his last breaths muted by the thick blanket of blood-flecked snow.

Jacob turned away as Spargo's body slumped to the frozen ground and then ran to Anna. On the horizon, Morgan and the armed policemen were running up to the monument. Over by the visitor centre Holloway, Innes and the two guards were also making their way towards them through the blizzard.

Jacob ripped off his peacoat and threw it over the top of Anna, wrapping his arms around her to keep her warm and out of the storm. "It's okay," he said. "I can see the ambulance. It's driving up through the snow."

She stared back, numb and terrified.

"It's over," he said. "He's dead and it's over now."

CHAPTER 44

Tuesday, 1ˢᵗ January

The following day, Jacob had quietly escaped from the press pack at the station and driven back to the Old Watermill. He had left Marcus Kent to explain to the world how he had solved the crime and taken the opportunity to get back home for the day. When he got there, he found the kitchen door unlocked and stepped inside to find Sophie Anderson pouring two glasses of wine.

"Hello stranger," she said.

"Make yourself at home."

"You *did* tell me where the key was."

"True."

"Wine?" she asked, hesitatingly. It looked like something was on her mind.

"Thanks – what's that amazing smell?"

"I'm cooking roast beef for dinner. Want some?"

"Count me in," he said.

They sat at the table and she finished pouring the merlot. "I heard about Anna," she said. "How is she now?"

"She's going to be all right. Just needs a few days in the hospital to get over the effects of the drug."

Sophie shuddered. "I can't imagine how awful that

must have been."

Jacob nodded. "Apparently, this drug freezes you but leaves you conscious, so the victims were aware of everything."

"Good God," she said. "That's horrible."

"It's called succinyl chloride, or SUX for short. Another word for it is suxamethonium chloride. According to Mia Francis, it's a medication used to induce temporary paralysis, usually as part of a general anaesthetic. Its trade names are Anectine or Quelicin. It's a serious drug used to cause paralysis as part of RSI."

"RSI?"

"Rapid sequence intubation. It's a protocol followed by doctors when a patient's airway is obstructed and immediate intubation is required. The normal procedure would be to administer the drug alongside sedation so the patient isn't conscious when the paralysis occurs, for obvious reasons. Not being able to move anything, including your eyes, would be extremely distressing for anyone. She's lucky to be alive."

The fire crackled in the kitchen hearth as she handed him the wine glass.

"It was a very brave thing you did, Jacob."

He took a sip and warmed his hands by the fire. "I did my job. That's all. She'd have done the same for me."

"How did Kent react when he found out about my being on the team?"

"He's not happy about it, but your work gave us some

critical leads. He could throw me out of the force or demote me or even bring criminal charges against me, but for now, he's going to make me wait. We'll find out soon enough. He wasn't best pleased about missing the action last night either, but apparently, his wife had put his phone on silent mode."

She went quiet for a moment.

"Don't worry about it," he said. "It was thanks to you we got Miranda Dunn."

"It's not that," she began. "Listen, there's something I need to tell you."

He set down his glass on the mantelpiece and walked over to her. "What is it? You look terrified."

She opened her bag and pulled out a small engagement ring box.

"I'm flattered but we only met a few days ago."

She managed a broken smile. "It's not a ring, Jacob. Look."

She opened it up to reveal a small silver coin with an image of a honeybee imprinted on it.

"What is it?"

"It's Charon's obol," she said quietly. "The ancients put them in the mouths of the dead so they could pay the ferryman."

He felt his heart quicken. "Just stay calm."

They both knew the significance of the coin, and now Sophie broke the silence.

"This is Charon's obol, Jacob! The currency the dead

had to pay for their crossing over the Styx or the Acheron. These were an important part of Keeley's ritual killing – he believed he was liberating their souls, not simply killing them."

He heard the fear in her voice.

"I know it was," he said calmly, "but that's not what this is."

"Keeley left these coins in the mouths of his victims because like the ancient Greeks and Romans he believed that when you die you have to cross a river – the Styx – to get from the land of the living to the land of the dead. Charon is the ferryman who takes you across, but you have to pay him to do it. That's why he left the coins in their mouths – because the ancients did it. I know it's him! It's Keeley, I just know it!"

"It's probably just a crank." Jacob turned the coin over in his hand. "Just take it easy."

With trembling hands, she turned the coin over and studied it with wide, terrified eyes. "I'm no expert on numismatics, but it looks exactly like the ones we found in his victims' mouths."

"Numismatics?" Jacob said.

"It's the study of currencies and coins. During the Keeley case, we hired a leading numismatist named Dr Belinda Thomas and she gave us everything she could on the coins used by him. They were authentic, ancient coins from around 500 BC and always uniface, meaning that the image was punched into one side only. In every case, the coins he used were gold foil and bearing the image of a honeybee. Exactly like this one!"

"I remember your expert from the trial. As I recall, she said in court that these obol coins are not particularly rare. You can pick them up online for a few hundred quid, so anyone could get hold of one of these. It doesn't mean it's him."

"I don't know, something about this isn't right. Could he have posted this to me from prison?"

He thought it over. "Prisoners are free to send letters and packages but unless they're to or from solicitors or the courts they're usually checked by officers, besides there's no postmark."

"Are there other ways he could have sent this to me?"

There were other ways, he thought. One of the most common these days was to use a drone to take the package in or out of the prison. He'd already imagined Keeley using just such a method to get the coin out of the prison, but that would require an accomplice and Keeley was renowned for working alone and never trusting anyone.

"He threatened to kill me if he ever got out of prison, Jacob."

"He's not going to get out of prison. He's locked up tight in the Monster Mansion and he's never getting out."

"The Monster Mansion?"

"Wakefield."

She shuddered. "Please, can you check he's still there?"

"I think we'd have heard if the Ferryman had escaped

from prison, Soph."

"Please!"

Jacob looked into her eyes. "Wait there and I'll make some calls."

He returned a moment later and set his mobile down on the sofa. "He's exactly where he's supposed to be, locked up in Wakefield."

"You're sure?"

He nodded. "It's the biggest high-security prison in the country and they're very good at what they do there. As I said, he's locked up and there's no postmark so it's almost certainly the work of a crank who saw you in the news because of the Russell case."

"Yes, you're probably right. It's a crank." She dropped the coin back into the box and snapped it shut, putting the box on the table and turning away from it.

"Try and forget about it. You can't let it ruin your life."

He saw her visibly relax in the knowledge it was just a crank. After a while, she sipped some of the red wine and gave him a mischievous smile. "You know, you called me Soph a minute ago."

"Did I?"

"Yes, you did."

"I can't think what came over me. Would you prefer Dr Anderson?"

"Soph's just fine," she said, taking a step towards him.

Jacob set down his wine glass and pulled her closer to him. "Here's to a brand new year."

"And a brand new start in life," she said.

They fell down on the sofa among the scatter cushions and kissed in front of the fire. Through the window, the storm began to break apart to reveal the setting sun, lighting the snow clouds a coral pink as it sank slowly towards the horizon.

EPILOGUE

In the darkness of his solitary confinement cell, Professor Alistair Keeley watched the news with feigned disinterest. They had caught those responsible for the murders on the downs. According to the reports there had been six of them in all, in some kind of a druidic grove. Engaged in an initiation ritual, they had killed one of their own and buried her in the woods where she had lain in the earth for over a quarter of a century.

He struck the match on the concrete floor and lit the tip of his cigarette. A new smoking ban had led to the creation of so-called Frankenstein fags, hideous contraband smokes made from anything anyone could lay their hands on, including tea leaves, nicotine patches and even pages torn out of the prison chapel's Bible.

Now, Keeley dragged on his cigarette with a grimace. He felt the hot smoke enter his body and breathed a sigh of relief as the sedation worked its way across his tense muscles. Staring at the television's ghostly digital flicker, he tried to imagine what had happened up in the woods on that autumn night so long ago. He silently admired the grove for the length of time they had evaded detection.

Most impressive.

According to police reports, their leader was a police doctor who called himself Magalos, the Celtic god of the hunt. A nice flourish and he smiled at the irony as he took another long drag on the foul cigarette. He pushed a pile of folded newspapers to the side to make way for an empty tobacco tin which he now used as an ashtray. He looked back up to the news. The television was on a bracket on the far side of the cell and he craned his neck up to see it. The sound was muted so as not to attract the attention of passing prison officers. He read the subtitles, but more captivating was the sight of a dead man being stretchered away from Stonehenge.

Fascinating.

Then he saw the face of Detective Chief Inspector Jacob as he explained how the case had been brought to a conclusion. *Justice has been served*, he said, and then on the subtitles, a name came up.

Dr Sophie Anderson.

She had apparently played a critical part in bringing the case to an end, just as she was responsible for his incarceration like an animal in this terrible place.

This was the woman who had destroyed his life, wrecked his academic career and deprived him even of his liberty. He felt his entire body tighten, and the blood began to rush into his head. Dizziness engulfed him. His heart pounded in his chest and his mouth went copper dry. He closed his eyes and visualised the Underworld. Here, his soul would live for eternity and finally, he would find the peace he so desperately craved. The peace that Sophie Anderson had denied him.

When he opened his eyes, he had calmed enough to

look at the television again. The news was over and had been replaced with a weather map. Atlantic cloud banks and sleet. A break in the storms but more on the way. He thought of the storm he had brought into Dr Anderson's life when he'd sent her the ancient coin and a grim, crooked smile danced on his gaunt, unshaven face. That would have surely put the cat among the pigeons.

He dragged the last of whatever was in the cigarette into his body and exhaled the noxious blue smoke into the darkness of his new universe.

Justice has been served.

Not yet it hasn't, he thought.

But soon.

AUTHOR'S NOTE

Dear Mystery Reader

I hope you enjoyed reading this novel as much as I did researching and writing it. If you did, I would be very grateful if you would consider leaving a review on Amazon. It only takes a few seconds and helps to increase the visibility of the novel to other online readers. A reader's personal recommendation is the most powerful way to introduce new readers to an author's work.

I welcome all genuine interaction with readers and if you would like to get in touch I would love to hear from you on Twitter, Facebook or on my website.

Kind regards

Rob

ABOUT THE AUTHOR

Rob Jones is an international bestselling author from England who today lives in Australia with his wife and children. He has written twenty-four books and is currently working on the next DCI Jacob novel, as well as the fifteenth Joe Hawke thriller.

Printed in Great Britain
by Amazon